Dance to the Piper

&

And Promenade Home

A TWO-PART AUTOBIOGRAPHY

Dance to the Piper

&

And Promenade Home

A TWO-PART AUTOBIOGRAPHY

AGNES de MILLE

New Preface by Cynthia Gregory

A DA CAPO PAPERBACK

Library of Congress Cataloging in Publication Data

De Mille, Agnes.
   Dance to the piper & And promenade home.

   (A Da Capo paperback)
   Reprint (2nd work). Originally published: Boston: Little, Brown,
1958.
   1. De Mille, Agnes. 2. Dancers—United States—Biography. 3.
Choreographers—United States—Biography. I. De Mille, Agnes. And
promenade home. 1982. II. Title.
GV1785.D36A3 1982   793.3'092'4   81-22160
ISBN 0-306-80161-2   AACR2

This Da Capo Press paperback edition of *Dance to the Piper* and
And Promenade Home is an unabridged republication of the two
volumes first published in Boston in 1952 and 1958, here supplemented
with a new preface by Cynthia Gregory. They are reprinted by arrangement
with the author.

Published by Da Capo Press, Inc.
A Subsidiary of Plenum Publishing Corporation
233 Spring Street, New York, N.Y. 10013

To the memory of my mother
ANNA GEORGE DE MILLE
and to my husband
WALTER FOY PRUDE

Preface

It is both a pleasure and an honor to write about Agnes de Mille, and yet not a little daunting. How to appraise objectively a woman I have always held in such high regard—even awe?

From my earliest days as a ballet student, I can remember hearing about the great Miss de Mille from my teacher, Carmelita Maracci. Already she was a legend to me. Since then, this revolutionary woman who has played such a big part in changing the whole conception of dance on Broadway, in films, and in ballet, has touched my life and my work many times.

To dance in her works is truly a special experience. Her gestures and movements, so real and down to earth, are far from the stylized mime used in the old classics. Her dancers are true-to-life characters —real people. One must dig into one's deepest feelings and hidden emotions to create one of Agnes' characters onstage. The focus of her works is always on the drama of the human situation. Audiences can certainly relate to this, and are often moved to tears.

Those of us fortunate enough to work with Miss de Mille personally find that her vast knowledge, her wit and charm, her clear, articulate corrections and descriptions, and her pioneer-woman determination are unmatched in the dance world today. These qualities, along with a deep spiritual beauty which her face and hands express so vividly, work miracles in bringing artistic potential to fruition—often beyond reasonable expectations.

During the run-through of my very first rehearsal of *Fall River Legend* with Agnes, her voice rang out, "Bravo, Cynthia!" I must say that that one spontaneous remark has meant far more to me than all the applause and laudatory reviews I've ever gotten for performing the ballet before audiences. Just that memory of her acceptance of my portrayal of Lizzie Borden can see me through all those horrible times when I feel inadequate or incompetent.

I could listen to Agnes de Mille speak for hours on end. I could watch her exciting ballets again and again. I could read her fascinating books over and over. (In fact, I have—over the years). To me, this is the true test of genius.

Now, with her two-volume autobiography available again, a whole generation of dance lovers—amateur and professional—can have the marvelous adventure of getting to know Agnes and the myriads of famous people who have passed through her life. It will be a learning experience, but a wonderfully rich and charming one, full of funny anecdotes and tense, heartrending situations from Europe, through Broadway, to the golden days of Hollywood. Welcome back, Agnes de Mille!

CYNTHIA GREGORY
New York City
November 1979

Foreword

MY BOOK was neither planned nor intended. Rather it accumulated out of memoranda jotted down haphazardly, intermittently and furtively. The diffidence I felt in attempting expression in a field strange to me, and one in which the men of my family had so distinguished themselves, was understandably extreme. For years I hid what I wrote. Begun during my pregnancy as a pastime, the notes were continued whenever I had fifteen minutes to spare, on buses, subways, in dressing rooms, in drugstores, at times in the waiting room of the Children's Hospital. The manuscript consisted of letter paper, wrapping paper, programs, envelopes, paper napkins — in short, whatever would take the imprint of a pencil. A great deal of it was written with a child crawling around my neck or being sick on my lap, and I dare say this may account for certain aspects of its style. I did not attempt to write during rehearsals though I have polished off a paragraph or two while doing a barre, a practice which I would heartily condemn in young dancers. At the end of five years a considerable mass of unsorted and chaotic material had been assembled in bureau drawers and hatboxes. At last, feeling that the time had come for either bettering or burning, I delivered the inchoate bulk into the hands of Edward Weeks of the Atlantic Monthly Press. He promptly bought the lot. I then informed my husband what I had done. My husband was somewhat taken aback and not a little apprehensive.

Bringing form out of the manuscripts was no light task — but Mr. Weeks was equipped with incomparable experience, great taste and energy. I cannot begin to thank him. He also calmed my fears and threw out my most cherished prose. His enthusiasm from the first has been a source of strength and comfort; his taste has been a schooling.

I would also like to thank Clinton Simpson and Theodore Amussen for their initial faith, for suggesting that I write and encouraging me through the years to continue. Without their belief and informed approval I should never have attempted or persisted in the work.

Because this story is neither complete nor chronologically exact there are many whose names have been deleted for the sake of brevity, but whose wisdom nonetheless, and timely aid, made possible the continuing progress toward achievement in my chosen field. Most gratefully I thank Dr. Hilde Maas, Dr. Florence Powdermaker, Dr. Sydney Rogers Burnap, Eda and John Gershgorn, Lise and Dan Folke, Beulah Dix Flebbe, Lily Oberwarth, Lily Bess Campbell, Trudy and Arthur Bliss, Margaret and David Hertz, Marigold Taylor, and Marian Graham for service known only to them but recorded in my heart.

This career was not made, this book was not written, without generous and magnificent help.

AGNES DE MILLE

August 1, 1951
MERRIEWOLD,
SULLIVAN COUNTY, NEW YORK

Contents

Dance to the Piper

Dancing is the loftiest, the most moving, the most beautiful of the arts, because it is no mere translation or abstraction from life; it is life itself.

— HAVELOCK ELLIS, The Dance of Life

CHAPTER 1

New York

THIS IS THE STORY of an American dancer, a spoiled egocentric wealthy girl, who learned with difficulty to become a worker, to set and meet standards, to brace a Victorian sensibility to contemporary roughhousing, and who, with happy good fortune, participated by the side of great colleagues in a renaissance of the most ancient and magical of all the arts.

When I started my training, there were no native ballet companies except the disreputable troupe at the Metropolitan Opera House. The only touring companies most of us had ever seen were Anna Pavlova's Russian Ballet, the Denishawn group, or very rarely Isadora Duncan. There were good ballet schools in only four cities and no dance critics whatever on the daily papers. Throughout our country an almost universal indifference to the art prevailed, reinforced and perpetuated by social taboo.

I was born into a middle-class family which was by their standards successful. My parents were well educated and fastidious. It was unusual for a daughter of such a household to choose dancing as a career. I was brought up, my mother hoped, a lady, and ladies, my father knew, did not dance. Consequently a good deal of discussion took place by articulate people under heated circumstances.

My father, William C. de Mille, was a New York playwright who had several brilliant successes with Belasco before he was thirty-five. My mother was the daughter of Henry George, the political economist, and had been born in San Francisco just after the writing of *Progress and Poverty*. She was an ardent Single-Taxer and a fearless crusader from her birth.

She was raised in New York and met Father when they were both pupils at the Horace Mann School on University Place. At eleven she proposed to him but was refused. Friendship, however, persisted since the two fathers, Henry de Mille and Henry George, were mutually admiring and maintained throughout their lives cordial relations. Henry Churchill de Mille was a playwright. A North Carolinian who had left the Episcopal pulpit to write dramas with a message, he became surprisingly one of Belasco's first collaborators, but broke partnership when the Wizard decided to place all his gifts at the service of Mrs. Leslie Carter.

Henry de Mille died when his sons, William and Cecil, were young but he had made it plain he did not wish the boys to go into the theater. And so Father dutifully set about becoming an engineer at Columbia University. He changed his mind just as his father feared he might and during the senior year threw himself at Brander Matthews's feet. In a class which included John Erskine and George Middleton, he studied playwriting and after graduation, at the age of twenty-five produced his first smash hit, *Strongheart*, in which Robert Edeson starred. Now he was able to take his bride from the attic wing of his mother's boarding school to a flat on Morningside Park. There both I and my sister were born.

Margaret and I passed our first years in the exact routine of New York children — head colds, walks in the park, curtailment of racing and screaming in the apartment. Father continued to write hit after hit, collaborating with Belasco as his father had done before him — *The Warrens of Virginia*, which gave a fourteen-year-old, Mary Pickford, her first role; *Classmates*, whose ingenue was Mary Boland; *The Genius*, and *The Woman*, which made theater history because in it a husband forgave his wife an infidelity committed ten years prior to their marriage, an act of tolerance not then current, at least not on the stage. His mother, Beatrice de Mille, or Bebe, became one of the first women playbrokers.

Since Father was a playwright, I determined to be an actress.

From time to time actresses in feathered hats made their appearance at our New York flat for small teas or evening receptions — Miss Mary Nash, who had just made her first success in Father's problem play, *The Woman,* and her sister Florence, the Misses Chrystal and Julie Herne, and Miss Charlotte Walker, who had been so enchanting in Pop's Civil War hit, *The Warrens of Virginia.* The sweep, the scented grace and vivacity of these ladies seemed to me the epitome of all that was romantic and lovely — and obviously my father and mother thought so too. Any approach on my part to the status of the hats was therefore desirable.

It was only after seeing the matinee performance of Adeline Genée, dainty, doll-like and impeccable, that I altered my choice of vocation. I declared on coming home that henceforth I would be a ballet dancer, and that Mother might arrange about lessons for the next day. There were, however, no lessons. But nevertheless I danced, and sometimes I was permitted to improvise dances for dinner guests, and I was encouraged by Mother to improvise nightly while she accompanied me on the Orchestrelle, these exercises becoming as much a part of the evening's program as brushing teeth.

Father took no notice. Father was busy with the real theater. Suddenly, unexpectedly, he had a flop, *After Five,* a comedy dealing with suicide. I remember seeing him in bed the morning after this opening, the bed and floor strewn with newspapers while he hunted for a bit of mercy in edition after edition.

"What's happened, Father?" I asked excitedly.

"Go away, dearie," said my mother, sweeping me in front of her muslins and adding with that smooth voice of studied unconcern which instantly signaled to me that the family was on the verge of ruin. "Your father is preoccupied." Father raised an ashen face over the top of the *Times.*

"Perhaps," she continued as the door shut on me, "Hollywood *would* be a good change. Tell Cecil 'yes.' You needn't stay long. You can have a complete rest. I don't think it will damage your New York reputation — besides, it will be so good for the children's colds."

C H A P T E R 2

Early Hollywood

FATHER'S BROTHER, Uncle Cecil, had gone to California the year
before, in 1913, an adventure considered by the rest of the family
as the purest folly. But Cecil had little to lose. He had had uneven
success in acting and playwrighting, and his ventures with business
had failed as well. On departure for the West he asked Father for
five thousand dollars. But Father had staked him too often fruit-
lessly and this time was being cautious. It has since become clear
that Father's decision was not a profitable one, that five thousand
dollars would have entitled him to one-eighth interest in Paramount
Pictures, Inc. The company was founded around a lunch table in
New York. Jesse Lasky, an ex-cornet player who had made a small
name in vaudeville with his band of beautiful red-headed girls,
gave his name — The Jesse L. Lasky Feature Play Co.; Sam Gold-
fish, a glove merchant and Lasky's brother-in-law, lent his talents
as business manager. He later changed his name to Goldwyn.

Uncle Cecil went West, young, good-looking, open-minded, and
furnished with very nearly unlimited ambition. He raised the cash
he needed for his partnership in bits and pieces. His staff he picked
up haphazardly wherever he thought he'd found ability. His assistant director, for instance, sold Navaho jewelry for Fred Harvey on
board the Santa Fe trains until the day his peddling brought him
into contact with Uncle Cecil.

The plan was to establish the new company in Flagstaff, Arizona, but when the train arrived Cecil walked into a snowstorm, which did not seem propitious to a business depending chiefly on sunlight, so he stepped back on again and proceeded to the Coast.

The tales that drifted back from the West were hair-raising: Uncle Cecil had bitter rivals who were intent on doing him down; the exposed film had been trod underfoot and he had sat up all night covering the developers with loaded guns; he had been shot at in the dark as he hurried home with the reels under his coat to the bungalow he shared with a pet wolf (these were not press stories; these were Uncle Ce's letters to his anxious wife); he had overcome his rivals and the first full-length feature was finished; he sent for real actors from the East and for his wife and child.

In New York, I was taken to a movie theater to see my cousin Cecilia abducted by the Indians, while my handsome aunt was carried off in a back-bend over an Indian saddlebow, her mane of brown hair sweeping the sagebrush. I very much admired my aunt's back-bend and practiced it over a chair so that I should be ready for what was wanted. I was not a little piqued to see that Cecilia had stolen the professional jump on me, but it was some balm to my jealous spirit to note that she had muffed her opportunities, indulging in hardly any screaming and no spasms. I practiced acting every night in bed — dreadful scenes of having both my legs amputated, dying at the scaffold, coming upon the family unexpectedly stark and dead on the dining room rug, and when the tears were rolling down my pillow I fell asleep in the happy satisfaction that when my chance came, I would be more than ready. I also practiced nightly knee-bends of my own invention and prayed hard for those that didn't — "God bless Father and Mother and make them strong and flexible."

Cecil, who established himself immediately as Director General of the Lasky company, begged Father to join him. They were settled very nicely, he wrote, in what had been a stable on Vine Street. Business was expanding rapidly; the work was pioneering and picturesque; Father was literate and would, therefore, Cecil pointed out, find unique opportunities. So Father agreed to go.

He wrote back every single day from Hollywood and sent photographs: Cecil and himself in director's costumes, riding breeches, and puttees to protect their legs on location work. Cecil in his early thirties, balding already, stocky, with the dynamism of a young bull, his head lowered to gaze straight into the camera, his beautiful teeth flashing; Father, the older brother, thoughtful, intelligent, practiced, waiting slightly to the rear. There were photographs of rattlesnakes crawling over the dressing-room steps, of Hollywood and cowboys, of actresses in tangles of hair, their black-rimmed eyes squinting in the white sun.

Mother decided to close up the New York flat and follow him out with my sister and me. We planned to stay for six months and then we would come back so that Father, well rested, could write another successful play.

Mother started to pack: I looked ahead. I would, I hoped, go to school with an Indian boy. I would have a horse and ride with the cowboys. I would, please God, be allowed to act in the movies.

Hollywood was different from what I thought, anticlimactic after the momentous trip west. Where were the deserts cut and gullied by pale blue rivers? The red and orange Indian mountains we had left behind in Arizona? The ancient villages glimpsed fleetingly as the tracks clicked behind too fast? From a Pullman window I had seen two Navahos, scarlet and purple, riding quietly down a path to the shadowed arroyo, just as though it had been three hundred years ago, just as though a train were not going by in front of them with little girls eating their lunch of lettuce and Thousand Island dressing en route to join their handsome young father in Hollywood.

The trip was a belated homecoming for Mother. For Father, Margaret and me it was a voyage into pure adventure. We stayed the first few nights with Uncle Cecil but Mother quickly found us a dear little ugly house of our own, snuggling at the foot of a hill and boasting a banana tree and a rose garden.

Hollywood was merely a country town, like many in the East, with palms instead of maples and chestnuts. The hills, though steep, were plain colored. The people were just ordinary.

There were absolutely no Indians, but there was a hermit, which was even rarer, complete with sackcloth, bare feet and staff. Kids said he lived in a cave in the hills.

There were also a good many theosophists and folk of religious bent whose costume was not so easily discernible. I learned to know them by their batik scarves, their strings of beads, their unpowdered noses, their nervous, cheerful expressions and their readiness to come to Mother's teas.

And there were some cowboys. They kept largely to themselves out on the Lasky ranch, coming in only occasionally to the studio to play *caballeros* or knights or Civil War cavalry or themselves. Occasionally they would show up in a group of six or eight in Uncle Ce's back yard and take us for a good thumping gallop around the block astride their saddlebows. They smelled of sweat and leather and they laughed with great male laughs which we found pleasantly terrifying. We used to come upon groups of them riding down the back streets where the asphalt was soft under their horses' feet.

The scenery was unrefreshing to an Easterner. Geraniums hung unnaturally out of the palm branches. Magenta bougainvillea matted the shingles and waved shoots and tendrils over the roof tops, struggling in suffocating embrace with the Cherokee roses. Roses flattened the poinsettias against the windowpanes. The gross, succulent grass grew rank to one's calves unless one mowed and mowed, and as long as one watered. But right where the last drop of moisture fell there the green comfort stopped, the bare earth showed. Not a clover leaf, not a bit of moss vouchsafed spontaneous relief, not one tender unearned green blade offered itself. A gray, scratching growth took over, unlovely to the foreign eye and terrible to the ankle, which concealed no part of the uncompromising earth.

The main thoroughfare, Hollywood Boulevard, was a shambling, drowsy street of box stores and shingled houses under the dusty crackling palms and pepper trees. The stores had been thrown together in a week, but the houses were substantial, built by citizens of the Middle West who had come to the Coast to die at ease in the sun. A cross between Swiss chalet and Japanese temple, they reflected a cautious exoticism not in evidence in the Tudor-Moorish villas with striped awnings and plentiful cross-timbering which later replaced them. The houses seemed taken unaware by a business street across their front lawns. Backed up into their trees they appeared to yield yard by dusty yard of grass before the crowding of upstart shops. A trolley clanged down the eight miles from Laurel Canyon to the heart of Los Angeles, and this was the only public conveyance. On it every morning rode the entire working staff of the studio carrying their lunch boxes. Only the Director General, my uncle, and the producer, Jesse Lasky, rode to work in cars. Actors, directors and writers went by trolley. And when the family had Uncle Cecil's car or when he came home to dinner with Pop, they walked. I used to see them, crossing the vacant lot in the red sunset, their putteed legs scratching through the dried yellow grass. They carried briefcases and talked with head lowered.

"Anne," called Father, "I've brought Cecil home."

"Cecil?" said Mother in a fluster. His effect on the womenfolk was always that of a cock in a barnyard, and Mother, like all his female relatives, looked upon every chance to serve him as an indulgence on his part.

"William," she said, "you might have warned me." And she rushed to make the table look prettier.

They sat long after dinner and talked of the studio. I was asleep by then, but I woke to hear their voices. They talked with fervor. They were in love with their new work. In the first year, Pop stayed away from the studio only seventeen days, including Sundays.

The studio was a converted stable on Vine Street, a pleasant broad avenue, beautiful with pepper trees that hung in cascades of feathery fronds, pluming and pouring down before the great fruit gardens and arched date palms. The studio building itself was a dingy, dark green wood, soiled with the droppings of the pepper bark. At the little wooden railing which fenced petitioners from the Promised Land sat a brash kid with his feet on the rail. He was usually called Mervyn Le Roy, and insisted on greeting persons by their first names instead of addressing the daughters of studio executives properly as "Miss de Mille." In the wooden wall were wickets labeled CASTING DIRECTOR, and CASHIER. People lined up in front of them at appropriate times, but the daughters of executives swept through, snubbing Mervyn Le Roy.

Crossing the hall, one came right out into the open air again. There, in a great rectangle of wooden shacks, carpenter shops, dressing rooms, and such, were broad, low wooden platforms, the stages, open to the weather, and protected from the skies only by long awnings of white muslin called diffusers that pulled back and forth on guide wires. To a certain extent the sunlight could be regulated by the manipulation of these canvases. The rain could not be. When it poured the scenery got sopping and stood dripping and drenched under tarpaulins. The worn boards of the stage collected pools, and shooting was suspended. The first glass-covered stage was not erected until we had been there a year and was the exhibition piece of the company. All the shops went up in a fine blaze one Tuesday afternoon and were prudently rebuilt of cement. There being no walls of any kind around the sets, any studio member who wanted to could stop and watch and invite family and friends to join. Mary Pickford was the first actress to insist on privacy and was regarded as antisocial as well as temperamental and self-indulgent for doing so, but she was too expensive ($10,000 per week) to be gainsaid. Where the neighbors' houses overlooked the back lot the neighbors' kids and their friends formed a regular gallery whenever there was anything worth their attention.

Direction was largely improvisation, and acting consisted mainly of following, without showing irritation or fluster, signals shouted through a megaphone. To supply the rhythm which set dialogue or timed pantomime might have furnished and which everyone instinctively felt was needed, a couple of musicians stood by. They played anything they liked, appropriate or not, and they played without cease, through hammering, sawing, dragging, calling, banging, whispering and sobbing. In moments of intense passion, the violinist generally moved in close to the scene of operations like a good anesthetist, carefully feeding the efforts of the earnest young woman who was attempting to pull emotional significance out of thin air. She was given no build-up, no springboard of audience excitement, no pattern even — just told to pump out raw emotion under a blazing sky while she watched the yelling director or the chicken hawks overhead circling down from the hills and back.

The stories were generally settled in a day or two of conference. A list of sets and props was handed to the carpenters, a list of costumes to the dressmakers. The location man was told to hunt up a good place in the San Fernando Valley for a massacre. The camera man loaded his box, and they were ready to begin. It was my father who, coming from the tradition of a literate theater, suggested that it might be useful to write out in detail beforehand what they planned doing. He wrote complete little synopses for Cecil. Then he asked a writer friend, Margaret Turnbull, to come west to help him. The two of them wrote synopses sitting at desks in a small wooden house with screen doors on the lot. Pop got the studio painter to make him a sign which he hung on the doorknob, SCENARIO DEPARTMENT. And this was the first time these words appeared in Hollywood.

If there was no loitering, a feature full-length (five-reel) film could be shot in two weeks; with one week for preparation and one week for editing and cutting, a picture could be finished for the first running in about four weeks. The runnings or first showings occurred on Wednesday and Saturday nights. Every employee had the privilege of attending with his family. Everyone told the director what he thought of the work and offered his suggestions for improvement. Everyone was proud at the prospect of success, everyone saddened by a failure. New inventions were the boast of all, the first large close-up, for instance, or the daring sequence of a man leaving one house and arriving at another, omitting the intervening explanatory scene of his walking down the street.

It has become a vogue to run off old films — always on machines which were never geared to exhibit them — at dishonestly quickened tempi, and to howl at the inept stupidity of the technique. But I believe, by and large, there was more genuine invention in those days, more daring of untried devices, more zest, more hope, more fervor. Stomach ulcers and alcoholism were not the recognized concomitants of scenario writing. The men who made the early films did not despise their work nor hate their bosses. They had not come to accept frustration as their almost inevitable lot. Each picture was a challenge. They worked as individualists. They worked on their own as artists. And although very few of them were artists, they all had the pleasure and pride of believing they might be and worked accordingly. Some of their exuberance found its way into the productions and many of these films have the zest and sincerity of true primitives.

In those early days the citizens of Hollywood were openly contemptuous of the infant industry. Every now and then the comfortable maggot domesticity of Hollywood Boulevard was interrupted by a moving-picture unit, which arbitrarily roped off a section of sidewalk and made use of whatever portion of the town suited their story needs while the citizenry gaped in good-natured disdain or raw curiosity. A carload of Keystone cops would debouch in the leading thoroughfare, beat their victims on the head with cotton clubs, and effect a departure before the authentic constabulary of the town were aware of what happened. The townsfolk were amused but not surprised, since nothing the "movies" did surprised them. Picturesque, irresponsible people of precarious ways and bizarre tastes, they were considered no social threat as long as they were kept in their place. And they had a place; movies were not invited to join the better Los Angeles clubs. The contempt of the real estate operator for the movie was without blemish; it was his one perfect characteristic.

The citizens went to the picture theaters about twice a week. They went to church on Sundays. They took drives to Beverly Hills to see the nurseries where poinsettias grew naturally in the ground. There were no art galleries. The theaters were way off in Los Angeles. There was one public library, and a Woman's Club which imported visiting lecturers. And that was all culturally. The citizens spent long parts of the afternoons moving the sprinkler from one section of the lawn to another. They gossiped. They rode about. The whole town seemed to drowse between its orange and avocado gardens, under its trolley wires and telegraph poles, under its raucous signboards, under its hills.

Behind this street of sultry, social make-believe and inflamed ambition, behind this tiny empire-building, the hills rose suddenly, untamed, pre-Spanish, coarse with desert weed and wild tearing sagebrush, riven with flood, blind with dust storm, formed and burnt in an endless sun, and hard and promising that the future was as unknown and terrible as the past, that there was enough strength and brutal promise in the land to stir the earth underfoot until the windows rattled and the people knelt in their little stucco churches and conversed urgently with God. And over all stretched the bare sky, the original sky, the peeled and exposed sky, blind and endless.

Very few were aware of what the hills meant in their lives. If they thought at all of such matters it was to note that another milkman had drowned at the corner of Cahuenga and Franklin and to decide that something had better be done about a bridge. It was to stop suddenly on a December morning and remark that the hills had turned green with a veiling of grass and flowers, that there was a smell of wild lilac in the air, and from beyond the orchard country when the wind turned a hint of snow. The rains had come! The blackened slopes were now meadows of blowing, moving blossom. The children grew unmanageable and took to the highlands, returning after long forays, scratched and bitten, with armfuls of dying lupine and brodea or an entire yucca, twelve feet tall, which they presented to their perplexed mothers.

Once, years later when I was grown and far away, someone placed a sprig of sagebrush under my nose. I burst into tears. The hills, the breathing hills! Veiled with purple in the hazy canyons, powdered with gold where the mustard and the eschscholtzia tangled in the strong grass, the crests glowing and moving with promise beyond and beyond and beyond to where old San Jacinto stood in a final cold wall against the desert! My grandfather knew the hills when California was in truth a promised land, and rode their slopes with shining heart. My grandmother turned her head to them as she stood a schoolgirl in the cloisters of the Los Angeles Mission (La Puebla de Nuestra Señora la Reina de Los Angeles). I had seen the wheels of the Spanish ox-carts rotting in the grass. I had walked through the old molding adobe halls and stared into the blind reduced belltowers, so small and quiet beneath the terrible blue sky. I had smelled the box hedges around the graves. It seemed to me as I stood on the top of the hills that I heard the bells again, the pious Spanish bells, forged in another country and carried here with so much pride and care, now stolen or broken and forever stilled, the bronze bells that had brought my grandmother to her knees and roused the Indians in the San Fernando fields with apprehension. It seemed to me as I stood on the hills that my whole life lay before me. The descending grassy slopes filled me with a passion to run, to roll in delirium, to wreck my body on the earth. Space means this to a dancer — or to a child! The descent through the air, the finding of earth-footage, the embracing and struggle with the fundamental ground. These are to a dancer what strong scents are to an animal.

It is no accident that California produced our greatest dancers, Duncan and Graham, and fostered the work of St. Denis, Doris Humphrey, Maracci and Collins. The Eastern states sit in their folded scenery, tamed and remembering, but in California the earth and sky clash, and space is dynamic. When people speak of Hollywood I am not minded of the goings-on in the hot studios, nor the pleasant social life of cheap oranges and easy swims, but of the untouched country behind the town, pagan, pantheistic, where mountain cats still prowl, the little deer start and tremble at human approach, coyotes scream and the beneficent rain comes down in the eucalyptus groves.

C H A P T E R   3

The Industry

I HAD COUNTED on a week or two to get acclimated, to look around, but Mother with her fatiguing energy found and settled on a school within two days of arrival and we once more had to take up our good mornings with that sort of thing. The Hollywood School for Girls was held out of doors in a garden. We sat under the trees, moving from spot to spot for classes as it seemed pleasant to do so. When it rained we studied in long shacks. Very nice young ladies attended, mingled quite democratically with the moving picture daughters. Douglas Fairbanks, Jr., and Joel McCrea were our two male pupils. Doug, Jr., was a fat youngster in a sailor suit. He stood on his head too often and hung by his heels from the lower branches of trees. His father's reputation weighed heavily on him.

Several of us had famous fathers and none of us was unaware of the responsibility. Among the young ladies were the two daughters of Louis B. Mayer, Edith and Irene. They were dark-eyed friendly girls distinguished by mistaken enthusiasm for their father's achievements. Our loyalties remained throughout the school years violent and competitive. *Noblesse oblige* alone kept me from telling them outright what my family thought about their family's films.

The attitude of my family toward all competition strikes me today as remarkably haughty. When Cecil made *Carmen* with Geraldine Farrar and Fox quickly rushed out a rival version entitled *Carmen as It Should Be* with Theda Bara, it was automatically taken for granted by all de Milles that this second interpretation would be spurious. Naturally, all inner family councils were championed by me on playground and pavement. "Have you seen *The Birth of a Nation?*" asked Luigina Carpenter in rebuttal. I had not seen it for moral reasons. Nothing Mr. Griffith ever directed was considered by Mother suitable for a growing girl. But ignorance never stopped my tongue. "That's nothing," I said, "wait until you see my uncle's picture *The Arab* — three hundred horsemen galloping across the burning Arabian sands and massacring a whole town full of people."

"That's nothing," retorted the maddening Luigina. "In *The Klansman* there's the Ku-Klux Klan and fiery crosses and thousands, simply thousands of Negroes and Southern gentlemen lynching one another."

"My mother says that's not nice," I answered, slamming the front gate.

But in the Mayer girls I had tougher antagonists. For all their father's lack of orthodox theatrical training (he had salvaged ships in a Canadian harbor), he seemed to be doing very well indeed.

The one person in the school I made no attempt to bully or dominate was a beautiful, dark-haired child named Mary Hunter. She alone remained uncowed, though friendly, and played with me when and as it suited her and when her mother permitted, which was not too often. Mary was reminded quite peremptorily that we were movies. Nevertheless, we declared ourselves inseparable for life. Oddly enough, we have been.

Her aunt was Mary Austin, the writer. Mrs. Austin occasionally visited Mary's home and told us remarkable stories and worked out our fortunes in cards. She kept a strong protective watch over her niece and advised her about her studies, admonishing her as to behavior in long, strongly expressed letters about how to conduct herself in a manner becoming the famous Mrs. Austin's niece. Although not her niece, I was also given strongly expressed advice then and later.

The class I enjoyed most was pantomime. We had dancing too

but Mother refused to let me take this as possibly confusing to my
native gifts. But I watched the other little girls learning Ruth St.
Denis's and Isadora's dances third-hand.

I existed for the afternoons. We had at first no car so Mother
gave me the garage. In this I built a castle out of boxes, crates,
sawed-off palm branches and old furniture. I plotted my walk to
school by one series of dumps and refuse heaps and my return by
another, and I gleaned from all a most astonishing and repugnant
collection of furnishings. After I had returned one day with two
not very presentable pieces of crockery, Mother put a stop to these
garnerings and undertook to have a real carpenter with fresh
lumber build me a balcony, a table and two chairs. The little girls
of the neighborhood were quickly commandeered as workmen and,
bonded by God knows what tacit agreement, built every afternoon
with the sweat pouring down their faces for two hours or more
before I would let them play. Even when we moved, and one
would have thought distance might deliver them from my tyranny,
I summoned them from across Hollywood to come build an inn
with a thatched roof, to come lay the bricks of a floor, to come in
the broiling sun and tote a log that would have given pause to
grown men. They came. At that, it was probably more amusing
than playing tag or swapping pictures of Carlyle Blackwell or
Bessie Barriscale. Only my kid sister put down her hammer and
nails and looking at me with a small dirty face rivered by sweat
spoke up at last: "I don't see why we're doing this. It's hot. I'm
tired. I'm going to the house and get a cool drink and read a
magazine." And what's more, she had the effrontery to follow suit.
I watched her back march away under the orange trees that fairly
jumped in the dazzle. But despite her defection I saw to it that
the inn was completed with brick floors, a stone fireplace (impractical), a courtyard, a thatched roof and a wing two stories high.
Mary Hunter participated in all these enterprises, but largely in
an advisory capacity.

Sometimes the garage was a castle or an inn and sometimes a
theater. We made the scenery by stacking sawed-off palm branches

against the rafters and roof braces. Anyone who has lived in the subtropics knows that the base fronds of the date palm are as sharp and hard as stilettos and quite capable of piercing a man's riding boot. My little playmates did not wear leather riding boots to school. They wore ankle-length socks. Exits, entrances and retreats were punctuated by shrill cries and moans. These I disregarded as unprofessional.

I continued to pray fervently every night to be allowed to act in pictures.

Our second summer, Uncle Cecil brought Farrar to Hollywood to play *Carmen* and I had my first model to aspire to. The world-famous Geraldine was the first great international star to try the Western experiment. Grand Opera meant far more in those days than it does now or possibly ever will again. It represented the ultimate in theatrical grandeur, honor, permanence and splendor and Farrar was among its most dazzling names. She had trod the oldest and most glorious stages. She had graced courts. An emperor had been at her feet. The studio hummed with anticipation! It was in a sense like the excitement that preceded Mary Anderson's first visit to a mining town. The first star dressing room to grace Hollywood was erected, lined with chintz and furnished with comfortable wicker chairs and couches. A Steinway piano was procured for the set. She came west with her mother, her father, her French maid, her business manager, her hairdresser and two lady companions, all at the expense of the studio. That was quite proper. If she had come in any lesser manner we would have been disappointed.

She visited the studio first on a Sunday morning and we were all on hand, the executives and their families, either to welcome or to stare. I was enthralled — jet-black hair with blue lights in it (her hair was naturally chestnut; she dyed it — not blond according to the habits of the time, but black), a glowing skin, deep Irish blue eyes, a figure rather dumpy but superbly held, a lovely provocative voice and the most dazzling smile we had ever seen. She gave each person she spoke to her entire momentary attention. She brought out all that was witty, sparkling and vital in them, even in us, gap-toothed children, even for the part of a minute when we limply took her hand and bobbed a curtsy. We had never seen such unutterably lovely clothes. She wore a blond straw hat with pink roses, pendant diamond earrings, a cool linen dress and white silk stockings with long pointed black patent-leather shoes and cutsteel buckles. ("They may be fashionable," said Mother, "but I don't think they're in good taste. Black stockings should go with black shoes.") Margaret and I vowed to love her all our lives. She became our crush, and the grownups, quick to turn to their own advantage any emotion that would serve them, even the most sacred, prevailed on us to go to bed on time because she did (tenthirty always when she was not singing); urged us to answer our letters because she replied to hers within twenty-four hours in her own hand; suggested that we might also grow to be loved if we, like her, remembered people's names. She gave us her picture and we kept it by the side of our bed and took it with us when traveling. The electricians, the carpenters, the cowboys also adored her. Every one at the studio, from executive to assistant prop-boy, spoke of her as "Our Gerry."

The second summer she came back to do *Joan of Arc*, Uncle Cecil's first big spectacle, and the amalgamation of the women I admired most produced in me an emotional climax that approached vocation. I had identified myself for some little time with Joan of Arc and confidently expected visions at puberty and a martyr's death at nineteen. I did not quite presume to identify myself with Farrar; the differences were too marked. For one thing, she was physically clean, kept her clothes neat and was always on time for appointments. It was also pointed out to me that she did not bite her nails. On these points I felt that the Savior of France and I would see more nearly eye to eye.

Farrar was given a suit of silver armor to spare her the weight of the men's irons. She spent days in the saddle and whole days in a fosse up to her waist in muddy water, a cowboy guard around her dressed in bobbed wigs and fourteenth-century hats, fending off broken spears, falling beams and masses of struggling extras. The Sunday the battle of Les Tourelles was shot out at the studio

ranch, every director on the Lasky lot was commandeered as a lieutenant to Cecil; George Melford, Frank Reicher, Donald Crisp,
James Young, Pop, all stood in full costume in the line. Each
director was responsible for the authentic appearance, acting, and
physical safety of a company of soldiers. Father, as the chief's
brother, in an iron hat and the cross of Saint George on his chest,
was placed exactly where the French cavalry took the stockade,
lances couchant, hoofs striking fire and splinters, swords and iron
stirrups akimbo. He came out with his sight and all his members
intact but Mother missed a couple of bites on her sandwich.
Farrar's understudy, an equestrienne of stamina, rode at the head
of four hundred men on a white horse carrying a white silk banner.
We sat around watching in open cars with picnic baskets. It was
something like an English hunt breakfast.

It was the same at the burning. We all went down to the studio
for that occasion. We all went whenever there was anything spectacular, as later when Uncle Cecil fed Gloria Swanson to the lions
or threw Conrad Nagel into a crocodile pit. We went through
curiosity and family pride. Not every family boasted like displays
with which to entertain and impress their friends from the East —
an uncle down in a pit, unarmed, kicking alligators out of his way,
with nothing to protect his legs but riding boots. We were very
proud of his courage which was always noticeable on these occasions. During the burning, Uncle Cecil stood at the stake for
hours trying out smoke. He never asked an actor to do what he
would not do himself. Farrar stood until she was obliterated by
smoke and flame although everyone said it would do her voice no
good at all. But when they burned the dummy and its hair caught
and flaked off in a single shower of fiery cinders, she turned sick
and had to go to her dressing room and lie down. I stayed throughout, transfixed. I was impressed by the horrible heat given off by
the burning pyre.

Once each summer she came to dinner at our house. I was not
permitted, of course, to eat with her, but very nearly ran a temperature at the prospect of having her under our roof.

After dinner there was music. Farrar never sang during the

summer, but she played the piano with great power and everyone else sang. She played brilliantly, improvising as she went, talking and laughing. Before she played she stripped her fingers of her black pearl rings as large as robin's eggs, and her great diamond and pearl bracelets, and threw them on the piano top. Then she sat down and played like a man. The sound of the music and the laughter woke my sister and me and we crept in our nightgowns to the stairs and sat there with faces pressed against the balustrade, shivering at the glory below.

C H A P T E R 4

"Do Something"

As THE DAUGHTER of Henry George, Mother had early settled for herself the causes of war, of economic depression, of unequal distribution of wealth, and so on, and she naturally found it a matter of no great effort to reach definite conclusions on hats, dresses, interior decoration, manners, painting, music, plays, cooking, the rearing of children, and sex.

We were brought up in a manner lively but stern. Father wanted us healthy, nontheatrical, and lettered. He didn't seem to care about much else. Mother, on the other hand, had comprehensive ideas about everything.

Margaret and I were not allowed to go to the studio often and never unchaperoned. We were never permitted to read the newspapers. We were allowed to look at the pictures in the Sunday supplements except during the Arbuckle scandal, and then we weren't. We knew few actors. Father did not like them extracurricularly and only about a dozen were invited to the house. Margaret and I dined alone until high school age. We went to bed at eight until then and at nine until college.

Mother's ideas of dress were rigid. My sister and I were dressed exactly alike to prevent jealousy. We wore Liberty smocks or little frocks of Japanese crepe embroidered and cross-stitched by her own hand. With the exception of hats and shoes, she never bought us store clothes. She considered these too ordinary, and, I suspect, given her remarkable moral scruples, too easy. She dressed herself with similar independence and with proud disdain for whatever anyone else might choose to wear. She had a penchant for tricornes and wore them in velvet, satin, felt, velours, straw, with cockades and without, with feathers, sometimes with flowers, and when I was old enough I wore them. Never at any point in my growing up did they bear relationship to the current vogue. My sister, with greater independence of spirit, began making personal decisions about her own clothes by the time she was ten. It is no accident that she became one of the leading style experts in this country. I never gainsaid Mother about so much as a color or a ruffle. Mother liked red satin heels on her slippers because Louis XIV and XV had worn them, and when I was old enough I wore red heels. She liked eighteenth-century evening dresses, but made in useful, comfortable, twentieth-century materials like chiffon and China silk. She had definite ideas about hair — curls on the forehead, curls down the back, curls on the side. She curled me every morning before school while I read aloud to her, usually in French. She did not understand French, but she thought it was good practice for me. When I started going to parties she piled a crown of curls on the top of my head surmounted with laurel leaves. This arrangement did much to militate against any social success I might have had. Her own hair was very lovely, a bright golden red which she wore coiled at the nape of her neck. My hair was red-gold, too, quite handsome but rather too thick and curly to be manageable. "The Circassian Ugly" my sister called me, and there were many family jokes of similar nature. It was part of our parents' plan to keep us from imagining that we were in any way attractive girls — lovable, yes, but attractive, never.

Mother's skin was snowy and the preservation of its dazzling transparency a real care. She devised a black silk bathing suit for the Santa Monica beaches, with long sleeves, high collar and stockings that caused as much comment in that land of semi-nakedness as though she had walked into the ocean stark. I have seen people rise from a prone position in the sand to stare. My life was made horrid with chivyings about scarfs, shade hats, gloves and collars, but I came through with a white skin and no freckles. She was tiny. She wore a size one shoe. And she took great pride in the fact that I had inherited her small foot. I wore a size one and a half point shoe when I was grown which broadened in width as my toes grew misshapen in battle. I nearly ruined my feet trying to maintain her unmatched pedal tradition.

Mother loved to entertain but invited always those people she thought ought to get on together with small regard as to whether they were likely to or not. She set a beautiful table, regulating the drinks according to her scruples: none at all, for instance, during prohibition, although she heartily disapproved of the law. "Don't break the law," she would say to her thirsty and disappointed friends, "change it!"

She had a horror of waste, a tie-over from an impoverished girlhood, and even when my father was earning four thousand dollars a week regularly the year around, she would go about the house turning out the lights to save the light bill. In fact, she would come into a room and turn off all the lights except the one in actual use for reading. She felt compelled to shop at the end-of-the-month bargain sales even when she could well afford more leisurely times, even when she needed nothing. She saved everything, old letters, old laces and ribbons, papers and strings. She saved time. She shortened her life saving time. She was always late because she was afraid she might have some extra spare time on her hands and accordingly arranged a daily schedule that ignored geography or delay. Resting she considered a waste unless it was done strenuously, that is, on a bed, on one's back, with one's eyes closed. "Don't just sit there, dearie," she would say coming into a room. "Do something!" To this hour I find it impossible to read a book before sundown unless it has some immediate connection with my work.

We were put on dress allowances from the time we were eight, and all our spendings were drawn from this and it was never enough. I lived in debt to Mother forever. But I considered this condition correct and scorned the financial irresponsibility of friends who trifled away their resources on movie magazines and ice-cream sodas. I never bought ice-cream sodas. There wasn't money, for one thing, and there wasn't time. When I left school each day, I entered instantly on some afternoon project. I never hung around. I did something.

We said our prayers in French — for practice; there was no field which her sense of economy overlooked. Nothing was ever counted by Mother as having any value unless it had a moral purpose, that is, unless it bettered life in some observable way. With pure esthetics she had neither understanding nor patience, and with extravagance or luxury of any sort she grew downright intolerant. She carried this feeling to such a pitch that she could not permit herself to do anything pleasant unless she felt she was doing it for someone else's sake. I have known her to eat a bunch of grapes over a period of days and never have a sound one, keeping exact pace with the mold. The force of her will and her impact on casual strangers cannot easily be reckoned. On the way to a Single Tax Conference in Edinburgh, which Mother once attended with Margaret and me, the locomotive broke down and all the passengers were detrained in the black rain at Carlisle and told to shift for themselves until morning. Everyone made off obediently in the downpour to the local inn — everyone but Mother. She straightway raised such hell that the LMS summoned an engine for our private use and dispatched us absolutely alone in a single car north to Scotland. American railroad officials do not believe this story. It is, however, the truth.

Her humor was irreverent, capricious, zany and delightful but modified and curtailed by her multiplicity of moral compulsions. She was always worrying about something. She felt she was not wringing the worth out of the moment unless she fretted a little. She gave the impression of being a dear, quaint, fussy, old-fashioned busybody until a question of principle was involved or a crisis, then suddenly one found oneself facing up to a personality with all the instability of Gibraltar. She was a rock. She was a fortress. It was as though the shadow of her father stood behind her and quietly laid his hand on her shoulder.

My mother was born late in her parents' life and knew her illustrious father only after he had attained world renown. The atmosphere of her home life was a preoccupation with the problems of mankind, dedication and high-mindedness. Statesmen came hat in hand to the door. The young men who cluttered up her parlor grew to be the leaders in their communities. The issues in her life were always real and of serious social consequence. A priest was excommunicated for her father's sake. The revolutionary leaders of Ireland conferred with him; Sun Yat-sen and Tolstoi paid homage. He died of exhaustion and overwork fighting civic corruption. One hundred thousand people walked in the funeral cortege.

All through her life Mother was honored as the daughter of a great man. Tolstoi's son came to pay his respects (not a chip off the old block, my sister and I decided). And once Karl Marx's granddaughter came to tea. The punctilious courtesy with which these two descendants of rival, mutually exclusive messiahs treated one another is among the most treasured memories of my early social life. With loyalties lashed tight, with eyes veiled and wary, they deferred to one another with a consideration almost Japanese in its suavity and lack of substance. My sister and I grew accustomed to standing with aching knees in the crowds while Mother laid wreaths on public monuments, to watching her enter parliaments and banquet halls which rose in tribute. We were ourselves occasionally toted about and treated like Holy Relics. We naturally responded to all this with mixed feelings — part embarrassment, part shyness, part vanity. It was hard to think of ourselves as just ordinary, as Mother told us to. Very little of it comes under the heading of a normal American upbringing.

Mother's veneration for her father bordered on the religious. Her compulsion to carry on his work, to promulgate his theories, she accepted as proof of her love. She chafed and fretted at her inadequacy to do anything conclusive, but she let no small opportunities pass, such as talking to friends at tea parties, giving public lectures, or leaving pamphlets with the grocer, the shoemaker, the studio electrician, the traffic cop. It was her tragedy that she had inherited her father's energy and passion to do good without his sense of organization or intellect. The great powers within her were never channeled. They ran at cross-purposes, directionless, tearing at her heart, hurrying her, driving her. They would have broken her early but for her constitution which, though deceptively veiled in fragility, was unusually durable. But they left her no peace. All her life she could never rest.

Nor could she let us rest. Having known one authentic genius, she took for granted that anyone in whom she placed her faith and love must stand head and shoulders above the surrounding multitudes. This was a bit tough on her husband and daughters, bright enough in their way, but none too eager to be judged by standards of absolute supremacy.

I, however, considered Pop an authentic genius. He was to me the master artist, the great scholar. I frequently wept when he spoke about his work. It was more than my nerves could stand, this communion in professional purpose which the others in the family could not share. My passion was to please him, never to fail his expectations, to bear his name proudly. I did all he asked eagerly. He was an excellent photographer; I learned photography. He sang well and half-joking suggested that I learn the piano in order to accompany him; my response ran to five hours' daily practicing in the summer and full-length recitals with my sister. He was a fine athlete and had been a track man at Columbia. He played brilliant tennis and worked out with Maurice McLoughlin and all the Suttons and Bundys on Sunday afternoons. I tried to learn tennis, making the semifinals always in the junior state tournaments. He told me what to read; I read. He told me what not to; a gun would not have persuaded me to open the book. He told me to write. I became editor of the school paper, and he took my best themes proudly back East with him to show Brander Matthews and John Erskine. He told me to stop bullying my little sister; I tried for a day or two at a time.

But, for all my veneration, I could be stuffy about his work. I adored him and I wished him to be perfect. I did not like him to make compromises, even the most trivial, and I used my small bits of knowledge to fly-speck his vanity. Anachronisms, for instance, drove me frantic. I was continually tugging at his sleeve. "Look, Pop, women's hair didn't show in the fifteenth century."

"And how many people do you think know this or care?" he answered.

"Well, I do, and now you do."

"That's not enough. I'm more concerned with the story."

I talked to the winds — after all, I was only eleven.

Father's great interest was first, and properly, with character and plot. But I never stopped arguing.

We talked long about tennis, about books and art — a great deal about books and the importance of fine work. He talked in detail every night at dinner about his work at the studio, inflaming me, exciting me, but never, never holding out any promise of a release for my professional yearnings. I kept hoping. I always believed that next month he would lead me through the gates of the studio and say, "Here is a new professional."

At this time our neighbor, Fred Stone, invited his little daughter, Dorothy, to dance with him as his partner at a big benefit performance. He taught her the steps and worked with her for hours. They had a great success. I ran with this example of paternal love to Pop. "But you see, my dear," he said, "I am not a dancer."

"Oh, Pop," I begged, "don't be horrid, don't tease. You know what I mean."

"No, my dear, I don't," he said, "and besides I want my daughter to have an education."

Mother believed in self-expression, but she could not go against his will, and he was particularly interested in not having us embrace the theater as a career. I dare say Mother would have liked me to be recognized as a child prodigy in every major artistic field, but without my ever suspecting that I was in any way unusual. Improvised dances were cultural, that was all there was to that. What went on inside Mother's heart, while she watched me hop and race, I do not know. I suspect she entertained some wild hopes. She admitted twenty years later that I was pretty damn good, but naturally she said nothing of the sort then.

She wanted me above all to be a fine, gentle, sweet-mannered, pure girl and this was what I was being raised as against every inclination in my nature.

C H A P T E R **5**

The Brothers

UNCLE CECIL is one of the most remarkable men I have ever met. His has been a marquee name since 1913 — a span of unbroken and successful effort which for sheer length has been without match in the history of moving pictures. Father, within the confines of our separate family group, may have been considered the intellectual, but Uncle Ce was taken by all, family, friends and admiring professionals, to be the type of success, the brilliant, decisive epitome of achievement. One did not contradict him because he was absolutely convinced, because his personality was compelling, and because he had been vindicated in his tastes by millions. Consequently, his idea of a star was accepted by almost all of us as axiomatically the recipe for a great performing artist. My desire to comply with this pattern and my subsequent rejection of it as unsuitable for myself have been among the strong shaping forces of my life. But he remained in the background, although perhaps not consciously for all of us, as the point of reference, the lodestar. We might say we did not like this or that or disagree in such and such a way, but the emotional impact of his position and power was enormous. We responded to him with a kind of reflex. There was no place in the family point of view for failure then or later; he had made it out of the question.

As younger men, both brothers, William Churchill and Cecil Blount de Mille, looked much alike, slender, dark and handsome,

Cecil very much the handsomer of the two. Father looked like a Spanish grandee, with melting brown eyes, dark curly hair, and the brow and nose of a thinking, proud man. His face was severe even in repose, and his mouth firm in preoccupation. But the lights blazed behind his eyes and his lids and his lips were cross-hatched with lurking smiles. His voice was an actor's voice, sharp and decisive but always quiet, drawing out soft and sibilant in his more wicked comments.

Pop's outstanding characteristic was his wit. Language was his delight and tool. He became known as one of the best after-dinner speakers in Hollywood. It is a pity he chose to spend the best years of his life working where no speech was wanted, for his dramatic satire was fine. He was as potent at the breakfast table, and I used to sit shivering in a mixture of admiration and terror as the barbed comments came closer and closer. Dinner with Father meant a real display of intellectual pyrotechnics to me. I sat with shining eyes, giggling and giggling. He never had a better audience, and he had many. My little playmates, on the other hand, were frankly scared out of their skins by him and ran and hid under beds at his approach while their mothers made him welcome in adoring delight.

Cecil also was a delightful conversationalist and an exuberant raconteur, but he leaned on exaggeration and flamboyance of statement, and although everything he talked about bubbled with excitement and fun, it was not Father's style. When Father said something, it was said for keeps. Pop could be dry and very brief.

Under a certain theatrical manner Uncle Cecil's attitude was patriarchal, loyal, and deep, but he lived with the grand gesture and exuded emotional protestations like eau de cologne. Pop never permitted himself demonstrations of any kind or even affectionate assurances. He was shy for all his articulateness and diffident and very proud. He treated us rather like puppies, for whom he had the fondest regard but whom he did not choose to fondle overmuch. He expressed himself in rude banter and awkward pats.

Cecil was always immaculate, a work of art. His valet garnished him. Pop was clean all right but frequently mussed, and he always smelled of cigars. Good Cuban cigars, mind you. Cecil stood stocky and straight, with his legs planted, like a wall, a barricade, a mounted gun, but Pop sprawled and crumpled. He developed out of pure laziness a slouch that rounded and sloped him down. This constant appearance of dejected lassitude was however deceptive. He could move when need arose with the speed of a track star. He had the co-ordination of a cat. He can still, at the age of seventy-two, wallop the daylights out of men decades his junior on the tennis courts.

Domestically Pop was incorrigibly lazy and totally spoiled. He never did anything at all around the house that was trouble. His chair, by choice a chaise longue, was sacrosanct; guests have been warned to get out of it. He called his car his toothbrush and the family would as soon have taken liberties with one as with the other. He drove with a carefulness that was nerve-shattering. He spent solid time keeping track of his belongings, tidying up and tabulating everything from loaded guns, of which he kept an arsenal, to postage stamps. The nursery, of course, was always hurricane struck, and he shuddered when he entered, but never scolded us; that was our domain. He was undeviating in all trivia, and his little household likings were ritual. First time of anything he liked established a habit, not broken thereafter for any but life-changing reasons.

In the tradition of his father, Henry de Mille, Pop was a liberal and a free-trader. He never hesitated to speak out for what he believed in, even buying space in the reactionary *Los Angeles Times* and more reactionary *Examiner*, to argue the case for the people. His political articles were brilliant. I remember one that particularly pleased me at the time, the concluding item in a campaign for tax reform: "Citizens of Los Angeles, you will either believe me or support me." He made excellent platform speeches and taught classes in economics. He even carried his feeling for justice into private life, and in cases where tried and loyal workers had been smashed by the Hollywood system of new efficiency and favoritism, provided financial support for years. His staff was chosen largely out of kindness and for sentimental reasons — as was also, sometimes fatally, his cast. Uncle Cecil was seldom troubled by these confusions.

Neither athlete nor sportsman like Father, Cecil went into life-long training to keep fit for his work; he drank and smoked with extreme moderation always, and during business conferences would not even chew gum lest some part of his watchfulness relax. He has always been physically extremely courageous. The great spectacles he produced, involving, as they so often did, wild carnivorous animals, flood, fire or catastrophe, kept him quite thoroughly exercised. He has never needed more than five hours' sleep a night, and his endurance during working hours, which frequently aggregated eighteen a day, became legendary.

Father didn't care how he looked on the set. He directed in his old clothes, an old battered tennis hat which he refused to change or throw away. He gave himself entirely to the business on hand and was extremely bad-tempered if he was interrupted, but he never raised his voice to his actors. With them he had endless patience, coaxing, cajoling, analyzing. He was adored by cast and technicians who usually called him "Bill" with familiarity and affection. Cecil, on the other hand, was always on show and appeared for work impeccably dressed, usually in well-cut riding breeches and leather boots. His manner was princely and courteous. He always made guests welcome, explained and chatted and showed off in a very satisfactory way. If he lost his temper it was in the grand manner, building up from a simple statement of displeasure, through long developments of sarcasm to a fulminating climax of operatic splendor which not infrequently terminated with dismissal. He held the belief that he got the best work from people when he had stripped their nerves raw, when they could no longer think, when they acted through an instinct of rage and desperation. If they turned in a fair piece of work and he struck them across the mouth, they'd turn in a better one the next day. He regularly set his entire staff by the ears by demanding publicly their individual opinions on one another's work while he sat aloof in Olympian calm until matters had reached a broth of discussion. He then stepped in and resolved the trouble by Jovian fiat.

He has often said to me that he thought ladies made poor actresses because, he reasoned, they had learned too much control. He had his own methods of breaking down that control. He generally got what he was after. When, however, he worked with skilled technicians he was quiet and patient. And he was very much more often charming than not, and humorous, and whatever he did he did with colossal zest, and it was never dull working for him. Although I suppose every member of his staff has from time to time resented his tyranny, they have stuck with fierce loyalty and pride, some of them for thirty years. They called him "Chief," and his theory that he was the greatest director alive they accepted as their party slogan.

And certainly, as a director of mass movement, this century has not seen his like. I have worked with many, including Reinhardt, Mamoulian, Cukor and Kazan, and I know. He surpassed in this respect by long odds D. W. Griffith, who many think invented and developed the technique of screen spectacle. The sense of rhythm, the eye for detail, the dynamic power with which he hypnotized a mob standing for hours in the open sun, kept them from sitting down, scattering, chewing gum or even growing mechanical in their response at the end of the exhausting rehearsals; his faculty for invention; his endless patience despite weather or wear to stop the whole enormous mechanism, as elaborate as an advancing army in attack, because some fool man on a balcony in the middle distance had thrown off his toga and put on his pince-nez; his courage to re-rehearse the whole scene, hearten his assistants, whip up the actors again to performance pitch and straighten out all technical difficulties before the sun dropped and the shadows changed, knowing that every five minutes the cash register ticked up thousands, were a source of never-ending astonishment to me. The power to dominate the mob came out of his guts, the very core of his nervous life. When I began to direct I recognized what went into these spectacular displays of endurance. He talked to me about it. "If one takes one's focus off the crowd for the space of even a few sentences to an assistant, if one leaves the set for five minutes, to go to the bathroom for instance, it takes an hour and a half to get the crowd back to where one broke off." I might have added from the depths of my own experience, "Or if one is doubtful or afraid or uncertain." But such ideas never occurred to him in his whole career. The strength for this domination came from his undeviating belief in what he was doing and from his enormous pride of position.

His beginnings were modest enough. While Pop was at the Gymnasium in Freiburg, Cecil attended the Pennsylvania Military College in Chester, Pennsylvania. It was this institution that gave him his first honorary Doctor of Laws. He left this college to play Osric to E. H. Sothern's Hamlet and while touring in *Hearts Are Trumps* met and courted Constance Adams, a svelte, cool, dark-haired actress, the daughter of the Judge of the Supreme Court of New Jersey. There followed years of trying to get a real foothold in his father's and brother's trade. He was in and out of every office on Broadway. He played Mary Pickford's big brother in Father's play *The Warrens of Virginia*. He claims to have written *The Return of Peter Grimm* but Belasco reduced his name on the program and thereby deprived him of the best fruits of that fine achievement. Uncle Ce says, however, that he felt no bitterness but on the contrary loved and respected the old man to the day of his death.

And certainly Belasco has been a dominant influence in his professional life. Much has been written about Cecil's Hollywood office, the Gothic windows, the deep fur rugs, the armor standing in the corners, the cases of mementoes, the great carved desk behind which the master sat studying his victim in a third degree police light rigged to unnerve and harass the prospective employee into giving the worst possible accounting of himself. I think it was Belasco's office they were writing about, stained-glass windows, fur rugs and all. It was the Jew in the clerical collar who sat behind the desk. It was Cecil who waited anxiously in the victim's seat, desperate with ambition, desperate to earn a living for his wife and infant daughter, driven, harassed, and apprehensive. The day Belasco's death was announced, Cecil put in his bid for the purchase of the Belasco theater, the scene of so many of my father's triumphs, the stage where *Peter Grimm* was launched on its spectacular run. Katharine Cornell beat him in the market by two hours.

But for all the Hollywood beginnings were strenuous, success came quickly. Everything he undertook professionally as director or man of business was enormous and exciting. Everything that transpired in his home was gracious, opulent, and shot through always with the excitement of his personality, the note of danger he injected, the sense of change and adventure. In spite of his heritage he is, by conviction, a deeply grounded conservative, an old-style Republican, a capitalist, in all that term has come popularly to mean. By nature he is a revolutionary, a buccaneer! Although a young man when he went to Hollywood, uncertain and insecure, with his whole life's fortune at stake, he was then, as he has been since, domineering, vital, shrewd, ruthless even, a fighter who worked with the instinct to take hold and never let go — but at the same time debonnaire and curious about everything — an adventurer-dictator!

He lived like a prince potentate. Periodically, there was the crisis of production, but the household under the control of my extraordinary aunt remained serene and ordered. She kept all in balance. Three children were adopted and later, in turn, all the grandchildren were given asylum and care. She liked children and so did Cecil, and this is rare for a man of his enormous egocentric drive. Tides of young people passed through those large flower-filled rooms, bringing their storms and turmoils and passions. Aunt Constance quieted the clamor and kept the place ready for the master. Frederik, the beautiful Norwegian butler, and Helja, the Finnish maid, helped. They were with her for twenty-five years. Her enchanting hospitality was open to all of us throughout our growing up.

My aunt moved through this luxury and excitement with un-
ruffled poise. She was ready for all eventualities. I remember one
April afternoon began for her with a children's hospital committee
meeting that was interrupted by a hysterical summons from across
Los Feliz Boulevard because of the drowning of a child in a nearby
reservoir. She went to the victim's home, cleaned the house, prepared supper for the brothers and sisters, comforted the mother,
returned, bathed and dressed, put in a brisk half hour hunting flies
and ants for her small son's neglected alligator, presided at the dinner table of her own children, sat with them while they studied,
and at midnight was found trailing alone around the cellar in a
red velvet negligee in search of the special Liebfraumilch which
Cecil liked with his late supper.

Uncle Cecil seldom came home to dinner before ten or eleven
at night. His table stood ready before the living room fireplace
set with Italian lace and crystal; the double boilers waited on
the stove. Aunt Constance gave him his dinner every night herself, prepared it and served it no matter what hour he came in,
and sat and talked to him until he grew rested enough to sleep. At
seven the next morning, the children were crawling over his bed.
At seven-thirty he was choosing his suit and tie and by eight-thirty
he was en route to the studio — often on foot.

There were always big plans. There were always important
people and projects in the offing. He has been the admiration of
many great businessmen; he performs with money like a virtuoso.

Success was power; success was comfort and fun for everyone.
He had acquired besides his home in Laughlin Park a large ranch,
"Paradise," a yacht, name jewels, a Rubens, a fine library, several
show horses for his daughter, a superb cellar, as well as the more
usual paraphernalia of a great Hollywood producer — swimming
pool, tennis court, cars, gardens, and Lord knows what real-estate
holdings and investments that were not apparent to a child's eye.
Laughlin Park was policed by a night watchman, and Uncle Ce
went to bed with a loaded gun as did my father always. These
circumstances I grew up with; they were the atmosphere of my

childhood — the direct antiphonal counterpoint to Mother's pre-occupation with economies and her unallayed guilt about owning anything at all while half the world went hungry.

He always talked over all of his business plans with his wife. He talked with excitement.

"I am not good at business," I once said. "I cannot take zest in bargaining. I cannot forget it's people's bread and butter."

"Don't think of it that way," he said, chuckling and jingling the twenty-dollar gold pieces he always kept in his pocket, "or you are lost. It's a game. Highest score wins." He played like a champion.

This expert attention to reality was accompanied but not diminished by a fervid attachment to mysticism. He considers himself a theologian. He believes with sincerity that he is spreading the word of God and fostering the brotherhood of man. He believes himself a dedicated person and his pictures, partially at least, instruments of religious faith. Zest for business and passion for religion have been combined many times before with happy results. Cecil is sincere in both. He has personally been a source of spiritual strength to many — even at deathbeds has held hands *in extremis* and the bereaved in his arms. This is a role few of the public know him in — but they do sense the real conviction in what he does, and this is one of the reasons they respond at the box office. Another is that what interests him interests millions. And another is that he is a superb craftsman.

Always on Thanksgiving and Christmas we went up on the hill to celebrate. Cecil took the whole morning to open his presents. They were piled on five or six tables around him as he sat before the great fireplace, gifts that grew most costly and elaborate with each year's success. He always waited until the children had opened theirs and then the real excitement began. The family sat around watching and gasping with admiration. The process sometimes lasted three or four hours.

This is the Hollywood way of celebrating the festival, and I had first been introduced to it at our initial Christmas there. It was very different from New York. Back East Christmas had always been a season of fearful excitement, of whisperings up the chimney, catalogued demands left on the hearth and unexplained rustlings. We had all this in Hollywood and we had a large amount of nice presents and an enormous tree. But what was my surprise to find the center of attention somewhat shifted away from me and my parents and focused on Uncle Cecil. Every worker in the studio had sent a token of affection and respect. Likewise, Cecilia, as heir apparent, was favored with a memento from every employee, and was only saved from throwing up with excitement by being marched off to take a nap. As one might imagine, our presents to him posed quite a problem. But he always pushed the more professional treasures aside and gave our gifts his whole attention and his enthusiastic and courteous gratitude. This was one of his characteristics — he could be gallant to children. He also gave all our early theatrical efforts similar grown-up attention and interest, much more than did Father. For Christmas Uncle Cecil gave us French perfume or lingerie which Mother discouraged us from using, for although she always liked us to under-dress nicely in case, as she explained, we should ever be run over, she saw no reason for French handmade lingerie. Father gave us books and suggested soap instead of scent.

We sat down to Christmas dinner twenty strong with Cecil like a Pasha at the head of the table carving the roast pig. All the females lined the sides murmuring and attentive, with Father, the older brother, somewhat sardonic, tucked away among them.

Uncle Cecil was always a princely host dominating the conversation with graciousness.

They ran pictures every single night up at Cecil's on the hill, and we were welcome to come. We gathered in his office which was also his library, and waited. When his dinner was over, he came in with his guests and family. The picture was run. Cecil told us, always wittily, whether it was good or bad. We went home.

I have said it was difficult, even impossible, to contradict Uncle

Cecil, his conviction being total and unassailable, but before his mother, Bebe, his spirit sometimes quailed. She talked to him about all his work. She would sit opposite him at dinner decked in the extraordinary collection of laces and beads and flowers with which she covered her beautiful gray curls and talk to him sometimes very sternly. He always listened. He listened more to her than to the critics, who at first were fairly rough. Cecil undoubtedly minded as all people do, but he never said as much. He would chuckle and jingle his twenty-dollar gold pieces: "The critics can write as they choose; it is the public who will give the final verdict. The public through the box office. Good pictures succeed; bad pictures fail." But at the praise or condemnation of his mother, his heart jumped. She remained critical, hard to please, and enormously proud of her extraordinary son.

The critics have come around a good bit since then, and Uncle Cecil has mellowed both in his technique of work and his point of view, but at that period "the critics" grew to be, in our estimation, synonymous with a poor sniveling lot of disappointed professionals back in New York who wrote entirely out of frustration and spleen and could scarcely make a living doing even that. But when Bob Benchley and Robert Sherwood took to hailing my father as "the subtle and intelligent member of the de Mille family," I began to view them in a better light. "I wish they would not use me as a hammer with which to whack Cecil," said Pop. The only thing that invariably made Father lose his temper and talk in an irrational way was a breath of criticism against Cecil, artistic, moral or spiritual. He had often staked him and had helped him out in every way he could. He simply would not have his kid brother picked on, no, not even when kid brother sat astride Hollywood, had been decorated by the Pope, and was one of the very rich men in his business.

C H A P T E R   6

Pavlova

ANNA PAVLOVA! My life stops as I write that name. Across the daily preoccupation of lessons, lunch boxes, tooth brushings and quarrelings with Margaret flashed this bright, unworldly experience and burned in a single afternoon a path over which I could never retrace my steps. I had witnessed the power of beauty, and in some chamber of my heart I lost forever my irresponsibility. I was as clearly marked as though she had looked me in the face and called my name. For generations my father's family had loved and served the theater. All my life I had seen actors and actresses and had heard theater jargon at the dinner table and business talk of box-office grosses. I had thrilled at Father's projects and watched fascinated his picturesque occupations. I took a proprietary pride in the profitable and hasty growth of "The Industry." But nothing in his world or my uncle's prepared me for theater as I saw it that Saturday afternoon.

Since that day I have gained some knowledge in my trade and I recognize that her technique was limited; that her arabesques were not as pure or classically correct as Markova's, that her jumps and batterie were paltry, her turns not to be compared in strength and number with the strenuous durability of Baronova or Toumanova. I know that her scenery was designed by second-rate artists, her music was on a level with restaurant orchestrations, her company definitely inferior to all the standards we insist on today, and her choreography mostly hack. And yet I say that she was in her person the quintessence of theatrical excitement.

As her little bird body revealed itself on the scene, either immobile in trembling mystery or tense in the incredible arc which was her lift, her instep stretched ahead in an arch never before seen, the tiny bones of her hands in ceaseless vibration, her face radiant, diamonds glittering under her dark hair, her little waist encased in silk, the great tutu balancing, quickening and flashing over her beating, flashing, quivering legs, every man and woman sat forward, every pulse quickened. She never appeared to rest static, some part of her trembled, vibrated, beat like a heart. Before our dazzled eyes, she flashed with the sudden sweetness of a hummingbird in action too quick for understanding by our gross utilitarian standards, in action sensed rather than seen. The movie cameras of her day could not record her allegro. Her feet and hands photographed as a blur.

Bright little bird bones, delicate bird sinews! She was all fire and steel wire. There was not an ounce of spare flesh on her skeleton, and the life force used and used her body until she died of the fever of moving, gasping for breath, much too young.

She was small, about five feet. She wore a size one and a half slipper, but her feet and hands were large in proportion to her height. Her hand could cover her whole face. Her trunk was small and stripped of all anatomy but the ciphers of adolescence, her arms and legs relatively long, the neck extraordinarily long and mobile. All her gestures were liquid and possessed of an inner rhythm that flowed to inevitable completion with the finality of architecture or music. Her arms seemed to lift not from the elbow or the arm socket, but from the base of the spine. Her legs seemed to function from the waist. When she bent her head her whole spine moved and the motion was completed the length of the arm through the elongation of her slender hand and the quivering reaching fingers. I believe there has never been a foot like hers, slender, delicate and of such an astonishing aggressiveness when arched as to suggest the ultimate in human vitality. Without in any way being sensual, being, in fact, almost sexless, she suggested all exhilaration, gaiety and delight. She jumped, and we broke bonds with reality. We flew. We hung over the earth, spread in the air as we do in dreams, our hands turning in the air as in water — the strong forthright taut plunging leg balanced on the poised arc of the foot, the other leg stretched to the horizon like the wing of a bird. We lay balancing, quivering, turning, and all things were possible, even to us, the ordinary people.

I have seen two dancers as great or greater since, Alicia Markova and Margot Fonteyn, and many other women who have kicked higher, balanced longer or turned faster. These are poor substitutes for passion. In spite of her flimsy dances, the bald and blatant virtuosity, there was an intoxicated rapture, a focus of energy, Dionysian in its physical intensity, that I have never seen equaled by a performer in any theater of the world. Also she was the *first* of the truly great in our experience.

I sat with the blood beating in my throat. As I walked into the bright glare of the afternoon, my head ached and I could scarcely swallow. I didn't wish to cry. I certainly couldn't speak. I sat in a daze in the car oblivious to the grownups' ceaseless prattle. At home I climbed the stairs slowly to my bedroom and, shutting myself in, placed both hands on the brass rail at the foot of my bed, then rising laboriously to the tips of my white buttoned shoes I stumped the width of the bed and back again. My toes throbbed with pain, my knees shook, my legs quivered with weakness. I repeated the exercise. The blessed, relieving tears stuck at last on my lashes. Only by hurting my feet could I ease the pain in my throat.

It is a source of sadness to me that few of our contemporary ballet dancers ever saw Anna Pavlova. At the time of which I write, her name was synonymous with the art — Pavlova, the Incomparable, was an internationally known slogan. She was as famous as Caruso and her position as unique. No one today approaches her power over the popular imagination. She half-hypnotized audiences, partaking almost of the nature of a divinity.

My life was wholly altered by her — so I wonder, casting about in vain for similar dazzling influences, what first drove Kaye, Alonso, Fonteyn, Toumanova and Helpmann to the barre.

Anna Pavlova was born in St. Petersburg of a Jewish mother and an unknown father, reputedly a laundress and a peasant. She was a graduate of the Imperial School and one of the last five ranking ballerinas of the Maryinski Theater.[1] Pavlova was the first great star to leave the Czarist confines and toured Scandinavia one summer with Adolph Bolm. They forfeited their pensions for doing so. The Scandinavians had never before seen any dancing like it.

Years later Bolm used to sit on the long Pullman jumps of his last American tour beguiling beginners like me with tales of the great days. There were dinners, banquets, torchlight processions, horses unhitched from the carriage, mobs outside the hotel windows, flowers thrown down on their heads. And in the winter, in the snows, when they went touring through the Russian provinces, trainloads of balletomanes followed them from city to city, rich and enthusiastic young men bringing their own servants and wine and horses, and in some cases furniture, along with them, and laughing with a flask of vodka in their hands and the snow matted on their fur coats, to see the darling, the great new ballerina, Anna Pavlova, rolling like a kitten in the snow, frost glinting on her dark curls, frost on her fur cap, frisking and waving her incredible little feet like deer's hoofs.

The short tour through Scandinavia gave her a taste for the outer

---

[1] The term *prima ballerina* has been bandied about by ignorant pressmen until it has lost all meaning, and is now applicable to any girl who has had ballet lessons. In the great days of the Italian, French, and Russian State Theaters, the ballet was divided into a hierarchy as rigid as the army and the classifications rose from *corps de ballet* or private no grade to *prima ballerina assoluta*, to which there is no corresponding military position. Protocol was iron and there was never any passing back and forth or jumping a rank. The roles were determined by prerogative. And there was absolutely never any democracy or fraternization. The Russians at the time of the First War recognized five ballerinas, Anna Pavlova, Tamara Karsavina, Olga Preobrajenska, Vera Trefilova, and Lubov Egorova, and one *prima ballerina assoluta*, Mathilde Kchessinska, the autocrat of the Maryinski Theater and before his marriage, the Czar's mistress. It was from her palace balcony that Lenin made his first great speech to the revolting crowds in November 1917.

world and in 1905 she followed Diaghilev to Paris and danced opposite Nijinsky in the initial, legendary season at the Théâtre du Châtelet. I am told their waltz in *Les Sylphides* was the lightest, most aerial and brilliant dancing ever seen by living eye. She shortly broke away, however, to become star in her company and thereafter toured the world, back and forth, around and around, and never stopped.

In 1910, she came to New York partnered by the first great male star this country had ever seen, Michael Mordkin, and aroused a popular response no one this century had commanded. When she tore across the Metropolitan Opera House stage that first midnight performance in *Coppélia* and then in the *Autumn Bacchanal* and *The Swan* women wept and ripped the violets out of their muffs and hurled them on the stage.

Few Americans had seen great dancing before they saw her, although they have always been responsive to foreigners. When Fanny Elssler came in the 'forties of the last century the members of congress unhitched the horses of her carriage and dragged her through the capital cheering. Bonfanti, a plump, unimportant Italian, danced with acclaim at Niblo's Garden in the mid-sixties and there were a few more visiting fatties, both French and Italian, but dancing consisted mainly of skirt dancing or twiddling about on toes. In 1898, Isadora Duncan, the great revolutionist, unknown and nearly starving, left via a cattle boat to try her fortunes abroad. St. Denis, only a little less neglected, followed soon after. They did not return for a long time and not until after their reputations had been firmly established in Paris and London. When they came back years later, their influence within their craft proved deep, lasting and incalculably productive. Under their leadership the dance once more was put to high purpose. But they never commanded the audience that flocked to see Pavlova.

When she had gone back to the mysterious regions whence she came, and the memory of her was less immediate and more indulgent, I turned to action. It seemed imperative that we give dance pageants. I summoned the gang and announced this to them. I don't think it particularly relevant to remark that not one of us had had dancing lessons. We wrote down a program on a piece of yellow paper and informed my mother how many costumes we should need, and the date of the performance — eight days later to be precise. With remarkable ingenuity and a minimum of purchase my mother coped, and very creditable and suitable little outfits they turned out to be, although the assembling cost her many weary walks, up and down hill in the neighborhood. "Have you got anything around the house that my child could wear as an Egyptian crown of the middle dynasty?" she would say, sinking into a chair and sipping a welcome cup of tea as Aunt Mildred Smith leaned forward all breathless eagerness to sacrifice any part of her furnishings or wardrobe, her dear face puckered in consideration. From Aunt Mildred Smith she got three deerskin rugs to clothe the shepherds in the Pastorale.

The dance program or pageant was performed under the banana tree in the back yard. The audience (ten- and fifteen-cent admissions) sat in the lee of the house. Mother stayed upstairs frantically changing the little girls. Since Anna Pavlova always began her *divertissements* with a Slavic folk dance, I accordingly opened with a polka, presumably of Polish origin, in an Italian dress borrowed from Luigina and a great wreath made of real poppies and straw about the size and consistency of a partridge nest. There followed minuets, shepherd dances, Ruth St. Denis's yogi dance, St. Denis's Japanese geisha, a Duncan finale with tossed oranges and a classic *pas de deux* done on point in unblocked shoes on the grass. (I could stay on point, with pain, of course, only as long as I walked in the grass.) There was also a sea nymph danced by Eleanor Worthington, a dazzlingly pretty child, who hadn't given a thought to anything but her costume before running out on the lawn, but whose beauty elicited audible pleasure from the audience. This made me mad. It was the first time I had run up against biology in my professional life and I found it unreasonable.

Aunt Mildred Smith sat in a corner by the fuchsia bush with a small portable Victrola and a catholic selection of records. There having been no music or dress rehearsal, some strain was entailed during performance as I shot her signals from mid-stage. At any mistake, all action suspended and the aggregate stare of the cast turned on her in angry dismay until she grasped what was wanted next. At afternoon's close she confessed the need of a strong cup of tea.

Since Mother refused lessons, all I learned about dancing I learned through reading and looking at pictures. I cut out photographs of every dancer I could find and pasted them in a scrapbook. The Diaghilev Ballet Russe came to Los Angeles. Mother went and even had supper with them, afterwards, mentioning it to me in an offhand way when the week was nearly up. It seems she had been seated next to a very nice gentleman named Adolph Bolm who was interested to hear her little girl liked to dance. I was as staggered as though she had casually announced breakfast with the President of the United States. I set up a clamor to be taken to every remaining performance. But they were at night and of course I couldn't stay up for them. Besides, Mother said, they were very disappointing, full of silly things. The Butterfly in *Carnaval* wore white kid gloves, idiotically enough, with blue ribbons on her wrists. And there was something about *Afternoon of a Faun* which was, morally speaking, not quite fine. However, we were all taken to the Saturday matinee. *Sylphides* proved exquisite. Mother said if she had known they could do graceful and pretty things like this, she would have taken us more often. She urged me to look at all the colors and costumes in *Scheherazade*, hoping no doubt that the point of the piece would escape me. She was quite right. I grew so confused by the concentric circles of the debauchees, the platters of fruit, the turbans and the glitter, that I lost track about why the Shah got so mad at his wife that he killed everyone within reach. That afternoon I saw Nijinsky. I have nothing to say of that. He whirled and moved his head like a cat and the audience applauded. I was too young to know what I was looking at.

I saw Duncan shortly after. She likewise held no interest for me. A fat, cross-eyed woman in dull costumes made of material like portieres, she resembled not one little bit Anna Pavlova. Mother explained that the reason she looked so sad was because her little children had been drowned in an automobile accident. Mother said she found her dull too, but I noticed she sat with the tears streaming down her cheeks as she watched. "Why are you crying?" I asked. "I don't know," said Mother, "this dance is very long" (it was an entire Beethoven symphony) "but I can't bear to think of her losing her children." Isadora came before the curtain at the end and urged us all to run barefoot over the hills. I did the next afternoon, and Mother sat for some time picking cactus spines out of me.

But when the plays and pageants were done, when Mother's friends had stopped talking and had gone home filled with her tea and cookies, when the costumes were put away, then what? Then I spent an evening twisting before the truth. My dance pageants were only makeshifts. Father came home to dinner and talked of the real theater. His work went on and on, month by month, undisturbed by these nursery flurries. I wanted so much to study. I wanted to be part of a real professional company where grown-ups worked. But Mother and Father were obdurate; Father did not wish me to get involved any further with dancing. And Mother, living in an age where self-expression was considered paramount, was afraid of the stultifying effect of training. It was then the proudest boast a mother could make — "Entirely self-taught, my dear, never had a lesson in her life."

Once Ruth St. Denis was invited to the house to look me over. With gigantic *sang-froid* I performed one of her own dances for her. She paid me the serious compliment of growing exasperated, kicked off her shoes and sat on the carpet beside me going through the entire routine twice correctly. She then left recommending that I be trained at once, preferably in her own school. But it came to nothing. St. Denis and Shawn, however, grew to be devoted and close friends of my parents. Father repeatedly said that, although dancers, they were very intelligent people indeed. But he refused to attend a single performance.

Matters might have gone on this way for years if my sister's arches hadn't providentially fallen. She was taken to a great orthopedist who advised, of all things, ballet dancing. He advised it for her, not for me, but what one sister did in our family the other always shared. We went straight away to the Theodore Kosloff School of Imperial Russian Ballet.

The Kosloff School

THEODORE KOSLOFF had been a member of the original Diaghilev Ballet Russe. He had an enchanting smile, crooked, childish and slightly cruel. He was slender at the time, lithe and thatched with a mop of soft wavy brown hair. He had been trained at the Moscow Imperial School and had appeared at the Maryinski. Thence he had gone to Paris with Diaghilev and danced in the initial seasons with Nijinsky and Karsavina. Although he played only minor bits in this company, he had a remembering eye and the time he put in during these seasons paid off more than well in his subsequent choreography.

Gertrude Hoffman, an enterprising American, who saw the value of beating the Russians to New York with their own ballets, summoned him over. He came with his wife, Maria Baldina, and Fokine's best repertoire. For Hoffman he staged among other things a peppery version of *Scheherazade*. There being no copyright for choreography, Fokine could raise no legal objections. After this success, Kosloff shrewdly decided to have his own company and acquired for this purpose two exquisite young dancers, Vera Fredova, an English girl from Pavlova's company, and Natacha Rambova, née Winifred Hudnut. They toured in vaudeville throughout the country, reaching Los Angeles in due course, where they were seen by Uncle Cecil's scouts and promptly hired. Cecil at this time was producing one of Farrar's later pictures, *The Woman*

God Forgot, the story of Alvarado and an Aztec princess. When I first saw Kosloff he was naked in feathers, leaning on a feathered spear. He had painted himself horned eyebrows in the Russian Ballet style, and his gestures were real classic pantomime, involving clenched fists and the whites of the eyeballs, a positive style which gave the camera something substantial to focus on. Here was passion and here certainly was sincerity in amounts. Every expression was performed with a force that could have carried him across the room and over the wall. I was awe-struck. I went home and doubled the number of knee-bends I performed every night before bed.

Kosloff liked pictures and Hollywood very much indeed. He settled down quickly with his two lovely assistants, his wife and small daughter, and started to accumulate real estate and glamour. He also acquired pupils. He continued to act. The assistants on the other hand were forbidden to work in movies. They were set rather to keeping the school running, making costumes, doing his accounts, ordering his housekeeping and rehearsing all his ballets. Before them he dangled the promise of a return to the ballet world, New York, Paris and London and a great career as his ballerinas. But the nearest they got to this dream after years of waiting was a couple of vaudeville tours. Miss Rambova lost patience after a time and married Rudolph Valentino. Miss Fredova stuck it, loyal, devoted soul that she was, until all hope of a personal career was past.

Kosloff agreed to take us as pupils and out of courtesy to Uncle Cecil he took us free without pay of any sort for as long or as often as we wished to go to his school.

We went down for our audition on a summer morning. The studio was an enormous bare room with folding chairs pushed against the white walls for the mothers to sit on while they watched their daughters sweat. Across one end of the hall hung a large mirror. Around the other three sides stretched the traditional barre. I gave my audition in a bathing suit. Kosloff himself put me through the test. He did not say how talented I was or how naturally graceful. He said my knees were weak, my spine curved, that I was heavy for my age and had "no juice." By this he meant, I came to learn, that my muscles were dry, stubborn and unresilient. He said I was a bit old to start training; I was at the time thirteen. I looked at him in mild surprise. I hardly knew what emotion to give way to, the astonishment of hurt vanity or gratitude for professional help. I was sent off (I keep saying "I" — my sister of course was with me but from the start I took for granted that these lessons were mine. She just came along). We were sent off to buy blocked toe slippers, fitted right to the very ends of our toes, and to prepare proper practice dresses.

The first lesson was a private one conducted by Miss Fredova. Miss Fredova was born Winifred Edwards and had received her training in London from Anna Pavlova. She was as slim as a sapling and always wore white like a trained nurse. She parted her dark hair in the center and drew it to the nape of her neck in glossy wings, Russian style. She was shod in low-heeled sandals. She taught standing erect as a guardsman, and beat time with a long pole. First she picked up a watering can and sprinkled water on the floor in a sunny corner by the barre. This she explained was so that we should not slip. Then she placed our hands on the barre and showed us how to turn out our feet ninety degrees from their normal walking stance into first position. Then she told us to *plier* or bend our knees deeply, keeping our heels as long as possible on the floor. I naturally stuck out behind. I found the pole placed rigidly against my spine. I naturally pressed forward on my insteps. Her leg and knee planted against my foot curbed this tendency. "I can't move," I said, laughing with winning helplessness.

"Don't talk," she said. "Down-ee, two-ee, three-ee, four-ee. Down the heels, don't rock on your feet."

At the end of ten minutes the sweat stuck in beads on my forehead. "May I sit down?" I asked.

"You must never sit during practice. It ruins the thigh muscles. If you sit down you may not continue with class." I of course would have submitted to a beating with whips rather than stop. I was taking the first steps into the promised land. The path might be thorny but it led straight to Paradise. "Down-ee, two-ee, three-ee, four-ee. *Nuca.* Give me this fourth position. Repeat the exercise."

So she began every lesson. So I have begun every practice period since. It is part of the inviolable ritual of ballet dancing. Every ballet student that has ever trained in the classic technique in any part of the world begins just this way, never any other. They were dreary exercises and I was very bad at them but these were the exercises that built Taglioni's leg. These repeated stretches and pulls gave Pavlova her magic foot and Legnani hers and Kchessinska hers. This was the very secret of how to dance, the tradition handed down from teacher to pupil for three hundred years. A king had patterned the style and named the steps, the king who built Versailles. Here was an ancient and enduring art whose technique stood like the rules of harmony. All other kinds of performance in our Western theater had faded or changed. What were movies to this? Or Broadway plays?

I, a complacent child, who had been flattered into believing I could do without what had gone before, now inherited the labor of centuries. I had come into my birthright. I was fourteen, and I had found my life's work. I felt superior to other adolescents as I stood beside the adults serene and strong, reassured by my vision.

I bent to the discipline. I learned to relax with my head between my knees when I felt sick or faint. I learned how to rest my insteps by lying on my back with my feet vertically up against the wall. I learned how to bind up my toes so that they would not bleed through the satin shoes. But I never sat down. I learned the first and all-important dictate of ballet dancing — never to miss the daily practice, hell or high water, sickness or health, never to miss the barre practice; to miss meals, sleep, rehearsals even but not the practice, not for one day ever under any circumstances, except on Sundays and during childbirth.

I seemed, however, to have little aptitude for the business. What had all this talk about God-given talent amounted to? It was like trying to wiggle my ears. I strained and strained. Nothing perceptible happened. A terrible sense of frustration drove me to striving with masochistic frenzy. Twice I fainted in class. My calves used to ache until tears stuck in my eyes. I learned every possible manipulation of the shoe to ease the aching tendons of my insteps. I used to get abominable stitches in my sides from attempting continuous jumps. But I never sat down. I learned to cool my forehead against the plaster of the walls. I licked the perspiration off from around my mouth. I breathed through my nose though my eyes bugged. But I did not sit and I did not stop.

Ballet technique is arbitrary and very difficult. It never becomes easy; it becomes possible. The effort involved in making a dancer's body is so long and relentless, in many instances so painful, the effort to maintain the technique so grueling that unless a certain satisfaction is derived from the disciplining and punishing, the pace could not be maintained. Most dancers are to an extent masochists. "What a good pain! What a profitable pain!" said Miss Fredova as she stretched her insteps in her two strong hands. "I have practiced for three hours. I am exhausted, and I feel wonderful."

My strongest impression of the Kosloff studio was, beside the sunlight on the floor and the white walls, the smell of sweat, the salty smell of clean sweat, the musty smell of old sweat on unwashed dresses, the smell of kitchen soap and sweat on the fresh dresses. Every dance studio smells of this — moist flesh, moist hair, hot glue in the shoes, hot socks and feet, and soap.

Paradoxically enough ballet dancing is designed to give the impression of lightness and ease. Nothing in classic dancing should be convulsive or tormented. Derived from the seventeeth- and eighteenth-century court dances the style is kingly, a series of harmonious and balanced postures linked by serene movement. The style involves a total defiance of gravity, and because this must perforce be an illusion, the effect is achieved first by an enormous strengthening of the legs and feet to produce great resilient jumps and second by a co-ordination of arms and head in a rhythm slower than the rhythm of the legs which have no choice but to take the weight of the body when the body falls. But the slow relaxed movement of head and arms gives the illusion of sustained flight, gives the sense of effortless ease. The lungs may be bursting, the heart pounding in the throat, sweat springing from every pore, but hands must float in repose, the head stir gently as though swooning in delight. The diaphragm must be lifted to expand the chest fully, proudly; the abdomen pulled in flat. The knees must be taut and flat to give the extended leg every inch of length. The leg must be turned outward forty-five degrees in the hip socket so that the side of the knee and the long unbroken line of the leg are presented to view and never the lax, droopy line of a bent knee. The leg must look like a sword. The foot arches to prolong the line of extension. The supporting foot turns out forty-five degrees to enhance the line of the supporting leg, to keep the hips even, and to ensure the broadest possible base for the support and balancing of the body.

It should always be remembered that the court, and therefore the first, ballet dances were performed by expert swordsmen and derive much of their style from fencing positions. The discipline embraces the whole deportment. The lifted foot springs to attention the minute it leaves the floor. The supporting foot endures all; the instep must never give way even when the whole weight of the body drops and grinds on the single slim arch. The legs can be held in their turned position by the great muscles across the buttocks only by pulling the buttocks in flat. The spine should be steady, the expression of the face noble, the face of a king to whom all things are possible. The eyebrows may not go up, the shoulders may not lift, the neck may not stiffen, nor the mouth open like a hooked fish.

The five classic positions and the basic arm postures and steps were named at the request of Louis XIV by his great ballet master, Pécourt, Lully's collaborator, codified, described and fixed in the regimen of daily exercise which has become almost ceremonial with time. Since then the technique has expanded and diversified but the fundamental steps and nomenclature remain unchanged. The "Royale" is still the faked beaten jump it was when Louis XIV, not as nimble in the legs as he would have liked to appear, failed to achieve a proper *entrechat quatre*.

The ideal ballet body is long limbed with a small compact torso This makes for beauty of line; the longer the arms and legs the more exciting the body line. The ideal ballet foot has a high taut instep and a wide stretch in the Achilles' tendon. This tendon is the spring on which a dancer pushes for his jump, the hinge on which he takes the shock of landing. If there is one tendon in a dancer's body more important than any other, it is this tendon. It is, I should say, the prerequisite for all great technique. When the heel does not stretch easily and softly like a cat's, as mine did not, almost to the point of malformation, the shock of running or jumping must be taken somewhere in the spine by sticking out behind, for instance, in a sitting posture after every jump. I seemed to be all rusty wire and safety pins. My torso was long with unusually broad hips, my legs and arms abnormally short, my hands and feet broad and short. I was besides fat. What I did not know was that I was constructed for endurance and that I developed through effort alone a capacity for outperforming far, far better technicians. Because I was built like a mustang, stocky, mettlesome and sturdy, I became a good jumper, growing special compensating muscles up the front of my shins for the lack of a helpful heel. But the long, cool, serene classic line was forever denied me.

And at first, of course, the compensations and adjustments were neither present nor indicated. Every dancer makes his own body. He is born only with certain physical tendencies. This making of a ballet leg takes approximately ten years and the initial stages are almost entirely discouraging, for even the best look awkward and paralyzed at the beginning.

My predicament was intensified by the fact that Mother and Father had no intention of permitting me to slight my other studies for this new enthusiasm. I was allowed one private lesson a week (forty-five minutes) and one class lesson (one hour). In between times I practiced at home alone, something no dancer, pupil or professional, ever does. One needs company to overcome the almost irresistible tendency to flag. One needs someone else's eye on awkward parts impossible to see. It is an unnatural and unprofitable strain for a child to practice without supervision. I practiced in Mother's bathroom where she had a little barre fitted for me. The floor was slippery and there was no mirror. And I hated to practice there. I flagellated myself into the daily grind. Mother thought I was overworking and forbade me to practice more than forty-five minutes. When I showed signs of resisting, she persuaded Kosloff to order me not to exceed this limit. All the other children practiced one hour a day in the studio and had a daily class lesson besides. They practically lived at the studio, practicing in the morning, taking lessons in the afternoon, sewing costumes and talking dancing in between times. Some of them even came back at night to practice alone. I cried myself to sleep because of the restraints imposed on me. Mother answered that dancing technique was not as important as education and health. We reached an impasse.

Why did I not simply disobey Mother? Because I cannot remember disobeying her in any single instance after the age of ten, never at any time. And because behind my mother stood my father, whom I loved with all my heart and whom I did not wish to flout.

Since I could not practice long, obviously I must practice harder. I strained and strained. Between the Monday lesson and the Thursday lesson, I developed and matured rigid bad habits. Every week I developed a new bad habit.

The plain truth is I was the worst pupil in the class. Having grown into adolescence feeling that I was remarkably gifted and destined to be great (I remember a friend asking Mother, "But do you want her to be a professional dancer?" and Mother's cool reply, "If she can be a Pavlova — not otherwise"), I now found I could not hold my own with any of the girls standing on the floor beside me. So I crept about at the rear of the group, found matters wrong with my shoes, with my knees, with my hair, resorted to any device to get away from the dreadful exposure.

Furthermore, the Kosloff method of teaching rather accentuated my dilemma. The accent was placed on force and duration instead of harmony. He was intent on disciplining the feet and legs, and paid almost no attention to the co-ordination of arms and facial expression. The girls grew as vigorous as Cossacks, leaping prodigiously, whirling without cease, flailing and thrashing as they went and contorting their necks and faces in a hideous effort to show the master how altogether hell-bent for beauty they were. The exercises he devised were little miracles of perverse difficulty, muscle-locking gut-busters, all of them. I have never since seen healthy girls faint in class, but in Kosloff's class they went down quite regularly and were dragged off with their heels bumping on the floor behind them. Kosloff barely stopped counting. He used to sit in a great armchair facing the room, stamping and roaring, whacking a cane in measure to the music. In the corner sat the man with the balalaika barely audible through the noise. All the girls adored the master and gladly fainted for him. It was Miss Fredova, however, who gave me my private lessons, quietly, patiently, kindly. Kosloff occasionally walked in, looked for a minute, said, "No juice, no juice. More *plié*. Do you know? More expression, more sowl," grinned suddenly with Tartar glee and lost interest. "Don't be discouraged," said the angel Fredova, "I wish though you could practice more regularly."

I was always late for class. We had a piano lesson before the dancing lesson and the traveling between required at least forty minutes and getting into practice clothes another ten. Mother allowed twenty minutes exactly from keyboard to barre and in three years she refused to adjust her timetable, always hoping that geography would somehow give way. As a consequence I always missed the preliminary warming-up exercises and started every class half through, cold and unprepared. I was not permitted ever to make the trip into town alone so I could not better the situation. Mother gave up two afternoons a week, a noteworthy sacrifice in a busy life, to driving us downtown. She never put off one class in three years, but she also was never on time.

Only once did I have a small bit of my share of success. On a single occasion Kosloff gave exercises in pantomime. He suddenly stopped the class and called me out from my position in the back of the room. I demonstrated the exercise to a hushed and watching group. I did, of course, the best I could, trembling a little. They applauded. Kosloff beamed on me. He told Uncle Cecil that I showed the finest talent for pantomime of any pupil he had ever taught. This remark was naturally not repeated to me until long after.

Ah but there was a glory in that room! Each day's class was important and a little frightening. When the master praised a pupil we shivered with envy and excitement. When he roared and denounced we blanched. When he made jokes we laughed although we rarely understood what he was saying — it nearly always had to do with teasing some wretch. When he talked about expression and "sowl" I, for one, wept. When he talked about fame, galas, "applows," and *réclame*, I slept poorly for nights after. We curtsied formally at the end of class. We were never late — that is, the others never were, I always was. When he talked of his triumphs with Diaghilev in Paris and how the pupils practice in Moscow with butter on the floor to make it harder, and how as a young man he could easily turn twenty pirouettes with a single push, we listened round-eyed, grabbing the chance to get our breaths before the next frantic series of jumps.

At Christmas there was a table covered with gifts, photographs for the first year pupils, gold pins for the second year, and pins with additional diamonds and wreaths and bars for the veterans. We were called out singly by name and given our gift. We then made a reverence, said "thank you" in Russian and retired. Kosloff kept open house on Christmas with magnificent Russian food and boundless Russian welcome.

There were books on a side table in the studio filled with pictures of the great ballerinas. We pored over them between classes. As

I stood shifting from one weary foot to the other trying to ease my cramped muscles, Miss Fredova used to tell about Legnani, the great Italian ballerina, who brought the *fouetté* pirouette to Russia — how a ruble used to be placed on the floor and a circle drawn around it — how she placed the toe of her left foot in this mark and then performed sixty-four consecutive *fouetté* pirouettes, stopping in perfect fifth position, the toe of her left foot exactly in the ruble mark; how her turnout was so extraordinary that she could balance a glass of wine on the flat of her instep as she revolved in second position — how her balance was so peerless that she could perform a complete adage, thirty-two measures long, standing in the middle of the floor on one point without support of any sort. "Will I be able to do this?" I asked breathlessly. "I doubt if you will be that good," she said smiling. "Oh," I sighed with deep disappointment, not realizing that no one else has ever been able to duplicate this feat, not realizing that it is unlikely indeed that Legnani herself performed it. But the legend spurred me on. "*Nuca*," said Miss Fredova, "give me this one pirouette and stop in some recognizable position."

My weeks were divided into two sections, the three days I prepared for the class lesson, and the three days I prepared for the private lesson. I woke on Monday saying happily, "Today I have a lesson, today I need not practice alone." I woke most blissfully on Thursday saying, "Today I have a lesson with Miss Fredova." Friday entailed disappointment since it introduced a whole week before the next private lesson. Three times during the first winter, Miss Fredova said "very good" and I recorded the event duly in my diary. On those nights I drove home with a singing heart and stood in the bedroom in the dark gripping the edge of my desk in excitement, so in love with dancing, so in love with her. "Oh God," I prayed, "let me be like her. Let me be a fine dancer." I took to wearing sandals because she did, even to parties, and when my schoolmates teased, I scoffed at their fashionably distorted toes and said proudly, "I have a use for *my* feet."

My well-filled curriculum — classes, homework, tennis, piano, editing — was ordered with just one thought: to make room for the dance practice. I rose at six-thirty and I studied and practiced at breakneck concentration until six in the evening when I was at last free to put on dancing dress and walk — to Mother's bathroom.

All through the lonely, drab exercises beside Mother's tub, without music or beat, proper floor or mirror, I had the joy of looking forward to dinner with Father, to hearing him talk about his scenarios and what was going on at the studio. Sometimes he talked about music and literature. Once he said he thought I was an artist. Sometimes after dinner he sang and I accompanied him. These evenings my cup ran over. I went to bed early planning next day's practice, praying to do better in class. And as I lay waiting for sleep, breathing in the moist garden smells with my fox terrier slowly pressing me from the comfortable center of the bed, I used to dream about dancing on the stage with Pavlova, dancing until I dropped in a faint at her feet so that she would notice me and say, "That girl has talent."

CHAPTER 8

Ballet and Sex

MY FATHER was quite aware of my infatuation but preferred to take no notice of it whatever. The mania which took possession of his daughter was not unique. No one could expect him, however, to understand it well or sympathize. The case was not by any means a simple one, dealing merely with choice of vocation. A kind of madness is involved. When pubescent girls have any inclination toward dancing at all, they are fairly driven by the frenzy. Indeed, nearly every woman has at some time known the desire to perform in public where people could see her, and it has usually been external circumstances that have prevented her doing so. Dancing appeals more strongly to women than to men; among its practitioners the expert women far outnumber the expert men. The audiences are largely female. Pavlova's effect on the women in her audience was to a recognized degree hypnotic.

The reasons for this are not hard to understand. Barring sport, which offers a minimal emotional outlet, it is the one physical performance possible to women that does not carry with it either moral responsibility or physical hazard. It constitutes a true recapturing of pagan freedom and childish play. It can be even a complete although unconscious substitute for physical love, and in the lives of the greatest dancers it usually assumes this function.

Ballet dancing particularly has an appeal to Western women, not because of the subject matter, I should imagine, nor the lavishness of production, the flowers, the dressed-up audiences and star system, although opulence is always seductive. Its power and appeal lie rather, I believe, in the actual quality of technique.

Ballet technique as opposed to the more modern dancing and even folk forms is less natural, if one can use such a word in relation to any art code, more arbitrary, more stylized, more impersonal. The body has been disciplined to look unlike a human body. It has taken on the elements of abstract design and on the surface at first seems to be used without regard to sex or emotional experience. Yet it must remain a body and can never be anything else. It therefore represents the body as we wish it were, not one of our bodies well-used, but a dream body liberated from trouble. It is the epitome of all the elements we consider most attractive — lightness, fleetness, strength, ease and, above all, fulfillment. Every joint and sinew is pulled long, the arms are wide and free, the foot arched in the utmost spasm of exaltation, the spine taut; from head to toe the body is one strong, positive assertion. In this way it constitutes probably the most erotic form of dancing known to us. But it is an appeal hidden and indirect under its impersonality and is, therefore, inoffensive to our puritanism. The elongated, erect, strong, vital line is music to our spirits, honey to our senses and God knows what to our subconscious.

I can well imagine that ballet dancing would not have much appeal to people of other cultures — the stretching up and out, the liberating jump, the racing over and away from the earth, is the western European expression. Flight, freedom, the spring into the air are our characteristics. With head lifted, we leap and race. The Oriental caresses and droops, turned inward, on one spot. Theirs is a dance of inner pattern and speaks of curtailed living and the search for hidden life. They've had no space for thousands of years; we've had aplenty.

André Levinson in his book on Argentina [1] has some extremely interesting comments to make on this subject. He indicates exactly how the two forms met and fused, exactly where the cultures

[1] *Paris Editions des Chroniques du Jour,* 1928.

clashed: in Spain — "the curves which swell and undulate in an internal rhythm, the rotating hips and the shielding, covering arms," represent the Oriental strain. The erect carriage of the spine, the head, the free use of the knees, the leaping, stamping feet — the European. He continues, "Whether at a social ball or on the stage, the Western dancer seeks a fashion that will permit motion to the arms and legs. The ballet-dancer has adopted the décolleté-bodice that leaves shoulders and arms uncovered, while the tulle flounces about the waist, so to speak, a mere abstraction of a skirt, do not in the least interfere with the action of the legs. The almeh will leave the abdomen uncovered, but prefers to veil the shoulders, the breast and face. The Spanish dancer tends to swathe herself. Over the low-cut neck of her bodice, she loves to throw a fringed scarf. She accentuates the mystery of her body. In this connection, it should be remarked in passing that what one might almost term the classic dancer, is purely functional, serving to facilitate the mechanism of her art. Hence its non-sexual appeal."

We have come to consider the stylized ballet figure with the exposed legs and the tutu as an abstraction of woman and not a particular woman — as long as she never wore garments familiar to everyday life. It was Antony Tudor who first put his women in long dresses, the Edwardian dresses his mother wore (*Lilac Garden* — 1936). The effect was startling and a real shock to the imagination. The audience was called upon to accept the balletic gesture as a form of simple dramatic communication. It was also asked to watch women who looked like their mothers and aunts kicking over their heads or wrapping their legs around men's bodies. The beauty of gesture cauterized the connotations at first, it seemed, but soon their full significance became apparent. We had been, we discovered, speaking quite freely in gesture for a long time on subjects that were barred from the language.

It matters not a jot what the classic dancer wears or leaves off, so deeply imbued with sexuality is the movement itself. The dancer need not be a beautiful woman; need not rely on the slightest personal coquetry — must not, in fact. What she is doing is the *thing* itself, not the reflection or indication through an individual personality. I expect to be disagreed with violently. This idea will be repugnant to anyone who has not danced.

Furthermore, there are very definite sexual etiquettes about what is permitted or not permitted. Women may use points — men not — and this is not entirely derived from the fact that they might hurt their feet because of the greater weight on the foot knuckles. The roles in an adage may not be reversed, not certainly because of relative strength but because it would not be seemly, nor may the solos, although technically in many instances they could be. All this talk about abstract design is invalid; we are always dealing with human bodies. No, the sexual connotations are there, but as Levinson speaks of Argentina, "Not the total sensation, in its brutal or troubling materialism, but the essence of that sensation, its spiritual perfume." And this is why so many women choose dancing instead of love.

Consider for a moment how the body of a dancer attaches to itself the attributes of love. It becomes the center of attention; it is the symbol of all that is most beautiful and powerful in physical life. Before the great sensitized and impersonal mass which is her audience the woman appears at her absolute best, infinitely desirable. She is beloved. She is cherished. But never at any moment is she threatened. Nothing this great impersonal lover can do or feel will compromise her physically. Her privacy can never be usurped. Free as a nymph with no earthy spoiling of her fresh strength, she will possess and be possessed by the integrated audience, fused and informed by her beauty into cohesive sympathy. She need not wait nor attend, she herself controls these great unions. She is the motivating force. She acts. The very physical stresses, the strengthening and bracing and tautening of her back and leg supply such a sense of driving power as to give her the illusion of male potency. The plunging leg, the arched, vital foot, the delicate mechanism of equilibrium and balancing with their attendant hypnotic reflection in the audience suspend her in a state of continuing power.

But she pays for this omnipotent duality dearly. The price is unflagging lifelong effort. She must abandon forever her natural female passivity. She is forced to relinquish her unique womanly power: her grasp of reality. She is rooted in air. The fruit of her womb is gestures. Dedicating her life to her own body, she sacrifices the reality of her children's bodies and in effect that of her husband's. Very few great dancers marry well. Literally and profoundly they wed their work.

There is a further simple economic reason for this. Dancing is by all odds the worst paid of the arts. Except in those countries where ballet is endowed by the state and the performer can be assured of a reasonably secure life, marriage for either the man or the woman is impractical. The life besides is exhausting, and the exigencies of touring, rehearsing and practicing make domesticity difficult. The dancers are always at the end of their strength. It is obvious, then, that anyone who deliberately chooses this profession feels herself by nature segregated from normal living and aloof from the group pattern. Concert or ballet dancing as opposed to Broadway or moving picture dancing tends in this country to attract the misfits both male and female.

Very few women dancers are homosexuals. They become, rather, a kind of neuter and lead a skimpy and incomplete sexual life — nearly all the great ones develop physiological aberrations of some sort and few risk motherhood, which must be understandable enough. Any healthy woman can bear children — dancers in fact much more easily than the rest — but the rearing of a child cuts into rehearsal time like nothing else I can mention.

I have written about women because from my own experience I know something of their psychological involvements. I know less about men. I suspect their motives in choosing dancing as a career to be quite different. But I do not know. Homosexuality was present but never prevalent in the European state-endowed theaters, and in Broadway musical shows. Wherever, in short, it has been possible to have a dance career at once commercially successful and socially acceptable men with the more usual inclinations toward family and security have functioned happily. There was nothing effeminate about the great hoofers of our theater and they would have been astonished at the suggestion. Let us hope that with the growth of opportunity and recognition of dancing in this country, more men will join the profession, as they would any other, without qualm or taint, and with hope for solid rewards on which to build their lives.

Women are seldom conscious of the sexual choice they make, and most particularly they are unaware at the time of the initial dedication in their early adolescence. They are apt to consider themselves the elect. Their friends and families, however, are more likely to look upon them as just queer.

It has long been a subject of some remark that the arts attract the curious, the crotchety and the quirked. But dancing seems to be practiced largely by the downright perverted and deranged. This is an odd condition for the oldest, the most virile and the most potent of the arts to have fallen to. Other arts may have had from time to time some strange champions but they have never at any one period been given over mainly into the keeping of fanatical women and emasculated men. In all primitive societies dancing is the chief concern of the warriors and the priests. Women are rarely permitted to participate and then only in a subsidiary fashion. What has happened?

The change, a basic curtailment of function, can be traced largely to the resistant attitude of the Christian Church. For one thousand years there has been (with a few trivial exceptions) no dancing in the Christian religion and it is the only great religion that has had none. It is obvious why — a religion that is based on the mortification of the flesh is not going to find the flesh and its attendant heats a suitable medium for expression. We owe to the Church our architecture, painting, music. It is the Church which developed polyphonic harmony together with the methods of notation, using five hundred years and the largest group of endowed scholars that have ever been put at a single task. The Church had need of music; it had no need of dancing. Quite the contrary. The rhythms of the

human body are a very different matter from a plaster wall or a
tonal scale. After a few clerical experiments in early medieval
times, it repudiated all manifestations entirely for a while and then,
when the traces of pagan exuberance were castigated forever, gave
its sanction only to the parlor forms, outside the cloister and only
as a social safety valve. Dancing, together with fancy eating and
dressing up in ribbons, became the accepted release for animal
spirits. It was also used as a minor aid in courtship. Naturally
it failed to develop as an art and gradually came to be reduced to
the unconscious expression of a folk form. Unlike all other arts
it lacked a recording medium and was therefore given no serious
recognition. It never occurred to men of intellect to express themselves through dancing except, of course, biologically. The women
of intellect were at this time in the kitchen and nursery. No absolutely first-class mind, on a par, let us say, with Shakespeare, Goethe
or Beethoven, has ever concerned itself with the business.

In the sixteenth century, after five hundred years of suppression,
a professional theater free of church influence revived; by that time
dancing had lost pace with its sister arts and could not be and
was not considered of equal importance with music or painting. It
was used at court or on the stage merely as trimming. But there
again it fared badly. The great architects and painters played at
scene designing. Dancing was the cult of the royal amateur, the
mountebank and the acrobat.

At the beginning of the eighteenth century, the stage had developed a separate class of performers, professionals trained to the
business, expert and barred from society by every kind of distinction. Their life was erratic, financially unstable, and morally capricious, and from the less acceptable of these ranks were drawn
the dancers. The Romantic movement found its dance expressions
in a light, incorporeal, fragile, aerial style that was eminently more
suitable to women than to men. During the nineteenth century
dancing became plainly and simply a woman's medium. Men
became the women's servants, lifting, supporting, carrying, bearing and catching. When granted a few minutes to themselves on a

stage, they could think of nothing better to do as a match for their bodyless partners than outfloat, outhover, outfly them. A man's business is not constantly floating away from the earth. It is getting down to work on it. Small wonder that a man of any health or force found nothing responsive in a technique that denied all he found lusty and good in life. His religion ignored it. It was without history or tradition. The practices he saw and the practitioners did not arouse his admiration. He let it alone.

Women were welcome to try their hand because, simply, men had not sufficient liking for the job to bar them away. Choreography is probably the only field where women have run up against no male resentment, and I think it is no accident that the great dance revolutionaries have been largely women.

The nineteenth-century ballet girl, however, found herself in something of a quandary. She had wandered a long way from dances of passion and purpose. She was being a fairy these days — once up in the air there was nothing to do but stay there or come down. Finding the vantage point flattering to her legs, she stayed up. But her reasons ceased to be spiritual. And while the short skirt shortened and the extended leg lifted, the motivating ideas grew plainer and uglier. During the golden era of the Opéra the terms "ballet dancer" and "courtesan" were synonymous.

At the end of a thousand years of growing refinements and ceaseless effort, dancing had completed its course from altar to gutter.[2]

My father, like all educated men, considered dancing at best ex-

---

[2] "She is a wonderful artist; but there is something unutterably sad to me in the contemplation of such a career. The blending in most unnatural union of the elements of degradation and moral misery with such exquisite perceptions of beauty, grace, and refinement, produces the impression of a sort of monstrosity, a deformity of the whole higher nature, which fills one with poignant compassion and regret. Poor, fair, admired, despised, flattered, forlorn souls! Mrs. Grote . . . had undertaken, under some singular impulse of mistaken enthusiasm, to make what she called 'an honest woman' of the celebrated dancer, Fanny Elssler, and to introduce her into London society — neither of them very attainable results, even for as valiant and enterprising a woman as Mrs. Grote." — Fanny Kemble on Fanny Elssler — *Records of Later Life*, 1882,

hibitionistic acrobatics, and certainly a field that offered neither intellectual nor spiritual challenge ("serious dancing is a contradiction in terms," said Hogarth). Worse, the woman dancer entered a field long and closely associated with prostitution. Men did not want their women dancing publicly: they recognized in the performance an unconscious rivalry. Any dancer, man or woman, embraced a life that paid badly and guaranteed nothing. It was a serious business to see a daughter give herself to these lifelong risks. Had I been a son he would have marched me off to a doctor. And rightly. The young man who challenges the monumental taboo on this subject deliberately casts himself outside the security of our cultural and social sympathies. In setting his heart against dancing, my father was only following the pattern of all thoughtful and fastidious men for the past two thousand years.

Today all the factors still stand. But I think husbands and fathers have perhaps not so much to say about what their women do. If the girls continue to dance, and I think they will, there will have to be searching readjustments in the lives of all concerned.

CHAPTER 9

The Swan

POP WAS TOO SMART to forbid me outright to continue with my chosen work. He knew that direct frontal attack would only serve to crystallize my determination; he bored from within. He sought to make me doubt the validity of the art itself. And I listened to him in anguish because he was an artist, in my eyes — a genius. He counted on this deference. He refused to go to my classes, to go to any performance of dancers, to read about them or look at pictures. At mention of any incident in the ballet school and the daily doings there, ice would form on his mouth and he would sit silently sipping his cocktail until the subject had been dropped.

Occasionally we settled right down and talked problems through. One night in his study with brandy in one hand and a cigar in the other, he asked quietly, "Do you honestly think, my daughter, that dancing has progressed since the time of the Greeks?"

"No," I replied snappily. "Do you think you write any better than Euripides?" That ought to hold him, I figured.

He looked at me long and slow. "No, my dear," he said, "but we have Euripides's plays. They have lasted. A dancer ceases to exist the minute she sits down."

As Father spoke I understood death for the first time. I was a child of fourteen but I realized with melancholy that oblivion would be my collaborator no matter how fine my work. Mankind had never developed a reliable way of recording dances. Well — so much the worse for me. I was born a dancer.

Those days when I was called upon to dance in school plays I froze with inhibition. What if I should reveal myself as not truly great? I never showed off any more for Mother's guests. Showing-off also meant exposing. I sought refuge in study and daydreaming, and unconsciously all my private extracurricular resources led to the unnamable goal.

Uncle Cecil had a fine reference library in which he gave me permission to browse whenever I liked. So on Saturday afternoons when I was free from study, I used to walk up through the beautiful gardens and sit in the large room with the mullioned windows among his trophies, suits of armor and knives, silverwork, French battle flags, the Crown of Thorns on a red velvet pillow, and pore over the extraordinary volumes of old prints — Shakespeare, Doré — the entire portrait gallery of Versailles. How quiet and enriching those afternoons were to me! Hollywood lay below sparkling, here and there a window reflecting fire in the late day, the Italian cypress blackening in the lucent air. The garden suddenly intensified as it always does before dark, all the odors breathing out more poignantly with anticipatory pungent chill exhaling from the leaves, the great sky deepening and streaming with banners and banks of fire. And all these, the Italian garden, the Renaissance sky, the glint on the armor and the warm radiance cast by the blood-red curtains and the bowls of Uncle Cecil's dark roses, as I sat bowed over the books attempting to learn and memorize forever every detail of every costume, filled me with an enormous sense of excitement and latent power. I felt in truth I should amount to very much. The high excitements of the Renaissance were present again — whom might I not meet at the turn of the road or come upon standing in the garden as I went home through the dew? What had the great nights following upon other great baroque sunsets meant to these men and women under my hands? What pomp? What daring? What clashing of lives? What might the night mean to me who was alive, not dead, and very young and ready?

The night meant supper, trigonometry and bed at nine o'clock. Or just possibly a corner movie with Margaret and Rita, the house-maid, in attendance.

About this time, Anna Pavlova came back. I heard of the return with a mixture of excitement and dread. What if she was not as I remembered her? What if I looked at her and saw her as Father would see her? I knew a great deal more about technique now; I would look at her with a critical eye.

Mr. Kosloff, Miss Fredova and the leading girls of the studio went on opening night. I was not permitted to go, of course, until the matinee. "Watch carefully," I said to the girls after class. "Tell me everything. Every little detail." And the next time when I was in the studio I fairly gasped my curiosity, "How was she?"

Miss Fredova spoke with moderation. "Well, of course, there is only one Anna Pavlova. She is very graceful and lovely, but there is something not quite in order with her knees. And the joint of her right foot has enlarged with all this touring. Mr. Kosloff was very sorry to see that."

"Does she show signs of growing older?"

"Oh my, yes, how could it be otherwise?"

"She does not dance so perfectly as she used to?"

"Oh my goodness, no. She probably has not had the time to practice her barre carefully every day. And then — she is getting older. Still, she is very lovely."

My heart felt like iron.

We were excused from school for the Thursday afternoon matinee. I ate scarcely any lunch. I saw to it that we were in our seats twenty minutes before the curtain rose, Mother's first experience of the kind. The ballet was *Autumn Leaves* composed by Madame herself to music by Chopin. The curtain went up on a park scene. Two slim girls ran out chased by the autumn wind in a blue wig, and were whirled to the floor. Volinine played a poet with his left foot pointed behind and his right well turned out, showing that he was saddened by the indifference of his lady love who was paying him no mind in *demi contretemps* and *jetés battus*. He grew more and more disconsolate and finally sank on a bench in a *fondu*. This was plain ham, but I turned to Mother with glistening eyes. "It's wonderful, isn't it?"

"Hmm," said Mother. I waited.

She came on. What did she do? Does it matter? She was gone. The audience stirred. She was back and dancing. Right there in front of me in flesh and nerve. Oh, holy life! How could I have doubted her? She changed us while we sat there that Thursday afternoon; she made us less daily. I don't know what she did. I know and remember what she meant. The upturned face, the waiting listening face, the exposed heart, the shared rapture.

A friend touched my shoulder. "Would you like to meet her? I know her well." Mother answered for me. I was unable to speak. "She would. Yes." We filed backstage. I remember the dress I wore, dark blue silk taffeta, my first silk dress. I had a little blue hat to match with petals that curled up against the crown. My sister was an exact replica two sizes smaller. Madame had finished the program with a Russian dance. She stood in full *Boyarina* costume in the dressing room talking to friends. She spoke in light, twittering sounds and her dark eyes flashed incessantly with enormous alertness and inner excitement. Her clawlike hands played nervously with the pearls at her throat. They were the veined hands of an old woman or of an instrumentalist. I noticed her insteps jutting up under the straps of her buttoned slippers. The rocky arch was like a bird claw. There seemed to be no flesh on the foot; it was all bone and tendon. The toe was clubby, broadened and coarse. Her little thin shoulders lifted from the gathered peasant blouse. What was gross had been burnt and wasted off her. She had kept no part of her body that was not useful to her art, and there was about her the tragic aura of absolute decision. The high pale brow, her front against the world, the somber eyes, the mobile lips shut with humorous tolerance on God knows what tumult and violence caged within the little skull, marked her as one apart. She had the fascination of a martyr. We drew aside and looked at her with both reverence and relief, smug in our own freedom. Possibly I am reading back into her face the wisdom of my own bitterness learned later. Possibly as a girl I saw only the glory. But I think not. I knew enough to understand the cost of the beauty she achieved and to be terrified at the price.

"This is Kosloff's best pupil," said my friend, pushing me forward. An exaggeration, of course, but I was incapable of speech. Kosloff had undoubtedly presented his own candidate nights before.

"Ah! Brava! Brava!" chirped Madame. "Would you like some flowers?" She tore a handful of pink carnations and cherry blossoms from a basket that had just been handed to her across the footlights. Then she leaned down and kissed me. Anna Pavlova kissed me.

I wept.

Someone led me kindly from the room, maybe Mother. Someone stood beside me and lent me a pocket handkerchief while I fought to regain control of myself among the hurrying stagehands. Someone helped me into the car and asked no questions. I was weeping silently by this time.

"Well," said Margaret, "I must say I don't see what there is to cry about."

"Be quiet!" said Mother with the greatest severity I had ever heard her use in addressing my little sister.

When we reached home I ran through the garden without stopping to take off my coat and threw myself on the ground under the orchard trees.

O Father in Heaven make me worthy!

I kept the flowers she gave me for ten years in a box, shaming myself at last into throwing the little mummies away. Dear Madame, she kissed all the little girls that were brought backstage to her, gave them all flowers and altered their lives. One out of every dozen dancers of my generation has confessed to the same experience. This does not make it any less impressive — more so, I should say. She was an apostle. She had the power of conversion. That it may have come in time to seem a touch routine to members of her company does not mitigate the miracle. The recipients bear stigmata.

She returned again three years later, her last tour. By this time, my taste and judgment were forming. I looked with a professional eye. She had begun to develop real crotchets and mannerisms. For example, she held each pose until she got applause like a circus performer. It was this abominable trick that led one of our ablest critics to call her an acrobat. She roughhoused and savaged the music for any effect she wished. And the choreography — oh God, the choreography! Her own inventions, *California Poppy, Autumn Leaves, Blue Danube Waltz,* were probably the silliest and most tasteless items I have ever seen. She was incapable of creative imagination. And in the dances tailored for her, the Gavotte, *Coquetteries of Columbine, Don Quixote, Dragonfly,* she made use over and over again of a barren string of five ballet steps. I sat shocked. But then, after folding the orange silk petals of the poppy about her head and flopping over sideways to simulate sleep, she began to take bows and therewith performed a theatrical miracle. While bowing, not while dancing, she built a paltry hand to bravos and calls. She was known for this enchanted teasing; no one else has ever approached her technique in curtain calls. The applause never diminished. It rose instead to climactic screaming. The applause was purely for her, not so much for what she did. At the end of three bows, the audience had fallen in love.

Among these idiot pieces were three important works — *The Bacchanal, The Swan,* and *The Indian Suite,* the first choreography of an eighteen-year-old Hindu named Uday Shankar. Everyone has seen pictures of her in *The Bacchanal,* composed in 1904 by Fokine. She wore her hair fuzzed out in black curls, grapes over the ears, and a white tunic flecked with red. Her partner's arm about her, she entered skipping, the knees working like pistons to the chest and the feet driving through the earth. The dancers carried over their heads a scarlet veil, and the man held a large bunch of red paper roses with which he pelted her. Occasionally, she chewed a paper rose with her teeth. Corn? Thunder and fire. The working knees, the feet tearing the earth, the wild glance, the flamelike thrust and contraction of her back, the abandoned arms, her body broken and contorted on his thigh, the exhausted flame against the earth as he stood over her, the head moving, moving, in restless joy, the hands torn, stretching, fainting, unresting. Oh ancient ecstasy, passion beyond promise!

She danced *The Dying Swan*. Everyone has danced *The Swan*. What was it? A series of *pas de bourrées* around and around the stage with flutterings and undulations of the arms interspersed with broken staggers until the final collapse and folding away. Nothing else. Fokine composed it in half an hour for a charity performance, and it is probably the most famous solo in the history of dancing. When she trembled onto the stage it was a death agony, the voice in the dark, the final anonymous cry against annihilation. And when she lay doubled up and the last shudder passed through feathers and broken bones, drawing as an afterbeat when all was finished the shivering inert hand across her face in a gesture of final decency, everyone sat stricken. Death was upon each of us.

Death came to Anna Pavlova in 1931, when she was fifty. She had not stopped touring for a single season. Her knees had sustained some damage, but she would not rest, and she was in a state of exhaustion when the train that was carrying her to Holland was wrecked. She ran out into the snow in her nightgown and insisted on helping the wounded. When she reached The Hague she had double pneumonia. Her last spoken words were, "Get the *Swan* dress ready."

Standing on Ninth Avenue under the El, I saw the headlines on the front page of the *New York Times*. It did not seem possible. She was in essence the denial of death. My own life was rooted to her in a deep spiritual sense and had been during the whole of my growing up. It mattered not that I had only spoken to her once and that my work lay in a different direction. She was the vision and the impulse and the goal.

Her death touched off a world-wide hysteria among adolescent girls that is without precedent. Several young dancers identified themselves so completely with the star as to believe in fact that her soul had transmigrated into their own bodies. Each one felt that she had got the original or genuine soul and looked upon the other claimants as impostors. One poor girl went into a decline, shut herself in her room and refused to eat. She finally pressed confusion to the point where she failed to note the legal difference between Pavlova's dances and her own and wound up in a Paris law court with Madame's exceedingly angry husband and a dozen of Madame's indignant colleagues pointing it out. The Paris press had a bean feast.

Nor was this odd mania confined to mere fools. Alicia Markova, one of our two greatest living classic dancers, believes that Pavlova's spirit takes possession of her body when she dances and has said so many times, and despite the merciless teasing of her colleagues — "The spirit is doing fine tonight, eh, Alicia?" — persists in the belief and draws reaffirmation and comfort from it.

"It is doing fine, isn't it?" she says with perfect sweetness, flirts out her tutu and runs back on stage to dance peerlessly.

Pavlova's ashes were laid in the Golder's Green cemetery near her home, Ivy House, Hampstead Heath. All the glory of the last great Imperial days stood by. Karsavina was there, Lopokova, Massine.

But also in New York, in Los Angeles, in Paris, Berlin, Rome, San Francisco, wherever there was a Russian Orthodox Church, the dancers gathered, those that knew her and many more that didn't. I went in New York and all the dancers of the city were there. My mother came. She said she wished to, that she owed her a debt of many hours of joy. We stood. The Russians held lighted candles; the choir chanted with a high tonal insistency that wore down like rain on rock. The priest passed in and out of his painted, holy screens. A friend leaned to me. "They are singing," she whispered. "Receive the soul of Anna. Cherish our Anna. Bless and protect Anna." But I put my handkerchief to my mouth and heard the drums and the beating of feet and the cries she gave as she leaped. At the conclusion of the service, Fokine as senior friend, colleague, and Russian, received our condolences. He knew very few of us. We walked up silently, strangers, and shook his hand. His wife, Vera Fokina, in black from head to foot with sweeping veils, stood beside him.

We went out into the day. Wherever Pavlova had passed, hearts changed, flames sprang in the grass and girls ran out to a strange, wild, ancient dedication.

CHAPTER 10

Adolescence

ANYTHING CAN HAPPEN in adolescence. It is always a risky time. Ugly ducklings sometimes change into swans. The reverse is equally possible. The best-brought-up child is taken over by powers as divorced from daily habits as earthquake. And the important point is that what happens now is definitive, physically speaking. Up to this moment there has been margin for correction. Up to this moment it didn't really matter what went on inside your mouth, on the front of your skull, or down the length of your skeleton. After sixteen — this is it — for life. The chances are good you won't like it. I didn't.

I had been a pretty child. My nose was small and pert, my skin white. I was skinny, spider-legged and quick. I found myself suddenly imprisoned in someone else's body, heavy, deep-bosomed, large-hipped. My skin went muddy and on my face there developed seemingly overnight a large hooked nose, my father's nose. "Roman," my mother called it. "Aristocratic," the family said. "Full of character," people have told me since. But it would fool no girl. It was ugly. And it was mine for life. From that unmarked day when as a narcissistic youngster I looked in a mirror and realized I was not going to be a beautiful woman, I gave up caring how I looked — or thought I did. Except in costume.

I had Titian curly hair, but this was the time when girls wore their hair in fan-shape do's and mine wouldn't stay flat. The year following they shaved their heads like men. Though my figure was large it was good, but this was not the sweater era; girls were breaking their breasts deliberately with straps and tight flat brassières. The boyish figure was the ideal, probably the most decadent fashion in the history of women's dress. I received an anonymous note at school suggesting I wear tighter underclothing. It was couched in French, in the interest of delicacy. I did not get over that note in a hurry.

I considered my body a shame, a trap and a betrayal. But I could break it. I was a dancer.

Mother continued her losing battle to bring me up as a normal girl, and boys seemed indicated. I was juxtaposed to three or four pimply youths from the Hollywood High. It was my practice to challenge boys immediately to a trial of strength on the tennis court, beat the hell out of them and then dismiss them. They were never asked back. Indeed they seldom wanted to come. How I envied my sister, who hung on the telephone, mistress of the wisecrack and the ready laugh, talking nonsense for half hours at a time, while smoldering adolescents implored her to let them take her to the movies! She had serious suitors at eleven, and flowers and escorts right through her teens. She had become, it may seem redundant to add, an extremely pretty girl with a great sense of personal chic. Her complexion was a legend even in adolescence. At fifteen I began to fill the position of chaperone. No hanky-panky was possible in my presence and everyone knew it.

Mother signed me up for the Junior Cotillion and forced me to go. I used to enter the cotillion room clad in a pink or flowered crepe de Chine dress made by her, a little sash tying my precocious torso in two like a sack, a frill at my neck and frills at my elbow, pink silk socks and sandals (all the other girls wore taffeta frocks and silver cloth slippers with pointed toes). My hair was arranged by Mother in a nest of curls and crowned by a laurel wreath. How I hated my hair! All the excitement of putting it up was canceled out by the visual result. Mother elected to arrange it before every party and reserved time in her day to do this while I sat before the

glass sinking into deeper and deeper melancholy. Great tears stuck
in my eyes. My mouth grew sour with rage and disappointment.
I knew I would never look like the others. Then jabbing the final
pin into place with last-ditch conviction and remarking that I was
unco-operative and ungrateful, she would kiss me and dispatch me
to an evening of enchantment.

I always bobbed a curtsy when I met my partners until requested
to stop. They used to break into sweats of embarrassment. I was,
by general consensus, a perfectly rotten dancer, pointing my toes
and performing little variations on the basic shuffling that completely unnerved my doggedly pushing escort. I also snapped my
head smartly on every turn as one does in pirouettes. Indeed I responded to every musical suggestion so enthusiastically and vari-
ously as to take the boy off guard and leave him with no plan. He
generally suggested lemonade and talk. I began to talk.

"The music is excellent tonight. Don't you think?"

"Gee — yes!"

"The floor's good."

"Sure."

Pause.

"Do you play tennis?"

"A little."

"Oh — " Pause.

"Do you like music?"

"You mean what they're playing now — 'I'm Always Chasing
Rainbows'?"

"No, real music."

"Gee, I don't know much about that stuff."

Pause.

Very slowly — "I see."

I tried again.

"What grade are you in?"

"First year high."

"Oh, I'm finishing. I thought you were older."

"I guess I'm not bright like you."

I sat out alone as many as thirteen or fourteen dances in a row. I sat with that alert indifferent air of one who has too much on her mind of interest and charm to notice that she is bleeding to death at the heart. I held my head very high and turned it vigorously with an exaggerated interest in every single thing that was in no way connected with the stag line. I told myself with somber pride that when I was a great dancer with all the capitals of Europe at my feet, they would be very surprised indeed to remember they had passed me up. Very surprised. I used to go outside and look at the night sky and the line of hills against the stars and tell myself that these boys and girls never in their lives could know the deep emotions I felt. The next day I always practiced like a maniac.

Still, I was not unhappy. On the contrary I got through adolescence without a pang. I postponed it.

I lived in a gay bustling exciting household. There was never a minute when something entertaining or provocative was not going on. Our house at this time was a great old-fashioned rambling affair set in five acres of garden directly on Hollywood Boulevard. The garden was the core of Mother's heart. We had the largest collection of bulbs in Southern California. Every Easter we filled clothesbaskets of white iris for our church. In July the agapanthus stood six deep in solid borders the length of the driveway and the whole space was redolent with hot lavender, broom and amaryllis and the wonderful swooning smell of the camphor trees. We had an English spring that bloomed nowhere else on our side of the Rocky Mountains, hawthorn, primroses, bluebells, violets, narcissus, grape-hyacinth, apple, quince, cherry. Many a homesick Englishman has stood silent before those beds until Mother led him in to tea.

When my mother lay dying years later, I sat by her bedside and tried to recall the plants name by name as we traversed the paths in memory. "We didn't really use the garden enough," she whispered sadly.

Up and down the garden paths ran seven wire-haired fox terriers neurotic and shrill-voiced. They killed all the gophers, birds and neighbors' cats they possibly could, noisily. They took exception to every motorcycle and all the little boys who used to skate on the outside, rattling sticks against the wire fence. They also disliked Father's tennis and had to be locked in the house whenever he played, whence they tried to hurl themselves out windows. It was my job to keep them quiet. This proved difficult while practicing.

Besides dogs, the house was always full of people, friends for tea, Mother's Tuesday walking club, the frequent Single-Taxers and various aides in her plans to alter the state constitution. Each community project in Hollywood drifted through our parlor — the Bowl, the Woman's Club, the Studio Club, the Assistance League, Hospital Benefits, the Community Theater. Every out-of-luck artist and writer rang the bell to find Mother exactly what she was purported to be, gullible and kind. Our halls were hideous with the water colors of brokenhearted old men. Mother brought home every visiting lecturer of note to tea and a fire or tea and a garden. I passed it all by and went up to study or practice alone in her bathroom. She always caught me en route and begged me to stop, reminding me that I had practiced yesterday and might practice again tomorrow but that Rebecca West might never again in our lives return.

Sometimes I had to stop because the guests were there and Mother wasn't. She would dash in an hour late, her green tricorne slightly askew on her red curls, full of apologies and scattered orders for tea, muffins, tea out in the Blue Garden. (It was called the Blue Garden because Mother planted only blue flowers and marked the spots with blue sticks. Nothing ever flowered there but yellow Scotch broom, but Mother saw no cause in this to alter the name.) Or, if it was windy, tea was served in the house, explanations of the Single-Tax meeting that had caused her tardiness, followed by suggestions that they glance through the selection of pamphlets she immediately produced from her handbag.

Every Sunday evening we had guests for supper and then ran a studio movie on our projector in the living room. School friends

were invited and sat on pillows on the floor at the feet of the grownups. After the movie came music by the family, songs from Mother
and Father, piano pieces by Margaret and me or our teacher.
Occasionally, Mother would entice (using a trip through the studio
as bait) visiting concert artists like Rosa Ponselle, Mischa Levitzki,
Edward Johnson, the Zimbalists, Eva Gauthier, Reinald Werren-
rath, Lawrence Tibbett — then we had real music. They were
never asked to perform, of course, but they usually did. Ten
minutes of the family entertainment and the most reluctant went
rushing for his music case. But they also undoubtedly felt real
affection and gratitude toward Mother and Father and furthermore,
I believe, it was small effort to perform with Charlie Chaplin on a
pillow at one's feet.

My God, what an audience Chaplin was! Singers sang as at a
première. Folks talked with a wit they had never suspected — even
Margaret and I, even kids, as he sat giving us, the children, his
whole undivided interest and doing for us in a corner his incredible
imitations of disagreeable wives, nagging relatives, French actresses,
and so on. Yes, and by heaven, getting us to do them. I have never
been so dazzling since. Much has been written about his gifts as
a talker, his virtuosity of improvisation which made every parlor
stunt a miniature work of art, but has anyone paid him his due as
a courteous, enkindling listener? When Douglas Fairbanks came
(*père*, *fils* was still at school), they improvised one-act dramas in
fake languages. Alice Duer Miller was good at this also. But
when Chaplin talked about pictures we all sat still and listened
hard. We knew very well what we had among us. The greatest
actor of our time, unique, irreplaceable. He stood quite outside
the jurisdictions or embroilings of Hollywood. He was beyond
jealousy. He was an absolute.

The evenings manifested a kind of chemical frenzy if only be-
cause of the elements thrown together. There was always a famous
English author or two out West on a temporary contract, Somerset
Maugham, Elinor Glyn, Edward Knoblock, Rebecca West, Michael
Arlen, Robert Nichols, Cosmo Hamilton. (Edward Knoblock and

Cosmo Hamilton wrote a scenario each for Father. They were openly scornful of the medium and difficult to deal with. Knoblock handled one dramatic problem with exaggerated delicacy. "Words fail to describe the scene that follows," he wrote. "That," said Pop, "is a great help to any director." Hamilton contributed, "Not by accident they met alone in the mountain cabin." It took Father two weeks and five sets to shoot "not by accident." This last was for a picture entitled, not by Hamilton, *Midsummer Madness*.)

Madame Glyn was frequently present. She and Mother struck up an incongruous but ardent friendship, because I think each recognized in the other a vigorous and reliable family woman. Madame was an old darling although she looked like Semiramis. She wore her hair dyed red and coiled in a crown on her forehead. Her dresses were by her sister, Lady Duff Gordon, and they were terrific. Her posture would have made Eugénie sit up straighter. When she smiled enigmatically, which was her response to nearly every comment, there was a plenitude of gum. In an exquisite, refined, silken voice, she whispered incredible platitudes. But she had a good warm household heart, and we all loved her. We loved her wonderful posing and her crossed green eyes, and her manner of addressing men as though she'd come straight from a special session at Eleusis instead of a cup of tea and two Bath buns heavily buttered. Her eyes drove tigers absolutely mad, she claimed. They hurled themselves screaming at the bars of their cages. She also had a pulse that she could regulate at will, a trick taught her by a Yogi, and with a killing glance at the family doctor she asked him to verify the statement. "How do American men make love?" she would inquire in low pulsing tones as she momentarily uncrossed her eyes and focused gums and green gaze on her unprepared dinner partner. She alternated high passion with mysticism, piquant allusions to current royalty, wandering occasionally almost beyond reach in aeons of reincarnation. She made Mother pretty mad by reminiscing with half-shut eyes about her past lives with my father. But she had written *Three Weeks* to pay off her husband's debts and had reared two daughters unhelped, Mother reminded herself. There was much to be forgiven her. As for Elinor Glyn, she cherished Mother. She had traveled around enough to recognize a stanch spirit when she saw one.

There is not a stick of our house left. Public tennis courts occupy what was my mother's garden. The social and business life of the town has moved west and the site is shoddy and decrepit. Father is probably the only man who ever invested in Hollywood real estate and lost money. There is no trace of what we knew in the vicinity except the laughingstock across the street, the Frank Lloyd Wright group, Hollyhock House, on Olive Hill which turned out to be, to Mother's surprise, architectural history.

Ours was a bustling and benevolent house and in its gay time set the pulse of all the pleasant and invigorating activities in Hollywood. And Mother was the heart and pulse of the house. She never knew this. She thought it was only Father they wished to see because he was famous and witty. He thought so too, and so did I. We both know better now.

CHAPTER 11

Decision

As I GREW OLDER it became increasingly difficult to follow a routine of work at home. The house seemed to be always full of people. They were interesting people. I longed to join them. When I undressed and went into Mother's bathroom for my bootless workout, I could hear the sound of tennis rackets and laughter. I felt I was not getting anywhere with dancing: I knew I was not making technical progress. I began to dread the lonely practice morbidly. I thought about it at school all day, and on the way home I used to long for something beyond my control that would interrupt or delay it, an accident even. By the time I got through high school, dancing meant exhaustion and little else.

Father sat me down and told me in so many words that I had to give it my whole time or I must abandon it. Father was being quite honest. At this point had I chosen dancing he would have supported the decision. But the years of restraint had done their work. Gradually, I had grown disheartened. The dance studio seemed only the scene of endless unprogressing strain. To shut myself up with those dreary, hard-working girls away from the verve of Father's company, the house and its parties, away from Mother's activities, the friends, the conversations, meant a kind of death. There were no ballet companies in the United States at that time. The only opening lay in Kosloff's moving-picture troupe or in his vaudeville tour. My spirit quailed.

One morning toward the end of summer I walked into Father's bedroom while he was shaving. "Pop," I said, "I've decided to give up dancing and go to college." He replied without looking away from the mirror. "I'm glad you have, my dear. I don't think you would have been happy."

The next week I entered the university.

College opened a new life or so I intended. The University of California at Los Angeles was only a mile from the house. Mother wouldn't let me take the compulsory course in sex hygiene, but I was allowed to eat what I liked for lunch, and I lunched for one solid year off a hot dog and a bun, chocolate cake and a glass of milk — twenty cents. I also read the daily newspapers for the first time in my life, put my hair up and used a light lipstick.

I wore a large gray tricorne with a cockade and a gray cloak and pretended I was a young man out of Dumas's Antoinette romances attending the Sorbonne. I acted out the fantasy well into my junior year, except at those times when the actual presence of live men sitting in the class beside me excited me into forgetting.

I studied the way I danced — to the point of dropping. I worked. I did nothing but work. I'm told we had a fair football team. I never went to a game. There were dances. There were sorority teas. I was not asked to a single rush party. I did not have one date that first year.

But I was quite happy. As I had been the Artist during my school years, I was now the Scholar at the university, and I didn't miss dancing one little bit. The relief from the drudgery of the barre made my school term seem like a season of Sundays. Writing was hard, too. But one could do it sitting down. I was intoxicated by all the learning available and regularly signed up for more courses than I was permitted. I had to go repeatedly to Dean Charles Reiber for permission to take the extra hours. "Certainly," said that wise man, a pupil of William James, "it's a poor student that can't sleep through a couple of his classes."

My social life consisted of a tea party now and then with Dr. Lily Bess Campbell and other members of the English faculty.

My breeziness with the faculty did not simplify my relations with my fellow students much.

I fell in love with the young assistant professor who took me through my first poetry course. Really in love — that is, enough to alarm Mother. Although naturally I never breathed my feelings to a soul — although naturally the first time she suggested that I might invite him home for tea I went into my room and shook for forty minutes. So she may have noticed something. In any case, in order to patrol the situation, she enrolled in his courses. And, as we bore the same name, she was seated beside me where not the flickering of an eyelash escaped her attention. I never have heard of this happening to anyone else in the history of education.

I started the second year still in the gray cloak. Father gave me his cast-off Buick and I now drove to college, picking up stray members of the English department en route.

This second year I simply had to take the course in sex hygiene or I should not have been permitted to go on. I passed the test higher than any of the 1200 women in my class. For once Mother was without comment.

I learned three important things in college — to use a library, to memorize quickly and visually, to drop asleep at any time given a horizontal surface and fifteen minutes.

What I could not learn was to think creatively on schedule. At all my examinations involving any sort of improvisation I would sit biting my pencil and staring at blank paper until five minutes before the releasing bell. It is droll that my entire theater career has functioned within just those circumstances I instinctively found intolerable. The rehearsal of any Broadway show reproduces all the emotional hazards of a final examination. "How many hours of rehearsal time do you require?" I am asked as I sign for each new ballet — and the budget is scaled to my exact reply. How many hours does a novelist require to write a book? Supposing there were union rates and union restrictions controlling his reply and that the entire enterprise depended on his precise calculations. How many hours then? He can allow not more than six hours' waste in case he gets stuck for an idea. Learning to conform to these conditions has been an act of major discipline. My reputation and my job now depend on my not sitting biting a pencil for fifty-four minutes, but in cracking off at the starting bell. But in those merciful protected times the understanding professors dropped my blank examination books in the wastebasket without a thought and marked me on daily work.

Sometime during the beginning of the sophomore year a revue was put on in the college auditorium for the benefit of student victims of a campus fire. I volunteered and danced French *bergerettes* in the manner of Watteau and that was the first time in my life I stepped on a stage. The next day I was rushed by three sororities. I joined one which later became the Beta Xi chapter of Kappa Alpha Theta.

For four years this lovely life lasted. I continued in a happy somnambulistic state, blousy, disheveled, dropping hairpins, tennis balls, and notebooks wherever I went, drinking tea with Dr. Lily Campbell and the professors, lapping up talk of books and history, drinking tea with classmates and Elizabeth Boynton, the librarian, having dates or nearly dates with the two *M*'s on either side of me, Macon and Morgan, having dates with Leonarde Keeler, who was working out campus thefts and misdemeanors with the first lie detector, falling asleep in all afternoon lectures, late for every appointment (once when I entered English history on time the whole class burst out laughing). With the smell of iris and budding acacia coming through the windows, the sound of scholasticism filling my dreams with a reassuring hum, I sank deeper and deeper into a kind of cerebral miasma as I postponed all vital decisions. I had some vague, soothing fantasy of living in Mother's garden indefinitely, and studying until I slipped gracefully into old age while I wrote exquisitely about — what? No doubt it would all become apparent in time.

Occasionally I staged dances for the student rallies, mostly to Chopin, mostly about yearning for beauty and always accompanied by sorority sisters who were not trained. Campbell shook her head.

"This is not good," she said. "You simply haven't a dancer's body. I'd like you to write, but if you must go on the stage, act. I believe you're a tragic actress. Stop dancing. Look at yourself in the mirror."

In my junior year I presented a skit at the Press Club Vod based on the idea of how closely allied jazz dancing was to the jungle. I represented the jungle. Father for a wonder was in the house — he hadn't been up to this point — and was, along with the student body, markedly impressed. He told me next day with quiet gratification that my sketch made a real dramatic point, and that he thought it good enough to incorporate into his next picture. I went to bed dizzy. I lay awake hours planning each shot, thinking of lighting rhythm, camera angles, experiments that I have never seen to this day. I prepared to write it all down and present it to him. But the next night he came home to dinner with the announcement that he had given the idea to Kosloff and told him to get to work on it. Kosloff thought it was good, he added.

I can't remember whether I left the table or not. Probably not. I probably ate as usual. But if he had slapped me I couldn't have been more stunned. And yet I was not wholly unprepared. Father simply could not consider any member of his household as a professional with professional rights. He must have noticed something of my bitter disappointment. He was extremely uncomfortable for a few hours, but he came home the next night with everything solved: he had decided not to use the dance after all.

I usually danced about Beauty and how one should be ready to die for it. I did a good number of Petrarch's sonnets at one football rally when the men got their letters. I suspect the student body must have had pretty nearly enough of me. But this last performance had one happy aspect. I dressed the girls exactly like Botticelli nymphs with draperies split to the crotch and was forth-with summoned into the director's office to explain why. Dr. Moore knew all about Botticelli; he was also acquainted with eighteen-year-old glands. I listened with profound respect but refused to alter a stitch.

In order to get back up on my numb points, I had started exercising again. At first only for a couple of weeks before each show, but gradually, with God knows what contingency in mind, because I swear I had banished from conscious intention all thought of going back on the stage, I got to practicing every day. It could not be for very long and it was always late at night after I had finished studying. I used to fall asleep over my books, and then toward midnight force myself awake, and shaking with fatigue perform between the bureau and the closet mirrors, *relevés* in every position, on toes that went pins and needles with the unexpected pressure. I tried not to shake the floor out of concern for the sleeping family. Once, while I prodded along the upstairs hall in a particularly stumpy *pas de bourrée,* Father stepped out of his study, pipe in one hand, book in the other, and contemplated me. I kept going. I was in my petticoat, face blanched and wet with weariness. At length he spoke, "All this education and I'm still just the father of a circus." He went back in his room and shut the door.

At the Pasadena Playhouse, Margaret had spotted a young actor she thought she'd like to get better acquainted with. She engineered a meeting, that is, she gave out the order that he was to be brought to the house on a Sunday night, and he was brought. His name was Douglass Montgomery and he turned out to have good manners and a pleasant husky charm. Mag liked him fine. She arranged to take him through the Fairbanks studio, which was the second step in her softening-up routine. He came the following Sunday. Mag was dressed to kill in white silk, a dazzling white coat, a white cloche on her sleek dark hair. She sported gardenias and fake pearls. I thought she looked, as always, just ravishing. I was dressed in a dirty red practice tunic and I had all the living room rugs rolled back to the wall. Mag met him at the garden gate and whisked him around to the tennis court where the lively twanging of rackets and the yelping of our seven dogs gave evidence of Father's Sunday fun. "But what is that going on in the house?" said Douglass, turning his head. "Oh that," said Mag, "never mind about that. That is just my sister Agnes, who practices dancing on Sunday afternoon."

"I would like to see," said Douglass, and although she resisted, he maneuvered her back. There was no use in apologizing for the way I looked. Nobody looked the way I did who expected to be seen by anyone else. "Do you do this where people can watch you?" he asked.

"Well," I said with great misgiving. "This Friday . . . it's just amateur . . . "

"I'll come," said Dug.

Dug came. He stood backstage at the Friday Morning Club and looked me hard in the face. He trembled a little. There were tears of excitement in his eyes. (Dug was only seventeen.) He spoke in a very low voice. He put a cigarette in his mouth, but his lips shook. "Look here. You're no amateur. You're a very great performer. You belong to the world. Get out of the university. Stop this nonsense. Get into the theater. You've got a calling. You've got a duty. It's hard to say. Are you listening to me? You're a great dancer."

No trumpets sound when the important decisions of our life are made. Destiny is made known silently. The wheels turn within our hearts for years and suddenly everything meshes and we are lifted into the next level of progress. In a crowd of fussing clubwomen, overdressed, chattering, impatient to get to their chicken patties and ice cream, the laborious battlements my father had erected with all the sincerity of his heart and life care fell before one sentence. This boy simply said what I had waited all my life to hear.

I went constantly to Pasadena to see Douglass act. We came home afterwards and over hot chocolate analyzed every line, every turn of the head, every fold of the costume. Oh, this was my language for which I'd waited and yearned. This was my kind of talk.

Father was away from home as he so often was these days. Mother also. Nothing hindered our meetings. On and on through the long rustling afternoons, through the long evenings after his performance, in the still of midnight sitting decorously on opposite sides of the living room, we regarded one another's lives. We were young and passionately ambitious. "Do you believe you will be really great?" he asked with bated breath.

"I do," I answered, simply.

"I'm not sure," he said, "about myself, I mean." But he lied. He was sure.

I told him about Pavlova's kissing me. The silence tightened between us. My heart knocked and then muffled down in floods of waiting. The air stopped. He was going to kiss me.

"I like that," he said.

"Like what?"

"Like that in you — that you cried."

He hadn't moved. "Yes," I said and willfully destroyed the moment. It had passed. He wasn't going to kiss me.

"My God," he exclaimed, "look what's happened! It's morning." We ran to the porch doors and threw them open. There was the green garden aureoled in the dawn, the quince tree and the plum glowing in the waiting quiet. Mockingbirds threw out arabesques of sound. I walked with him to his car. He was a rich boy but the car door was tied together with clothesline, and that struck me as charming. Our feet on the gravel made the only sound in Hollywood beside the whirring and fluting of birds whose thin morning cacophony increased. Dug had a copy of *Romeo and Juliet* in his raincoat pocket — "never without it," he bashfully admitted. The car made a horrid noise starting. He was off in a cloud of gasoline fumes, and the sun tipped the mountains. I heard his husky voice as I climbed, so weary — so happy — the stairs to my strange bed. I was in love.

Mag seemed a bit taken aback at having lost her quarry. She had never had to move over for me before, but she no doubt soothed her pride by arguing that we were theater nuts with one-track minds, infatuated with our ambitions, not very good company to outsiders. Our romance seemed to get no forwarder — which was bewildering to me — but our professional sympathy grew frenzied.

Like a dog with a bone, Dug gnawed and mauled at my lethargy, chivying, imploring, worrying at me to go to New York, alone if possible (Mother would never in the world permit that, I said), and try my fortune. "I must study first," I argued. "I've lost so much ground."

"No, no," he said. "Get out from under. Go free. Don't wait. As for technique, you'll never have any. You've lost that chance." (This was bad advice, but I took it — because, obviously, I wished to.) "There are many great technicians. Your way lies in uncharted fields. You have to discover your own way, your own form of theater."

It gave me pause. I had to consider this. It was flattering; but it was vague. I'd wait for a bit.

Dug took me out to interview Gilmore Brown at the Pasadena Playhouse. Dug was now considered the white hope and he was listened to with deference. He claimed I was going to be one of the great figures of my age, and he suggested that Brown put me on in something quick which, out of affection, Brown did. I played the lead, choreographed the dances, found and trained the group. The play and the dancing, as I remember it, were dreadful, but the week made up my mind — I was going on the stage.

On Saturday I gave two performances. The following Monday I took a five-and-a-half-hour English comprehensive examination which I passed with high honors.

Pop had been away from home during the Pasadena session. He returned to find a *fait accompli*. Poor Pop had troubles of his own these days and could no longer fight my battles. He bowed to defeat gracefully, if a trifle wearily. Hadn't he done the same with his father's commands? If it was in my blood to dance, he said, he knew I would in the end.

But I had lost my body. This he had not reckoned on. I was heavy. I was soft. I was exhausted with study. My vitality ran very low, and what was worse my physical vanity had been hurt. I was at the age when Pavlova made her brilliant debut. I was at the point of emotional and mental development where I should step out in creative work, the childish drudgery of mechanics behind me. More, my body, having reached full development and maturity, should all the long while have been building into a dancer's body. I now was about to start my adolescence at nineteen with a brain labeled ripe by the university. My head raced my muscles.

It is a question of the greatest importance to dancers today in this country whether they can have a technique and/or education. Or whether education as it is taught in the universities is beneficial to them. I am inclined to think it is not. If one is going to be a professional in the arts one should start a professional apprenticeship at the age of thirteen or so. The painters of the Renaissance entered the masters' studios very young. They ground paint. They stretched canvases. They cleaned brushes. They handled as a matter of course the implements of their craft from childhood on. They painted as other people learn to write, first details of flowers, then animals, then angels' wings and lesser figures, and always with the example of the master at work beside them. By the time they tackled their first solo picture they knew what they were doing. And in the meanwhile in the workroom they had listened to the great artists and philosophers and civic leaders. They grew up educated men.

The Russians in their Imperial Ballet School worked out a similar scheme. Children were accepted into the school at the age of ten and became wards of the government. They were taught ballet and character dancing for hours every day, but they were also taught languages and history. And from their first year they performed in the Maryinski Theater as pages or fairies, or whatever. They saw the greatest singers and dancers in Russia at work. They learned music by watching Tchaikovsky, Rimski-Korsakov, Borodine, at their jobs. They learned art history, style, color, architecture from Benois and Bakst. And when at seventeen they were graduated, they moved into a world where every cultural door was open to them, and an endowed theater waited staffed with the best in the business.

What did paleontology matter to me who wanted to jump high? Or astronomy when I needed to understand the phrasing of music? And granted the exposure to learning outside of my restricted domain broadened and steadied me, what I needed above all things in the world was training in moving design, design in time-space, in the manipulation and staging of bodies, in choreography. And this was not taught anywhere at all in the world. Dancing is not taught as an art in any university. There it is still in the gymnasium. Where dancing is taught as an art, the halls are noisy and dirty and troops of ignorant driven children are put through their paces daily like animals by expert semiliterate trainers and rewarded with food at the proper intervals. And the milieu is cheap music and greedy, jealous mothers and loud gossip, and noise and weariness. And never, never a book or an objective idea. But the children learn to move. And the ones with great gifts pick up all they need to know, somehow, along the way.

Sarah Lawrence and Bennington Colleges have made attempts to solve the problem, but while they do give the student a sense of style and composition, they do not train the girls early enough or long enough to build a professional technique. Their graduates — in point of pure dancing — cannot compete with the sixteen-year-old athleticism produced by the professional studios. In all other colleges and universities, dancing is still in the gymnasium and is beneath professional consideration.

I was graduated *cum laude* and all I longed for was to dance the mazurka in *Sylphides,* and I knew I never could.

I turned my glazed eyes on the misty future. And suddenly the future was in my face.

The day after they had stood side by side watching me take my degree, Mother and Father told me they were going to be divorced.

C H A P T E R   1 2

Tryouts

THAT SUMMER we made a desperate pilgrimage through Europe, dragged at the tail of Mother's grief. The trip was so bleached by her anguish that I cannot recall any part of it without melancholy. No theaters. No restaurants. No dancing. Just evenings by the pension window, staring at the suicide wallpaper while Mother sat in her bedroom writing, writing endlessly home to Hollywood.

The summer was at length done and on a brilliant September morning we steamed up the Hudson, and I stared at New York busy with little smokes, the smokes that make the static laden island seem accessible and lively with morning bustle. I had arrived to change the American theater.

These were the days of speak-easy money on Broadway and speak-easy taste, of the active casting couch, of dancers hired on the sheen of the stocking and the wink of their agent, of the unmuted trumpet and the High Fish off the perilous pedestal, of the sexy rhinestone, the Texas Guinan holler, the zip, the boom, the guts, the speed, the hot-diggety-dirt. This was the profession of my choosing, this corrupt carnival.

And what were my qualifications?

I could speak meticulous English.

I could use a library.

I had never so much as bought a hat without my mother's advice.

I had never been kissed.

I was stiff in the joints, overweight and underpracticed.

I had a poor complexion.

No taste in dress.

I had never hunted a single day's work.

I was a snob.

I knew what I thought was beautiful.

Had I foreseen what lay ahead of me I think I should not have had the courage to go on.

I faced a theater which for sheer toughness and vulgarity had few counterparts in the history of the stage. Because I was a dancer I entered a branch of that theater which had almost no standing or opportunity. What dance companies existed were small, confined and dedicated to the personal exploitation of some star.

The Metropolitan Opera, our great lyric theater, in reality a national institution which should have housed the finest dancing as it housed the finest music, had in fact degraded dancing to a point it never sank to in any European community. The impresario, Gatti-Casazza, frankly despised ballet, and though, oddly enough, he married his chief ballerina, Rosina Galli, he used what influence he had, and as husband and director his influence was total, to suppress all dancing. The last full ballet to be presented under the auspices of the Met was *La Giara* (1927), a bit of peasant nonsense with a nice score by Casella. ; The ballets in the operas were cut as drastically as the music permitted and were a byword in the profession. No dancer would enter the *corps de ballet* of the Metropolitan unless every other avenue of opportunity was closed, and although our country had produced soloists and choreographers of world-changing power, our great lyric theater never once employed an American soloist of national importance, nor one single American choreographer of any caliber whatever. They did employ Balanchine for one season but hamstrung him with rehearsal restrictions. The condition begun under Gatti persisted to the advent of Rudolf Bing. The dance critics never reviewed the opera ballets; it was tacitly agreed among them that the dancing below Times Square was not worth a single line of comment.

Whatever one may think of the cultural viewpoint manifest in this line of action, it was certainly a poor one economically. At the time of Taglioni, the Opéra, that is, the Théâtre Nationale de Musique et de la Danse (please note the exact title), subsisted more on its balletic attractions than on its vocal. It would seem that the brilliant seasons of ballet which occurred later semiannually, under independent management, at the Met, in which the standees frequently crushed six deep, would have given the Metropolitan Board something to think about. But no. If there was one institution that blocked the progress of dancing in America more than any other, it was the Metropolitan Opera. Rudolf Bing, the new director, has inaugurated a new program, a change that was twenty-five years overdue. When I started dancing, the Met held out no opportunity.

The dances in musical shows were rarely true ballets but specialties, tap choruses, line routines, or precision work. There were ballets of sorts in moving picture houses, sometimes performed in scenery, usually performed in front of jazz bands with cut-glass or *diamanté* music stands. No concert manager booked American dancers with the single exception of the Denishawn troupe. In all the United States there was just one critic paid by a daily newspaper to write on dancing and qualified for the job, John Martin of the *New York Times*. The word "choreography" was not yet known. No educated adult was yet ashamed to preface his remarks with an unblushing, "Of course, I know nothing about dancing." It was the "of course" that used to make me despondent.

Two days after arrival Mother found us an apartment. Father had established a very generous allowance for my sister and me which was paid to us directly so that, as he explained, when this sad bookkeeping was first made clear, we could be independent and live and study and travel as we saw best. It was a splendid gesture and would have made sense if we had been raised to do anything at all, buy a dress even, without Mother's sanction. But Father overlooked the fact that money will not buy independence. He had allowed us to be shackled from early childhood with the cobweb loves of Mother's insistence. He said he could not lift his voice. I never understood why except that contradicting her on anything was a formidable undertaking.

The allowance he gave me would surely have been adequate to meet all costs of study and early rehearsals if I had lived like a student, dressed like a student and conducted myself as other young beginners do. But that was not the style Mrs. William de Mille had grown accustomed to. She leased a duplex apartment next door to Fannie Hurst and all of us pooled our income to pay the rent. She entertained a great deal and the shared upkeep and food bills came high. Moving out was inconceivable. At the time Father gave us financial independence — he had established a large trust fund for her — he also delivered into our arms a broken woman. To leave at any point during the next three years would have been an act of gross cruelty.

Furthermore, Mother made me comfortable. I had grown lazy domestically and fond of comfort. Her home, wherever located, was always seductively attractive. So we were installed together as a family in our large and opulent duplex. We also had a summer residence. In a further effort to make life easy and emancipated, Pop gave me the family cottage near Monticello. I could not, of course, pay the taxes, and Mother assumed all prerogatives and responsibilities as she had always done. But it was mine legally. He had made the gesture.

College had all but exhausted me. The divorce sapped the rest of my strength. Father arrived in New York and Mother's agony at his nearness grew acute and although I understood Father's point of view and the inevitability of separation and yearned in sympathy, I decided not to see my darling again and with great bitterness of heart told him so, cutting myself off not only from my chiefest source of fun and strength and stimulation but from whatever professional advice he might have given me. Mother, who, if anything, knew less of the world than I, undertook to go it alone.

I started out by seeing Father's friends, Dan Frohman, Brander Matthews, Walter Hampden, Edgar Selwyn. I wore for these occasions a crushed raspberry coat and hat I had bought in Paris, both hideous. With an unprecedented show of independence, I declined to have Mother accompany me. They looked me over carefully and, being gentlemen of the old school and friends of Father's, said they were sure I had something to offer. For instance, had I thought of writing? Archie Selwyn of a newer school and nobody's friend was more forthright. "You're too fat," he said, prodding me with a pudgy finger in the thigh. "There!" This was not what I had come to expect from the Dean of Letters and Science.

Dug was doing dandy. He had come to New York in August and had walked right into the juvenile lead of a Guthrie McClintic production called *God Loves Us*. He knew how to dress for managers and got himself up for an interview with as much strategy as though he were preparing a role. At the moment he was concentrating on being sincere. He cultivated a husky enthusiasm in his voice and an ingratiating giggle. He knew the name and inclinations of every manager in town. He knew the exact power of every agent. He knew which restaurants to eat at and which cocktail parties to go to. I marveled. He urged me to change my name. He didn't think "Agnes" would look well in front of a theater. He urged me to dye my hair which, although golden, was not brilliant enough, he said, for stage lights. He begged me to brace my jumbled teeth and cut off my nose. All these suggestions I resisted with unexpected stubbornness. I was determined to survive, if at all, as me. He thought this risky. He implored me to dress better. But I didn't know how. Mother was still inclining me to puffed sleeves and tricornes.

Dug's play was not a great success, but it did have a two-month run. I had bought a pale green beaded gown in Paris for the opening, and I went absolutely crazy with excitement. I had looked forward all summer to this because I figured that after the opening I would go back transfixed with the greatness of his acting and stand before him in blazing adoration. And under the impulse of this unforgettable moment he would surely take me in his arms and would, at last, kiss me. So I went back, and he looked up from his dressing table and said forlornly, "I wasn't very good, was I?" I had yet to tell my first lie. I said, "No, you weren't." That fixed that.

The school I had chosen to practice at was depressing. The hours alternated with tap-dancing and the rooms resounded to the clatter of steel-bottomed shoes, while the dressing rooms were given over to tiny children getting themselves into satin pants and diamond-studded brassières under the admonishings of their hard-eyed mothers. The older girls also wore, with greater cause, diamond-studded brassières. They performed pirouettes, adagio, and tap on toe. They all hollered and shouted and whined the whole time. The piano banged. Shoes clattered like gravel in a cement mixer. And not a heart under the sleazy satin or soiled lace but yearned and prayed for a spot on a night-club floor or, practically unobtainable heaven, a bit in a real Broadway musical.

Matters were not ordered as at the Kosloff School. Everybody was up on point from the very beginning. Everyone, even youngsters, turned *fouettés* pirouettes at the end of every class. Knees and ankles could take care of themselves. One had to have turns in order to finish a number. How else? So we turned. I learned to do fifty *fouettés* on spot in fair form without being able to maintain line in a single other exercise. This has been a source of some wonder to conscientious dancers. It was a comfort to me. I might dance like a pig, but I had one trick that Markova had difficulty in duplicating.

Dug thought it would be a good idea if I gave a concert, so I started working on a program. It was difficult to discipline myself. I had no schedule to meet, no coach, no teacher, no performance date. I was to make up a new kind of dancing, Dug said.

I hired a rehearsal hall. I hired a pianist. When I was ready I called Dug in. He sat alone in the studio tilting back on a folding chair, smoking vigorously to quiet his embarrassment. "What is your costume?" I told him. "What are your lights and props?" I explained. "Tell me when the curtain goes up," he said as the music started. These rehearsals nearly always occurred at midnight or later, of necessity, after Dug's shows. They were held in the empty Steinway building with no one but the night elevator man to let us in and out.

Dug was excited by these sessions. He held high hopes. I myself felt pretty secure and very hopeful. I don't think I have been quite so confident since. I stood breathless, private with immortality, as on the eve of birth. I felt myself familiar with greatness and other reassurances. Later, of course, came the anesthesia of activity, but I never again felt so deep, hoped so high. I was never again unconquered.

All I know about acting I learned from Dug and from my lonely experimenting. He taught me that every gesture must have some explicit meaning. He taught me to know exactly where the imaginary partners stood, how tall they were and what they were doing at every moment. It was an exercise of real discipline to establish the eye level of a six-foot partner moving rapidly around the room who, of course, existed only in the direction of my own eyes. But this was only the beginning. Any character actress could do this. He taught me to establish with a single gesture the atmosphere and inner rhythm of a personality. He forced me to establish mood with a posture.

The timing of pantomimic phrasing I found out for myself — how to attack with a real impulse, how to round the gesture on the musical line, how to make the point on the last down-beat. Timing comedy I seemed to know about always. The main thing was never to hurry, not to waste one second, but never to hurry. One had to make every stage of the thinking plain. One had to be brave just to stand still and be clear. Let the music race. One set one's teeth against hurry.

I aimed to do character studies where the dancing was a natural incident in the episode and a revelation of personality, using dance like costuming. The crux of the matter was the acted story. Since I couldn't dance very well and acted naturally, this seemed the course to follow. I had as helps twenty square feet of bare space, lighting, one costume, one piano, a provocative title, and choice of the world's music. I allowed myself eight bars after the curtain was up to establish who I was, when I lived, where I was at the moment and how I felt. I didn't realize it at the time but I was giving myself a stringent training in stage mechanics. I learned not to rely on scenery, quantities of people or lush orchestration. I learned what every true theater craftsman must know, that the actor and the gesture (or the word or the melodic line) talk. The rest is millinery.

At the time, of course, I was sore as hell that I couldn't get into a theater and play with all the goodies.

My pieces were not properly dances at all. They were realistic character sketches, dramatic rather than choreographic in form. What dancing there was derived from authentic folk or old-fashioned theatrical steps which I used as decoration and accouterment exactly like costumes, or lights, or music. For music I used bits of whatever seemed suitable, pasted together like an old moving-picture score. I avoided masterworks as having intrinsically too strong a form and atmosphere and because I had some decent compunction about scissoring up Chopin or Schumann. I liked folk music and popular pieces which, though cheap, frequently retained the body warmth of human living, and I clung to old dance steps as women cling to their grandmother's china.

My first group consisted of two Degas studies, a student and a performer, an eighteenth-century French courtier, an Elizabethan girl watching a parade, a forty-niner, and two romantic ballet waltzes quickly discarded. The next year's batch was to comprise an Irish reel, a *Schuhplattltanz* to Beethoven, a girl at a Broadway audition, a Civil War variety entertainer complete with musket and 38-star flag, and an Arabian *Ouled Naïl*. If the range seems eclectic, the point of view was native. I was meticulous as to exact reproduction of style, but the woman inside the trappings was what interested me, and that girl remained, of course, always recognizably myself.

The first dance I made up was '49, and this was, to my knowledge, the first use of American folk material on the concert stage. The second dance was *Stagefright* after Degas. I had seen the wax statuette of his twisted ballet child in the Metropolitan Museum of Art and thought she looked like me. The aching knees, the strained back, the dirty, smudgy face, the pride. I made five studies before I got what I wanted. The next dance was called *Ballet Class*.

I haunted upholstery and fabric departments. I flattened my face on the glass of the cheap jewelry shops on Broadway. Sometimes I hunted two months for the proper earrings. Everything I collected was put away as sacrosanct, never to be touched for any civilian purposes. Further, I took the stand that I was designing the costumes myself and needed no advice. As a matter of fact, I was downright rude about the matter, not to say implacable. After two or three years of attempting to influence me, Mother gave up — after her fashion that is, confining herself thereafter to innuendo, comment, persuasion, denunciation, entreaty and disobedience, and used to work off her blunted feeling in loving drudgery. For the next decade she entertained the Single-Taxers with eighteenth-century brocade in her lap while she stitched tiny spangles into the design or pleated gauzes. She was wonderfully skillful with ruffles, rosettes, laces and embroideries and invented and sewed far and away beyond the call of duty. My costumes were, as her mother used to say before her, sewn "with the red blood of time." They were miracles of hand-wrought detail.

Of course, at the time these costumes were only projected in my head. These costumes existed only for Dug and me. "How are you dressed?" said Dug.

"In a sunbonnet. In a calico dress limp from sun and weather, the shoes worn down from walking." And I put up my hand to shade my eyes against the long horizon.

I danced to Guion's *Walking to the Pasture*, a piece which as a girl I had practiced in Hollywood. It was a tedious tune and Father asked me to stop, rather peremptorily, I thought; it bothered his tennis. But as I had played, I had remembered how, as a little girl sitting in the Fred Harvey car, I had seen the prairies for the first time and recognized the meaning and the love of those large lands and realized things I had never personally known but which seemed clearer than the actual calendar experiences of school and home. The memory waited like a hunger for all my life to make itself known at the sympathetic time. "That's it!" cried Dug, watching. "That's how it was!"

This is the core of the matter. The rest one figures out with one's wits. This is why one dances.

ᴄ∿ᴏ

I began to give auditions for agents. I borrowed Walter Hampden's theater for the purpose. He was always extremely gracious about lending it to me. The Boys came — The Boys in every country look alike, something closely akin to newspaper reporters at an inquest. Their hats are a little higher in the crown, their ties and linen cleaner and more expensive, their hands more frequently manicured. About liquor, sex and money they feel the same. Also about art. The Boys are seldom producers, but they are always the men around producers and except in Hollywood, which is their Valhalla, they are never directors. Nowhere in the world are they writers, scene designers, composers or instrumentalists.

The Boys usually keep their hats and coats on during auditions. They smoke. They make their decisions standing in the aisle with lowered heads, hatted, and then they walk out quickly, leaving one or perhaps two to come soberly to the footlights and tell you. You stand, breathing hard, the sweat cold on your forehead, the make-up caking dry, leaning forward to see their faces, recognizing from the rhythm of their walk and their little irrelevant jokes that they are moving sideways toward an awkwardness.

Ben Boyar, who looked like Mr. Samuel Whiskers with eye-glasses, and who spoke for The Boys, was kind but final. The sum total of their opinion was "noncommercial — artistic and all that, but absolutely, totally, irrevocably noncommercial."

"All right, so you are," said Mother. "Let's plan on a concert quickly." "Gee, Ag, I'm sorry," said Dug, but he had a date that night and couldn't discuss it further.

It looked as though getting together a program of new dances was going to take the better part of a year, and in the meantime I wanted to get on a stage. So I continued to give auditions although it played havoc with my practice schedule. One audition was like another, I cannot even remember before whom I danced. In the course of time, however, I danced before every known manager and agent in New York.

I remember standing on an empty stage one noon warming up while a series of singers and specialty dancers milled around an upright piano. Out front in the dark were the boss and his henchmen. A dark, large-boned girl walked to the footlights and stood half insolently, half amusedly, with one foot on the coping. She spoke in a bass voice, "What do you want me to do?" I had practiced my dance for six months. I had foregone clothes so that I might have the tutu. It was beginning to wilt a little from lugging around. I had been up since eight packing and in the theater for an hour and a half applying make-up and doing a complete barre. "What shall I do?" she said with a languorous drawl, staring insolently at them. "Here, sing this," said a young man standing by the piano. Her voice sounded like hot chocolate. "Oh, nuts!" she said and threw the music down. "I didn't want to come here anyway this morning." The men laughed. "Come here and talk to me," said the young man and they went into a huddle behind the piano. The girl was Libby Holman, this was her first audition and the young man behind the piano was Howard Dietz.

Now it was my turn. I spoke in crisp accents, "My study is a satire based on the paintings of Hilaire Edgar Degas, 1834–1917. You know the paintings of Degas?" Silence. "Degas painted the ballet girls at the opera at the time of their greatest decadence — well, you must have seen them." A voice cut through — "Are you ready to dance?" "May I have the stage cleared, please, and silence?"

Silence was what I got. Not a titter; not a chuckle; not an indication of understanding. The quiet lasted for about a minute, then I could hear them talking. They'd put their heads together and were going right on with their business. They had stopped looking. An electrician carried a light across my path. I checked my jumps. "Aren't you through?" said a stage manager. "I'm sorry." As I was making my exit, before I had reached the edge of the stage, came the "thank you" from the front and the next girl walked down to the footlights. Two singers, numb with sympathy and terror, looked up from the bench on which they were waiting and said, "Very original, dear, really very original," and they smiled encouragingly.

As I write this, I realize none of it seems seriously distressing. I certainly had enough to eat and there was money to carry on for several recitals. But if I could not get into the commercial theater, I could not function. A dancer has only ten good years of performing life, and I had begun late. Also this was the first failure our family had known. Mag, before the end of her first term at Barnard, had taken honors in both history and English.

Dug of course continued to do brilliantly. He now was making a sensation in *Crime* with Sylvia Sidney. Urchins followed him down the streets, begging autographs; he was pointed out in restaurants; matinee girls formed a Douglass Montgomery club; they wrote letters, sent gifts, queued up backstage, waited in cars outside the theater. Spring was upon us. A whole winter had gone by. I stood at my window at night and watched the trees grow indistinct with leaf buds. South where the sky glowed hot was Times Square across which the women came hurrying through the sweet nights to court Dug. Sometimes he asked me to walk home from the theater with him as a kind of protection. He found me prophylactic because I had no sex appeal, that is, not off stage; on stage, a good deal. "Strange, isn't it?" he said, musing.

One warm night, we sat on a pile of lumber in Central Park West and took stock. "Your new numbers don't seem to have any commercial appeal, you have quality, but not the ability to sell an idea. Actually, you stand just where you stood when you finished your first dance." It had been raining and I remember the smell of the wet wood and the mild wild odor of forsythia, and I wondered if a dear little wet coffin would not be most comforting.

❧

Mother said a change of scene was indicated. We would go to Santa Fe and give a concert.

Why Santa Fe? It could have been any town, so long as there was a friend to help. In Santa Fe lived Mary Hunter and her aunt, the terrible old lady of the Indian country, Mary Austin. Also Santa Fe was on the way to the West Coast where Mother had to appear for her interlocutory decree.

The costumes went in one trunk with the music; our clothes in another. Mother undertook to find a theater, I a pianist. The theaters, the good ones, were used by movies. And who, pray, was Mrs. William de Mille — a relation of Cecil? And if he wanted something, why didn't he write a letter personally? They'd do plenty for him. There was a theater, a fair-sized one, but it had been used for prize fights for the last six years. It smelled rather high, and the stage had gone pulpy and rotten. Mother went right out to the local sawmill and got a man with a planing machine to ride over it and remove the fur of splinters. Then she bought putty and, crawling over the entire length of the floor on her hands and knees, puttied up the holes crack by crack. It's hot in Santa Fe in July. One goes white behind the eyes and feels for the nearest support. I returned from my practice in the parish house with the local piano teacher, whose daughter had been exposed to the measles, all tuckered out and a mite discouraged. "Have some iced tea," said Mother, sitting in a cool print dress in a cool hotel room. "Have some iced tea. I fixed the stage." And there was the iced tea clinking in a jug, and a bowl of garden flowers beside it and some little cookies bought at the local grocer's on a glass plate. "Have a cold bath and relax," said Mother, writing a letter to Hollywood. "It's all done."

She was a small red-haired woman with a lovely bosom, and she wore cool, sweetly printed cottons in summer with fresh white at the breast and inside her was the soul of General Montgomery.

There was nothing left to do but send a notice to the local paper, the *Santa Fe New Mexican,* which was edited by Brian Ború Dunne, to print tickets and deliver them for sale to the local drygoods store. And what makes people buy tickets? Why does anyone buy a ticket for a strange girl from New York who thinks she can dance? Why, a letter from Ruth St. Denis and Ted Shawn, and another from Edna St. Vincent Millay to some tubercular friends. (Why not go? In God's name, what else to do on a Saturday night in the middle of a long summer? If it's too bloody awful, one can sneak out and finish getting drunk at Mamie's Bar.) And by Mary Austin who was by no means to be brushed aside or disrespected, and by Mary Hunter driving up one street and down another and buttonholing friends, and by me saying to the Indians, "Now, I've seen your dances; come see mine." And handing out a couple of dozen passes. How does one sell cakes at a church bazaar? Anyhow, it was done. And the lady did not accompany me because her child did come down with the measles, but a young man did and he was a better pianist.

At six o'clock of the fateful night Mary burst into the hotel bathroom where I sat steaming in the tub collecting my wits. "We've done it! We've done it!" she exulted. "We're clear! Three hundred and sixty-four dollars in cold cash. The expenses are paid." Oh, how happy I was! There was no responsibility for me further except to be a great artist. But that seemed simple.

The program went from start to finish as planned and did not stop. Mother dressed me backstage, which was all right except that she very much minded my swearing and stopped to remonstrate. She also stopped whenever a stagehand came anywhere near, and lifted up a sheet until he had passed. This made the changes slow.

The poets said, pouring their cocktails next afternoon, they thought the first number showed wit, the second none. The painters liked the color of my third dress. The Sunday-school teacher wondered if I wouldn't come to a strawberry breakfast on Thursday. The Indians were convulsed. Why on the ends of the feet? Why, on the very ends? Didn't it hurt? What was the use? The *Santa Fe New Mexican* hailed me as Duncan's successor.

What did Mary think? She thought I was all right. And Mary Austin? She thought a lot of things. She thought a lot of things about every fact that came to her attention. We had supper at sundown on a slope under the Sangre de Cristo mountains, and wrapped in an Indian blanket against the chill of the evening she told me what she thought while she prodded a piece of meat on a sharpened stick into the campfire. She spoke like a sibyl. She always spoke like a sibyl, even when she was telling her niece how to make the jam, and a sibyl can be damned oppressive to have around the house. But there was prophecy in Aunt Mary's words and there was revelation. She was a startling old lady, a pioneer, "a foundered genius" said Rebecca West to me once. The Indians loved her. The anthropologists tried to despise her, but never quite succeeded in as much as she frequently turned out to be right, guessing what they proved and already waiting where their laborious searchings led them.

"In every Indian ceremonial," said Mary Austin, in the blue Santa Fe evening as we lay staring at the mountain line where the deserts began, staring out over the undefined precipices of color, down toward Albuquerque where twelve years before during a halt in the transcontinental trip I had seen my first Indians, my first cowmen lounging and walking among them, "in every ceremonial, there is the moment when the priest says the word that makes the magic. Up to that point, it has been ceremonial, after that it is potent. Your hands have that power. They make living contact with the audience. What you do becomes a living experience because of the potency of the gesture. . . . The Indians permit anything as long as the God is present. Anything — even the sex act — if the God is present. When He is absent, they consider everything obscene and not worth serious attention. They make great

fun of the white man's dances and plays because the God is almost
never there." She fastened me with the sharp steady look of a
frontier woman. "Never let the God be absent from your stage.
Say your prayers before you dance." The Spanish tortoise-shell comb
in her bun gleamed in the moonlight like a horny crown. She had
an arrogant, gray mustache, a drooping mouth and a dictatorial
manner. She did not converse — she issued bulls. She had broken
the wilderness.

She continued complacently scorching another piece of meat.
"This is the Mexican method of cooking. Mary, put on more sticks.
Not such green ones."

Mary Hunter, who was building an adobe house for her aunt
with her bare hands, under fire of frontier memories and suggestions, looked depressed and exhausted. Mother said nothing. She
wanted to get home to read the British land-values taxation report
before she went to sleep.

Like the real Indians, Mary Austin believed in living magic. She
was making magic between her and me. We both knew this. I
have not forgotten anything she said to me.

I went to her with my professional fears. "Bark your shins!" said
Aunt Mary. "It will toughen you up." Oh, pioneer! Aunt Mary
was very ill although she did not die until seven years later. She
did not spare herself, nor, of course, anyone else as she could not
abide squeamishness.

"Stop being sorry for yourself. We have all gone through this,"
she said. "Say your prayers and you will be a good dancer." And
she was apt to continue: "The activities and the expressions of men
are controlled by the land they live in — the American climate, the
topography, the mountains and plains have affected all inhabitants,
Indian, Spanish, Catholic, Protestant, Anglo-Saxon — all, no matter
how unlike, are stamped by the forces under which men live. You
must let the rhythm of the American earth come through what
you do."

"What beautiful hair you have, Aunt Mary," I said as I stood
saying good-by in her garden of flaked mud and dusty coarse holly-

hocks. Her hair lay like an unraveled blanket, gray and black, to her thighs.

"Men found it so," she replied with a leer of frightening archness and tottered back to bed. "Never let the God be absent," she said leaning her browned and gnarled hand on the doorjamb, "and don't be sorry for yourself."

C H A P T E R 13

The Profession

In december of our second winter, I heard that Jacques Cartier was going to give a recital and needed someone to share the program and expenses with him. I accordingly auditioned for Bela Blau, his manager, who agreed to take my three hundred dollars and give me time on the stage. Cartier was, quite naturally, to receive top billing and choice positions. Mother and I had heard that contracts were customary, but Blau himself never mentioned a contract — he only asked for the check.

We rehearsed in a large studio high up on Central Park South. It snowed a great deal and the black and white park below was lively with skaters and sleds, like a Brueghel landscape. As I splashed through the slush in my galoshes, a suitcase of music and practice clothes bumping my cold knees (skirts were high at this point), hearing the cries of children and everyone hustling along eager with holly and packages, I think I was the happiest girl I had ever been. There were regular hours of refining phrases, gestures, nuances; there was tea after the rehearsals with the maiden ladies who leased us the studio; there was the pause while Cartier pounded through an Indian dance and I waited with my nose frozen against the afternoon window, and the children below in the park merrily yelled and skidded and raced and everyone shopped and planned gay schemes for Christmas.

At home, the costumes were assembling, ruffle on ruffle, button on silk. The tutus sat on the sofas and on the chairs and they were in Mag's way when she entertained her boy friends. Mother laid her thimble by her dinner plate and Nettie Duff Reade, the seamstress, kept asking for a few more dollars for hooks or tape and disappearing with the money. She would show up now and again with wonderful things in a sheet, her moon fat face dewed with effort as she lugged the great bundle through the door. The throwaways were printed and we all sat around the living room addressing. Mother began to telephone all her friends to buy tickets. Pictures appeared in the papers and were brought with triumphant screams for my inspection.

At the last moment it seemed vital to me to throw out one of my dances. Cartier and Blau were naturally put out, but Cartier behaved well. Blau just fumed. I offered to substitute '49 and Blau auditioned me in it late in the afternoon on the day of the performance, then refused point-blank to consider it. At six-fifteen, Mag dragged me from the theater where she had been helping Nettie Reade hang up the costumes. Mag called a cab and pushed me in; I put my head on her shoulder and rode home unnerved — "that-son-of-a-bitch — that-son-of-a-bitch — we'll-show-him-that's-a-good-number — what-you-need-is-scrambled-eggs-and-a-hot-bath — wait-until-after-the-performance-and-I-have-the-leisure-to-express-myself-to-him — who-the-hell-does-he-think-is-paying-for-this-concert-anyway — don't-give-it-another-thought — where-did-you-put-the-extra-tights?"

Mother and Mag poured the eggs down me and at seven-fifteen Dug walked into the house. I was standing in the middle of the living room in evening dress, shaking. "I came to see you through these last few minutes," he said. He put his arm around me and walked me up and down. "I'm so frightened," I said and the tears poured down my cheeks. "Of course, my dear, of course, of course." He kept me walking. "Now go to the theater and warm up. There's nothing more to say. We all believe in you." He pushed me through the door — Mag had the elevator waiting.

There was a telegram at the theater from Father at Los Angeles: WELCOME, MY DAUGHTER, INTO THE PROFESSION.

The house was sold out. To this day, I don't know how Blau did it. Cartier was not too well known, and I was unheard of, and the audience was not paper. Mother and Dug bought their seats, and so did all the other friends.

The performance went on for thirty-five minutes of blue Indians, Japanese samurai and German elves before my cue to enter. Then suddenly, I was on the stage. I rushed on in my yellow tutu, swinging my watering can, and with the first gesture there was laughter. Intoxicated with power, I made point after point. Then suddenly I was through again and in the wings — fighting for breath, my eyes bugging for oxygen, my ribs bursting the seams of my yellow satin bodice. The applause was enormous and solid. But Blau had said no bows and so I took none. Not until intermission were we allowed to take a bow, Cartier and I together. Someone called my name, and I came out alone. This brought cheers and whistles. I was in. And to my dumfoundment, I found I was a comedian. The Degas *Ballet Class* which Mother had found too grim and heart-breaking to endure brought yells of mirth. It seems I was very funny, I who always wanted to die for beauty.

The next morning, John Martin said in the *New York Times*: "Here is undoubtedly one of the brightest stars now rising above our native horizon."

On waking I found I had lost my voice. I didn't regain it for a week.

At the repeat concert, I included '49 and stopped the show. After the third concert, there seemed to be no more money to go on. In fact, there seemed to be a loss, which was odd. No accounting was ever given, and we thought it rude to ask. Mother and I held long, anxious conferences. Would Blau take it unkindly if we demanded a full business statement? He volunteered nothing but a few unpaid bills.

That wound up the season. It had been an auspicious start. No managers or agents, however, had attended.

I began giving auditions again. In the late spring, Charles Cochran of London and Noel Coward came to New York to cast for a new revue. I arranged to audition, and went to this trial with high hopes. Cochran was supposed to be the most discriminating manager in Europe and Coward was, as we all knew, a genius. I did four dances in full costume and they were attentive and courteous but very suavely, very graciously, explained that I belonged in the concert hall. They were sure I would never find a place in the theater. "Had I ever seen Tilly Losch?" Cochran asked. That was the kind of dancing he wanted. I bowed my head. Mother and the pianist helped me get the costumes home. Dug was to come to tea and hear the news. It was an afternoon of great heat and sudden rains. I remember the rooms of our apartment were steamy with oppression. I stood in my bedroom tearing a comb through my matted hair, stiff with sweat and theatrical powder, staring with blank eyes through the mirror. Mother entered without one word and putting both arms around me drew my head down on her shoulder. This verdict had come from the top men of the trade. "My father used to say," she spoke quietly, "that a way would become apparent as we go along. In the end a door always opens."

I washed my face and went down to Dug. I made tea for him in the kitchen and told him. He said nothing. He looked at me for a long, long while. Dug came of a generation that believed in quick success. He was having it. At last he spoke. "Give up, Ag, give it up. You're good, but it's not working. You haven't the thing that will make people trust your talent." I put my head down on the table and the slow salt tears soaked through my fingers to the oilcloth. That was in 1928.

I spent the summer working on a new program of dances. The second program would be a greater test than the first, I realized, and I intended, very soberly, not to be a flash in the pan. I permitted myself only a few scattered week ends and devoted the hot days' time to practicing and trying to break my way into agents' offices. And I did land a two-week engagement at Roxy's which netted me some hard cash. I was held over which was encouraging. Unfortunately, this led nowhere. Leonidoff, the producer of all the stage shows, was on vacation, and during his absence Roxy got away with a number of unorthodox experiments he was never encouraged to repeat on Leon's return.

My second year's repertoire consisted almost entirely of dances about rape and seduction. By this time, it had become apparent that Dug was never going to kiss me. We had known each other intimately for four years and the most he had attempted was a peck on my left cheek one Christmas. I had fallen half-fainting against the wallpaper believing, like any Jane Austen young lady, that I was as good as betrothed. He drew back startled and kept himself thereafter in strict rein.

But I was in love and I had to let off steam somehow. *May Day* was a dance about a German girl who was infatuated with a boy who wanted only to eat. *Harvest Reel* was a rape. It was performed as a solo, of course, and it marked the first creative use I had made of pure dancing. For *Ouled Naïl*, a disappointed stomach dancer, I did research in the Greek coffeehouses of Eighth Avenue. Having no recollections, I was absolutely without inhibition. By the time I got through, experts believed I'd learned my stuff in Marrakech and the electrician on the downstage spot left had to leave the stage. Mother heard rumors and was considerably disturbed.

"I don't think that's quite fine for a young girl, do you?"

"What is?"

"A — well — a, a rape?"

"Yes, I think it's fine."

"You had better let me see these dances."

Now I submit that to dance a rape full-out for one's virgin mother is no simple order. I used guile. I invited Edward Johnson, whom she admired very much, to accompany her. He was plainly astonished, and she did not choose to fly in the face of his delight. He invited me out to lunch next day alone and gave me some fatherly advice. Not about dancing.

At the end of the summer, Adolph Bolm invited me to be a guest soloist on his autumn tour. I was to replace Ruth Page and perform three of my own pieces, an agreeable arrangement. The company numbered about fifteen and there was a small orchestra conducted by Louis Horst.

Bolm had been the great character dancer of the original Diaghilev season in Paris. He had created leading roles in *Prince Igor, Thamar, Sadko, Carnaval,* and had followed Nijinsky in *Scheherazade, Le Pavillon d'Armide,* and *Petrouchka.* In 1916, he had come to America with the troupe, and when the company returned to Europe stayed and took over the Metropolitan Opera Ballet and subsequently the Chicago Opera. He formed his "Ballet Intime" and toured with the Barrère Little Symphony, later making an extensive trip through South America and the States with Ruth Page as his leading dancer. For some years prior to the time I joined him, he had been established in Chicago, teaching and directing. His tour was an annual event.

The one I participated in was his last. He was once a great dancer, but had never been, I believe, a very great choreographer. Age, family responsibilities and the dreadful wear and tear of his profession had raveled him to loose ends. At the time I met him, he seemed incapable of coping with the distracting responsibilities of management. And with all the good will in the world, real kindliness and the reinforcement of his incomparable training, he achieved something always just short of his dreams.

So many of the great Russians have gone through this pathetic cycle. Cradled and reared in the enormous organization of their theater, served by the best minds of their generation, they were dismayed to find, on being set free, how much was achieved by the collaboration of others and how childishly helpless they had suddenly become. After Diaghilev's death, the Russian ballet fell completely to pieces and the performers wasted in scattered confusion for five whole years until Massine reorganized them. The stars' predicament was compounded by a haughtiness bred into them, a complete contempt for any other form of dancing which is the hallmark of the Russian Imperial Ballet School; no, let me be more exact — of any European ballet school whatsoever.

This haughtiness was a shield, I believe, for his dismay and bafflement. He had been given all the golden opportunities the United States had to offer — and here he was, inexplicably, with an ill-assorted group of pupils on a second-string tour. His great heart was breaking a little.

He was a warm, passionate man with a true paternal feeling for his charges. They were devoted to him, but that didn't make them dancers to be proud of.

What a sight he was, standing on the station platform, while the porter assembled the packages and boxes of his mongrel company. And the company, tired and chattering, struggled behind and drew lots for their berths. (The electrician and carpenter did not draw lots; they got lowers, by contract. My salary as solo star was fifteen dollars a week more than the carpenter's. But time has worked readjustments since then. The carpenter now gets considerably more than the soloists.) In Chicago, Des Moines, Louisville, Montgomery, Hollins, Macon, Pittsburgh, Bolm stood on the platform, his neck scarf loose, his shapeless felt hat pushed back from his waving hair, the sweat on his forehead still damp from haste and confusion, urging us to collect and trying to recall what he'd surely himself forgotten. He watched us half with affection, half with disappointment.

This should have been the Diaghilev company and they should be at the Gare du Nord. What dreary sequences and decrescendos had replaced Karsavina, Nijinsky, Pavlova, Rubinstein, Lopokova with Hattie, Tottie, Daisy and Bill? "The King of Spain . . . " he said, as the train started to jog, and the outskirts of some city slid by with its Negro slums, gasworks, and foundries lit up in frightening blue revelations. He dashed his hat on the seat opposite and put his arm in fatherly expansion around a ballet girl who cuddled, munching an oversize chocolate bar. His superb large mouth with the sensitive sensual lips curved in a smile of luxurious reminiscence. "The King of Spain led the cheering. That was in the bull ring in Madrid. There was no theater in the city large enough to house the audience." In Macon, Georgia, forty-five tickets had been sold in an auditorium seating four thousand. "For God's sake," said Bolm to me in the afternoon, "you are a university woman, call up the colleges and music schools and tell them this is art — this is culture — that they should come to see it."

In Paris, the opening night of *Prince Igor,* the audience had stormed right up over the footlights and carried him on their shoulders to his dressing room. He was so overcome by the violence of his performance, the intoxication of their response, that all he could do was lie back on a couch and gasp for breath. "Do you think," he said, turning to Louis Horst, "that the Pittsburgh management will ever pay what they owe?"

"No," said Louis, looking up from his detective story, "I don't."

"It will all come out of my pocket then," said Bolm, "the company salaries."

We had given the Pittsburgh performance in an atmosphere of rage, desperation, disappointment and contempt. He naturally refused to do any solos. His costumes went right back in the trunk unused. He never performed any solos where the audience was not large or responsive, and as his first solo preceded mine and I watched the stage manager repacking his white satin tunic, I knew exactly what to expect from front. "Save yourself," he said to me, as I did *relevés* in the wings to warm up my feet, "save yourself, don't throw yourself away. They haven't the faintest idea what you're doing."

"I don't suppose one could get a cup of coffee on this train at night? Naturally not," Bolm would continue, rolling his head against the sooty velours of the seat. "We always had such superb suppers after our galas — the Princesse de Polignac, Gabrielle Chanel, the Aga Khan, Lady Cunard. My dear, I will reconsider and have some of your chocolate bar if you don't mind."

He wandered around the car on the long day jumps, talking to this pair of girls and that, talking in Russian to Vira Mirova, the other guest soloist, coming back to where Louis sat trying to reinforce my aesthetics.

As an antidote for this *Cherry Orchard* atmosphere, Louis Horst talked of Duncan, of Mary Wigman in Germany, and of a young dancer, Martha Graham, who he believed would one day be good; he talked for hours and hours.

I had brought on tour a suitcase the size of a small trunk, and Louis helped me with it. Louis also helped me with finding hotels and places to eat. Nobody else did, and I plainly knew none of the ropes. Whatever town we came to Louis knew the best hotel, the best restaurant. He'd been there before. No matter where we went, he'd been there before.

I was not the first person he'd helped, nor the last. In the course of time, he has accompanied Ruth St. Denis (for twelve years), Ted Shawn, Ruth Page, Doris Niles, Martha Graham, Doris Humphrey, Charles Weidman, Harald Kreutzberg, Helen Tamiris and me. He has taught and composed for very nearly every concert dancer in the business. He has given all of us advice. More, reassurance and comfort and when need arose, money. Over the years he has influenced and helped the dancing in this country more than any other non-dancer, with the possible exception of John Martin and Lincoln Kirstein. The long talks he had with us worked like yeast in our creative thought.

Louis was a very large man, in appearance a cross between Silenus and a German Micawber. His hair had turned prematurely white which made him look old. He always sought to give the impression of a satyr, but he seemed to me from the first fatherly and kind. I've no doubt he will be outraged by this statement. Louis went traveling in a flat peaked tweed cap rather larger than a tam-o'-shanter. His overcoat was vast; his neck scarf long. He carried a music case and a bag which contained one dress suit, the nightly necessaries and a supply of paper-bound detective stories. He read one a day and he seldom read anything else. He had read good books in his youth, he said, and remembered. He never practiced, but an hour and a half before concert time he would try the keyboard and fuss with difficult passages, singing quite loudly to encourage himself. He sang throughout the recital and the alert ear could hear him through the playing. Since he never practiced, it followed he played many wrong notes, but these were of no consequence. Any delicately fingered passage he simply grabbed by the handful and tossed out of his way. He kept the beat and his beat was infallible, his pulse being in fact truer than the performer's.

When his piano constituted the only musical accompaniment, he arranged the instrument in the wings so that he had a clear view of the stage, hanging his coat over the back of his chair and playing in waistcoat and shirt sleeves. When everything was over, he put on his coat for the bow at the end, and then took it right off again and packed it. He turned his own music and gave every curtain cue and light direction. In short, he ran the stage from the keyboard. In between dances, he quietly read the detective story he kept propped on the music rack. On the Bolm tour he found very regretfully he couldn't read because he was on the podium.

When I first saw him sitting with bowed head before a concert, I surmised he was communing with his inner conscience — pulling himself together as I always did. I was very touched at the spectacle of the white-headed man sitting so quietly, meditating, and went up to him and put my hand on his shoulder. He leered at me; there was an Erle Stanley Gardner between the pages of the Scarlatti.

He was an able composer. His pieces for Martha Graham's *Primitive Mysteries, Frontier, Act of Judgment* are strong, inventive and apt. I do not think he has received proper recognition as a composer. His great function, however, has always been as teacher and coach. The long, heartening Pullman talks on the Bolm tour were the beginning of the Horst treatment.

Bolm used to slip into the seat beside us and listen for about four minutes. Then his impatience took the conversation over: Duncan had taught the Russians nothing new; why, he assured us, Fokine had been making researches in Greek archeology for years; she merely appeared at a moment when all the art and theater world was ripe to appreciate her; why, he and Pavlova had danced Greek dances on their first trip through Scandinavia; he had been the first, did we know, to take her out of Russia?

How Bolm loved her! How he cherished her! There would never

be anyone remotely like her and his times with her were golden and irrevocable with the beneficence of fine weather behind his mind.

"Martha writes," said Louis, "that she has seen Argentina and that she is very fine."

"Is she as great as they say?" I asked.

"Martha says very great — and she has had an unprecedented reception. The Spaniards got going with their *olés*, but the whole audience took it up. She is having a triumph." Bolm wandered off. He spoke back over his shoulder, "We did Spanish dancing — have you seen Massine's *Tricorne,* or my *Birthday of the Infanta?* There are dozens as good as Argentina in Spain — Diaghilev took us to see them when we were performing in Madrid. We learned all their dances."

"We must see Argentina as soon as we get back," said Louis.

"If there is another rude audience in Montgomery tomorrow," said Bolm, "I shall not do my mazurka. But I have a great project in mind for an enormous ballet company. Let me tell you."

"I want you to see Martha Graham," said Louis. "You watch her when we get to New York."

ᴄ⁓ᴏ

But it was to Argentina I raced when I got back. I managed to procure a seat at the top of Carnegie and saw a lone woman take the stage accompanied by a single female pianist and dance a whole evening. It was a gallant spectacle. And ordinary people, three thousand of them, laughed and clapped and sighed with delight.

Every detail of her program was effective. Callot had done her clothes. The program was beautifully planned and professional all the way. After the experimental, unevenly attended local entertainments, after the tarnished shabbiness of my recent adventures, this was a great comfort to see. It could happen. Beautiful, magnetic and superbly dressed, she danced as a star is supposed to dance, with fervor and excitement. And, oh, the sound of her castanets and the swing of her body! She released us. She carried us through the rhythms and they were enough. The gestures were enough. There was no part of us pent up, unexpressed to be taken home to ferment. Dancing was an honorable profession when it worked, which it so very seldom did. It was worth a lifetime of pain and sacrifice. In the middle of the third dance as I saw and heard the rhythms resolving and changing and merging so satisfactorily, so rich, so altogether lovely, I felt the blood rush back to my breast. How many young artists the world over took heart of grace from this single enchanting figure? She was a sign and a vindication.

What made her supreme?

First, her sense of rhythm, which has never been approached, not only in the castanets, but in the feet and arms and swinging skirts and the relation of all to the music. Second, in her classic, her architectural sense of composition. (Curiously Argentina could not compose for a group — something most choreographers find easier.) But above all, it was the utter womanliness of her presence. Behind her towered a tradition older than ballet dancing and she was schooled in the last etiquette of that tradition. Behind her loomed generation on generation of anonymous lovely women who had lived out their lives in obscurity and died decently and left no trace except in the innuendo of a fan or the turn of a flounce. She was what the northern European has always dreamed about, the Romantic, the Southern, the distant anonymous lady. She never for one moment seemed like a professional. She had the magic of great evocation and summoned up brilliant women, darling and unregenerate. There never was such a parade of ladies. When she lifted an arm, one felt like standing in recognition. And oh — her smile — the flashing of her dazzling teeth, sudden, free and audacious! She was utterly and completely bewitching, as easy as gardens, or wasted time, or skies. And this is a rare quality these days. Female dancers try too hard — their charm has all run to their tendons.

Bear in mind she came to town at a period when women were flattening their bosoms, shaving their heads, sheathing their trunks in tubes to reveal only the insect legs of the overmuscled athlete and you can imagine the effect of those perfumed skirts and antique veils. But the mystery and suavity of her technique, the lordliness of her creations you cannot imagine — and although sound film had been perfected before she dropped dead of a heart attack in 1936, not one foot of film was ever exposed of her dancing. The Rose of Spain! The irreplaceable lovely lady!

I was profoundly impressed and also no little disturbed by her. Here was lyric movement, nondramatic, without story or particularized character, in unbroken flowing design. The design moved the audience, as the design in music moves and compels, the phrasing, the choice and arrangement of gesture. The grave limitations of my own composition became by contrast shockingly apparent. I could not compose thirty-two bars of continuous dance without using character acting to give it interest. Argentina's creations were as intricately formed as a sonnet. All were delightful and several overwhelming. And although, I noted smugly, she was unbearably coy in her comedy, she was nevertheless a master in handling movement, and movement is the stuff of great communication. "We are interested in you," my theater friends used to say, "because you are more than a dancer. You are an actress." But I knew one could not be more than a dancer — being an actress was less. Of the two media of expression, except in the hands of the very great, dancing is the higher, and more evocative and powerful. I do not think this point can be argued. When Argentina crossed the stage, tears filled my eyes.

Louis Horst and I had been talking about Isadora because the year before her autobiography had appeared and everyone was talking about her. It is in many ways a great book. Perhaps, as some thought, the first statement in our literature of woman as artist, but it proved dreadfully unnerving to the young. Several virgins of my acquaintance went conscientiously astray in the hope of becoming great dancers.

The dance world argued her theories as violently as they had in 1905, and I too, like all beginners, searched for similarities.

Louis Horst

(Reproduced by kind permission of Aline Fruhauf)

Isadora went up to perfect strangers, declared that she was not only the greatest dancer in the world but she was changing all art and founding a new religion as well. She was sure of this at the age of twenty-two before she had once performed publicly. Isadora scorned scenery, costumes and all music except the greatest. She found a new heroic way of moving. She broke all the traditional moralities and lived like a bacchante. She indicated you couldn't be an artist unless you did. These ideas tortured me — I had been brought up to believe you must love the man you kissed, pay your bills, keep your word, be as modest as possible and work faithfully. If inspiration hit you along the way, so much the better, but it was not to be counted on. That was not bacchic. That was not Duncan. That, in fact, was everything she set her wild will against. I was not sure I was going to change anything including the shape of my legs. I would very much have liked to be heroic but it struck me that if I went against my instincts I would really be whoring.

Obviously I was not to follow the great pattern and I suffered dismay at the prospect of anything short of all that was most exalted. Louis sympathized with Isadora and urged revolution on all counts. But John Martin, whom I met just then, eased my doubts a little. "She disliked costumes and scenery and popular music. You like them. You belong to the theater. That's all there is to it. One can be very moving in the theater."

CHAPTER 14

Local Girl

IT IS GENERALLY RECKONED that the cost of launching any concert career is around forty thousand dollars, and the soloist who creates his own vehicles must of course count on spending more because the maturing process is doubly hard and much slower. In a brisk interview I had with Sol Hurok about this time, he named three thousand dollars as the overall cost for presenting me in a series of New York concerts, a very conservative estimate. I declined, hoping I could earn my way as I went and that no such frightening expenditure would ever be demanded in a lump sum. This was poor economy. Concert artists cannot pay their way for years and very substantial sums have to be risked without guarantee of any return. But I did not feel justified in losing three thousand dollars in a lump at this point.

The cost of a single concert in the early thirties was about twelve hundred dollars without rehearsal or costume expenses. Add to this a year's rehearsing, studio rental, pianists' fees and lessons and, on top of all, costumes. Multiply by four for the cost of every item today and you will see why so few dance recitals are given. Even with sold-out houses, the dancers lose heavily. In the late twenties and early thirties, the only dancer who could draw more than twelve hundred dollars a performance was Martha Graham. Mother began to lose several thousand a year on my career although I always hoped she wouldn't and never counted on the repeated expense.

Then, on short notice, I found myself engaged to choreograph and dance Christopher Morley's revival of *The Black Crook* in Hoboken. This was the first time I had ever arranged dances for a group.

Now I felt it was time to get a partner. Warren Leonard came to audition for me bringing an introduction from John Martin. He arrived in a blizzard, hatless, with the ice melting on his lashes and two ballet slippers stuck in pockets, one on either side of his great-coat. "I would like you to jump for me," I said. He took off his galoshes, removed his muffler and overcoat and, putting the slippers on his feet, started jiggling up and down. "Don't you want to change and warm up?" I asked.

"Why?" he said, staring at me blandly.

He jiggled twice more, rose vertically and touched his hand to the ceiling, then stood waiting for the next orders. "Anything else?"

"Jump like Kreutzberg."

He jumped like Kreutzberg.

"Can you do ballet dancing?"

"Sure."

"What else?"

"Tap, acrobatic, adagio, acrobatic tap, front overs, back overs."

"Can you lift me?"

"Depends on how much you weigh. I don't know how you dance, you know. You've got to show me a thing or two before I answer all your questions." With that, he fell to the floor and did twenty-five push-ups.

"Can you act?"

"Sure. Why not? What's there to acting?"

I confirmed all this with Martin. John said he could act. And he could. Very nicely, with a dry humor and an excellent, subtle sense of character.

We began to rehearse. Warren thought I was a mess, too fat, too slow, too timid.

"You depend on your personality to get by with murder," he said. "Never mind all that fancy feeling. You've missed your fall three times running now. And your back — how do you expect me to pick you up if you don't hold your back? Don't you care if you do a thing right?" This was an old-time vaudevillian speaking — one did one's tricks right or one got fired.

"I'm tired," I whimpered.

"What's that got to do with it? You're scared too. Why are you always so scared? Afraid I'm going to drop you? Here, I will drop you. It's not so bad." He dropped me. Deliberately. I hit on my chest.

"It's not bad, is it?"

"It's not good," I said quietly.

"Well, now you see? Now get up and do it again and do it right." I toughened up. He was tireless. He also despised food during rehearsal hours. Rehearsal hours were four hours at a stretch. No food, no rest, no conversation. Lots of argument. "Oh, honey," he said one day after a long workout, taking my face between his hands and gazing tenderly at me, "oh, honey, you're so lousy!"

He argued about music which was supposed to be my province, he not having had much experience with music outside of Orpheum orchestras. "No, no," he would say, his voice rising to falsetto with irritation. "You've done something bad with that phrase. It's not right. I won't let you do it."

He argued about language. I said one day very gently, "May I criticize something? You said 'I sing good.' That's not only untrue, it's ungrammatical."

"You pronounce 'apotheosis' wrong," he snapped.

He argued about clothes. He didn't like the way I dressed. Nobody ever had — but he began running around town to find suitable and attractive things for me to buy. Mother was appalled. "What right has this boy to make such suggestions?"

"He cares how I look."

"Don't you think I care how you look? Haven't I always?"

"Why doesn't she stay out of our rehearsals?" said Warren.

"What's he doing to your work?" said Mother.

"Please, don't be rude to her, Warren," I begged.

"Tell her not to be rude to me."

They were rude to one another from then on. Implacably. Never in all the time I worked with him did the tension between them slacken — until he stopped dancing with me, and then she converted him promptly to Single Tax and he became her lifelong friend and devoted correspondent.

I was being ripped from the placenta. I was being frog-marched into maturity — not a gentle process. Dug had tried somewhat and had even gone to the length of losing his temper once when Mother refused to let him take me to see *The Captive,* a play dealing with Lesbianism, which was causing a sensation in New York. But Dug gave way fast. He respected Mother, and he didn't want trouble. He did not care enough to do battle. Warren cared enough. He didn't think it was right that I should live in thrall, and when Warren didn't think it was right he just planted his feet and squared off. He was pugnacious, stubborn and mercilessly idealistic. Tact to him was compromise. All intercourse was apt to be sterling and uncomfortable; rehearsals above all were rigorous.

Whenever, for instance, I showed him a passage on which I had been working, he studied it stonily. Then:

"That's rotten."

"Have you nothing more to say?"

"No, what should I say? It's no good."

"I've been working for days, surely it has something."

"What are you trying to do? Wear me down? I'm sorry to hurt your feelings. It's no good."

Tears.

Twenty minutes later, after stampings up and down the studio, a couple of false exits, and tea, would come an intelligent and helpful criticism. We both would by this time be quite exhausted. My dance technique, however, began to improve. He was just as harsh with himself.

The Black Crook turned out to be great fun but the production was disorganized. The dress rehearsal lasted two days and they never did get around to timing the last act. I remember I tore all the blankets and pillows from my local hotel room and bedded down my dancing girls on the floor of the theater boxes for the two nights of dress rehearsal.

The opening performance endured five and a half hours, from eight-thirty until two in the morning. The audience that came in at eight-thirty went home at twelve, and a brand-new audience off the streets and from the Hofbraus and other Hoboken theaters, sauntered in free and filled up the emptying seats. Of course, they didn't know what the play was about, but that didn't matter. The dramatic critics went home at eleven and so missed all my work. John Martin stuck it out and came tottering backstage, with his wife, at two-fifteen. Not only that, but he took Warren and me out for food and cheer — and he did cheer us. He thought we were splendid, and he wrote long columns about us in the Sunday *Times*. But no agent or manager ever read a dance critic, so it didn't help commercially.

During the course of the season, Warren inadvertently kicked me in the face (an error due to my absent-mindedness) and broke my nose. The sound, a kind of wet scrunch, carried to the back of the theater, but, I am proud to say, neither of us missed step. This did not improve my nose. Neither did it hurt it. It remained the same, but the episode (I danced with splints up my nostrils) fatigued me and I was galled at doing the same thing every night, and I decided to quit after three months. The experience, in any case, had degenerated. People crossed the Hudson in the spring evenings to eat German food and drink beer spiked with ether. They arrived late at the theater, very high, not to say a little crazy. I danced through a barrage of peanuts, popcorn, beer coasters, chewing-gum wrappers and programs and a tumult of catcalls, whistles and drunken singing. I didn't like it. I handed in my notice.

Then for a period that seemed endless I tried to break my way through into any possible kind of entertainment. I appeared in third-rate moving-picture houses in Baltimore, Max Reinhardt's

Chorus, a stock company (I had agreed to play anything given me and was handed a piano off stage), a movie short, private parties, third-rate night clubs. All I balked at was jigging on the sidewalk with a tambourine. There was no stone I didn't turn, no door I didn't beat against. From time to time, well-meaning friends would suggest something. Whatever it was I had tried it. Absolutely nothing worked — nothing lasted — nothing led to anything else. And yet whenever I put foot to stage under proper conditions I could make an audience rock with laughter. It seemed inexplicable. I continued to give auditions. One for Billy Rose lasted four hours. He saw nine of my dances in full costume — a concert. He thanked me very courteously afterwards.

Margaret had in the meantime abandoned college and obtained jobs on a single reading with George Cukor's stock company and the Theatre Guild. Thereafter she was never without theater work when she wished to have it; all she had to do was ask.

I continued to audition.

Although it is always most difficult to triumph in the city of your childhood, it was in Hollywood, which had become the Mecca of the theatrical world, that I believed I should find appreciation. I suspect, in addition, the prospect of going back and showing off was irresistible. So Mother cashed a couple of bonds and back we went, the three of us and Warren.

I begged her not to let the family know of our advent, thinking to keep myself concentrated by an ascetic seclusion, but she wrote Aunt Constance and there was a delegation of aunts and cousins at the station. I, however, refused to dismount to be kissed. I wished to be considered as a star and sneaked out the back of the train, but my presence was discovered by the five-and-a-half-foot Civil War musket I carried on my shoulder. As it happened, no other passenger had one. So the cousins, gawking and snickering and looking back over their shoulders, though in deference to my feelings not one of them durst wave or call, were herded by the aunts into the family limousines and driven away by family chauffeurs.

Mother and I holed up in a hotel on Vine Street in the precise

location of the beautiful fruit gardens that had once graced this
loveliest of thoroughfares, cater-cornered from the old Lasky studio,
gone now and replaced by the aggressive and thankless stores and
filling stations of the southwestern boom town. It was a commercial
hotel full of noise and heat. Mother found it depressing and longed
for the suave hospitality of the guest suite at Aunt Constance's
where she could look out over arbors of jasmine and Cecile Brunner
roses toward the hills and where Frederik, the butler, would serve
her breakfast and kindly reminiscences in the Italian garden. But
I was adamant. I felt my professionalism would be jeopardized if
I put one foot inside that soft and seductive manse. I begged
Mother to go but she refused to leave me alone in a hotel in Hollywood under the same roof with a male dancing partner. That I was
old enough to vote made no matter.

We hired a theater — the Music Box — and a stage manager. We
hired a press agent, a brilliant woman, Agnes O'Malley, whose other
client was Oscar Hammerstein II. Our preparations took about
eight days. During this time I phoned my father once but refused
to see anyone except two college professors. Lily Campbell came to
the lighting rehearsal and forgave me on the spot for persisting in
this career. I was excited, but not frightened. I'd done all the dances
before, and I knew they were good.

The house was sold out. All the schoolmates, college friends,
teachers and playmates of my lifetime and all Mother's and Father's
friends came to see if their girl had the family spark. The lobby
was banked with flowers.

Mother's divorce had been a sad and shocking surprise to large
numbers of people. It was not an easy or so-called civilized divorce.
They had been husband and wife and they did not remain friends.
Mother's heart broke. To the day of her death, she did not understand what had happened. For five years after the separation, she
did not enter a room or a theater where she might encounter him.
It was ten years before she could communicate more or less casually
on business matters. Both Mother and Father were deeply loved.
The marriage had lasted twenty-three years and had been con-

sidered one of the happiest in Hollywood. Our home, as I have tried to indicate, had been a center for all kinds of gay and interesting enterprises. Our home was for many a real hearth. Now, on this night hundreds turned out, not merely to see a dance recital by a beginner, nor out of vulgar curiosity, but rather, I think, as an affectionate tribute to both of them and well-wishing toward me as the daughter of beloved friends and a symbol of past lovely times. Half the audience waved to Mother and blew her kisses; everyone in the balcony leaned forward. On the arm of Cecil she came down the aisle nodding right and left and bravely trying not to see Pop. She looked very well, but of course she was not happy.

Father had married the brilliant scenario writer Clara Beranger and they sat quietly where I'd given them seats as far away from Mother as was consistent with his position.

And I was backstage warming up. My father had never seen me dance professionally. He had set his life and heart against my dancing. Now he was out front as one member of a very large paying audience, three quarters of which were professional. I tried to think of the audience and not of him.

As for him, he must have been nervous indeed. Bear in mind, he had seen only two amateur shows in college and nothing since; if I were going to let down the family name, I had chosen the most public possible means of doing so, and the most poignant locality. The emotional circus in the theater was difficult also for him. He sat rigid.

The curtain went up and I rushed on in my yellow tutu swinging the watering pot. There was an immediate laugh from the house. Pop slouched to his normal sitting position on the middle of his spine, turned to Clara, his wife, and nodded. At the end of the number, he appeared considerably relieved. Adjacent friends leaned over and patted him on the shoulder.

Being largely professional, the audience behaved splendidly — quick, responsive, astute and affectionate. I don't suppose I ever danced better.

O'Malley brought Hammerstein backstage and he stood by the

side of his handsome wife and gazed with benevolence and kindly enthusiasm. My pieces showed marked talent, he said. The problem was how to use it. This was July 1930 — it took him twelve years to think of a way. In October 1942, when he was planning *Oklahoma!,* I jogged his elbow and suggested one.

After I'd talked to friends, separated Mother and Warren who were having a violent quarrel about something unimportant, packed all the costumes, collected the music, paid off the dressers, bawled out the stage managers and tipped the stagehands, I dried off and tried to pull myself together. In the frenzy, during performance, my evening dress had fallen on the floor, one stocking had sprung a run, I had forgotten to bring the proper brassière. Mother and Warren finally cleaned me up and got me to a car. I looked as I always looked off stage — exhausted, unkempt, not exactly clean, and harried.

I went up to Uncle Cecil's for a party. The big house was wide open with lights. The table shone in crystal and silver. Everyone I knew circled around: Mary Smith who had played Castle, the girls at school, the Mayer girls, Irene Mayer, now Mrs. David Selznick, Edith Mayer, now Mrs. William Goetz (Edith said to me, "I am surprised, I always thought you'd be artistic and things like that. I never thought you'd be original"), Joel McCrea, my piano teacher, the boys who had flanked me at college, Macon and Morgan, Boynton, the librarian, my professors and all the old guard from the Lasky studio — all were there — and new brilliant moving-picture stars and Dug who was having a fine moving-picture career.

Frederik, the Norwegian butler, blushing with pleasure, told Mother that this night was what he had waited for all the years he'd watched me dancing in the parlor. Father, of course, had not been invited.

Oh, but it was a success! All the Los Angeles newspapers ran columns with banner headlines — "De Mille girl makes good." I trusted everyone at the studios was talking. Now, I would get a job, now, quickly.

The next day, Father sent his car to take me to M-G-M where he was working. I went alone. He had sent no message of what he thought or how he liked it — just that he wanted to see me.

When I entered his office, he was sitting at his desk by the window. He swung around and looked at me without speaking and I saw him again. Pop, older, much older, furrowed with sadness and endurance. But the face I had grown up with, the familiar face, my father, the love, the honored one of my childhood and youth. He opened his arms — I rushed to him. I had been caught between two heartbreaks. I couldn't serve both with equal fervor. All the time I had been serving one — now I served the other a little.

I went to live in his home. I became reconciled to the new situation. His wife, Clara, proved herself a generous, wise, and kind friend and throughout the years has never stinted help. This I had to accept with discretion because of Mother's refusal to recognize the marriage as anything but an outrage to her heart and life.

On the strength of the first success we gave a repeat concert and Father bought hundreds of dollars of tickets and saw to it that every important producer and agent was in the house. But there was no professional result from the effort.

I saw Uncle Cecil. Not since Gloria Swanson, he said, had he met with a young woman of such promise. He proposed to road-show me through the United States with my own large company, my own manager, my own press agent, his idea being exploitation on a circus scale. "Do you think you could be ready in two months?" My jaw dropped. "Perhaps in two years," I said numbly. Since it had taken me three years to compose six good dances, and since furthermore I knew almost nothing about choreography for groups, I doubted how soon I could learn. I obviously needed time. I needed most importantly not to be hurried. I wished to be endowed while I learned. "In two years I'll retrieve your offer. I'm not ready yet." Cecil was dumfounded. He was also very disappointed. Star careers were made of brilliant showmanship, not time. In the years that would pass while I was getting ready my youth would go and the novelty and surprise value of my style would diminish.

"Now is the time," he said. "There is such a thing as the right moment."

He never made the offer again.

But perhaps he would give me a job, I thought, if not as a dancer ("You can't be photographed," he said. "Teeth and nose you know"), then as a dance director, costume researcher, music researcher, assistant director.

At the request for a job, he looked at me square — "But you are my brother's daughter. I cannot put you in a job in pictures. That's nepotism."

"Is that important?"

Yes, he said, it was. Because of his position.

When he had seen me perform, he explained, he had been deeply impressed and had thought to himself, "There's a fascinating and interesting woman," but then I had come to his party, stockings wrinkled, hair falling down, dress rumpled and ill-fitting, make-up smeared — a frump. "This is just a dowdy girl," he'd thought. Too bad. And if he thought that, every man would think so.

"But, Uncle Ce, I look fine on stage."

"Splendid. But that's not all that counts."

Indeed, indeed it wasn't. My costumes were minor works of art, down to the last hairpin and button. Couldn't he accept this as enough? Must I also exhibit the coquetry of the women I have seen at his knees all my life? Did not my relationship, did not my achievement, have some claim on his pity? No. Cecil was regarding me undomestically. I had asked to be a professional; I was being treated like a professional.

I told him I was exhausted after concerts and before them, that I was always exhausted. Then I was to arrange matters better.

"If I had twenty-five dollars a week of earned money, I think I could keep my stockings unwrinkled."

"Keep them unwrinkled anyway. You do not lack money. Your father takes good care of you."

"I lack confidence."

"That no one can give you. Do you think anyone gave me confidence when I first came to Hollywood?"

He terminated the interview by signing a personal check for seventy-eight thousand dollars made out to Irving Thalberg on some bond transaction. He showed this to me with a wry smile and picked up the phone.

Then Father indicated that he also was ready to talk business and I began to shake immediately. Our family has always been very tense about money. I didn't want his money; I wanted him — the father-director — to make a star of me. But he said he would give me six thousand dollars, that he considered I had proved myself worthy of help.

No tours in America being possible for lack of an American impresario, we decided to put the money toward a European tour. I had found a European manager and I emptied my own bank account as an earnest of my intentions, then asked for some of the promised six thousand to wire to Europe. But in the meantime, having discussed the matter with his old crony and classmate, John Erskine, who as head of the Juilliard was in a position to know about these matters, he had been dissuaded from participating in the swindle of another American debutante. The exploitation of American artists, Erskine claimed, was the chief source of income of unscrupulous European managers. Father drew back affrighted, his venture in the concert business having lasted just seventy-two hours. None of his money was to be offered managers to waste, European or otherwise.

"But Pop," I wailed, "my own five hundred has gone."

"Get it back," he said. I never got it back.

"What shall I do then?"

"Women's clubs, concert tours —

"I cannot have a tour. No manager will touch an American. There are no ballet companies. I cannot get on Broadway. I have auditioned for every single person in the business. You yourself have seen what's happened in Hollywood. I'll never become a dancer performing only twice a year. I'm going through Mother's entire savings. I cannot bear it."

"Well, keep trying," said Pop.

"How? What shall I do that I haven't done?"

"I don't know. I know nothing of concert business. John Erskine says it's a racket — Just keep trying."

What I could not accept was that Father in truth did not know how to help. He was having trouble in Hollywood in pictures (1930 was a desperate year, and the turnover in the studios was dictated by panic) and he did not in fact know anything of the concert business. But what I wanted, what I had always wanted, was to have him take over. Mother and I were obviously botching the business. That he was not the qualified person made no matter. There is no reasonable answer to "I want."

There was one concrete result of our Hollywood trip. Pop took me to interview Bernard P. Fineman at M-G-M with the thought that he might find a job for me, and Margaret, as usual, was along, and, as usual, looked very smart. As we left Fineman's office, she remarked quietly, "I think I'll marry that man." She did six weeks later.

When I returned to New York I moved from Mother's apartment. She stopped eating for a few days and wept every night, but I stuck it out. I moved to a faded and extremely dubious uptown hotel where all manner of disreputable things happened in the corridors. By taking inside rooms I was able to afford a suite. I couldn't tell midnight from noon, there was no air, and the furniture was early Pullman. But it was mine. Absolutely, entirely mine, with total privacy. I found for the first time in my life that I could work without effort. I worked half the night and no one said, "Put out the light, dearie."

C H A P T E R   1 5

Martha Graham

I WENT, as Louis Horst urged, one Sunday night, to see Martha Graham.[1] She performed with the assistance of three of her pupils from the Eastman School. She was impressive, certainly, but I found myself neither charmed nor moved. All of the dance public was arrested, but, at first, very few became enthusiasts. Martha, however, continued giving concerts, and no one of us ever stayed away. Each time I saw her, I saw more.

This was a stirring period in American dance history — a period of revolution and adventure. There were at least ten soloists working in New York, each making experiments. There were a score or more imitators expanding and developing our discoveries. Every Sunday, throughout the winter season, at least two dance concerts were given, frequently more, and the two dance critics, *Times* and *Tribune,* spent the afternoon and evening zigzagging through the forties in an effort to keep up. We all turned out en bloc for every occasion, wrangling and fighting in the lobbies as though at a political meeting.

Louis Horst played for a great portion of the concerts, sometimes

---

[1] All dance concerts except those given at Town or Carnegie Hall took place on Sunday nights. It was strictly against the law to dance in New York State on Sunday, but this was the only day theaters were available for rental. We broke the law until we were threatened, at the instigation of the Sabbath League, with arrest. Then the dancers organized and, headed by Helen Tamiris and me, we went to Albany and changed the law.

accompanying Tamiris in the afternoon, dashing off to Doris Humphrey in the evening and working all night on the score of Martha's new *première*.

The dance seasons these days are quite different. They are more professional and vastly more expensive, and the elegants show up in full dress, something they never did before, but the atmosphere then was crisp with daring. We risked everything. Every one of us had thrown overboard all our traditions, ballet, Duncan, Denishawn, or what not, and were out to remodel our entire craft. No one helped us, and there were no rules. We worked alone. We struck sparks from one another. It was a kind of gigantic jam session and it lasted nine years, until the end of WPA. There are brilliant young dancer-choreographers today, but no one with the power of Graham or Humphrey, and all of them are derived from and imitative of the styles launched in the 'thirties or earlier.

I am glad I participated in the period of the originators. There is a force and wonder in first revelation that has no duplicate. Greater dancers may be coming, greater and more subtle choreography, but we worked when there was no interest, no pattern, no precedent, no chance. We made it all as we went along, and every concert was a perilous test for all of us, a perilous, portentous challenge. The whole subsequent flowering of concert dance had its seed in this period. But from the first Martha was the most startling inventor, and by all odds the greatest performer that trod our native stage.

In the early days when I first got to know her, there was a good deal of talk about Graham, a lot of it unfriendly. People wondered what she was about. They always rushed like crazy to see at the next concert. Folks resented her unorthodoxy — the cult of her students, her temper, her tyranny, the expression of her face, the cut of her hair and, not least, her success.

The first time I saw her off stage, she was sitting in a New York theater in a melancholy which I had been told was her characteristic public pose. I had not met her, but I could not take my eyes off her. Heads were turning all around. Martha's presence, no matter how passive, cuts through attention, arrests speech, interrupts ideas. At the moment, she was sitting unmoving and silent. Her dark head with its cavernous cheeks and sunken eyes drooped on one shoulder. She held a single rose in her right hand which she sniffed from time to time. Louis Horst, to whom she did not address a word, sat stolidly beside her. She looked half starved, tragic and self-conscious. Two of these things she certainly was not. She ate enough for three. And while she was, from time to time, quite thoroughly unhappy, she was not ever, I learned, self-pitying. But she was unquestionably aloof. The first theatrical tradition she broke was that of being a good egg — one of the gang. She foresaw she had a lot to think out, and she arranged to have the privacy to do it in. This people resented. They said she was queer and arty. She wasn't queer; she just wasn't around.

I got to know her in a quite plain, folksy way because Louis Horst took us to dinner occasionally at Hugo Bergamasco's restaurant. Hugo was our flutist and served Italian dinners cooked in the back room by his mother and wife. Hugo made fine prohibition red wine and discoursed on modern music as he served the spaghetti. On the dining room walls hung signed photographs of Martha and me, the sexiest ones we could find. I almost always thought of her as a girl friend — almost, but not quite always; one does not domesticate a prophetess.

From the beginning, Graham knew what she wanted to do and did it. She was born in Pittsburgh of Scotch Presbyterian parents, and raised in Santa Barbara, California. Her father was a physician who specialized in mental ailments. So from an early age she grew accustomed to the idea that people move as they do for reasons. Her father, for instance, used to detect lying by the manner in which people held their hands. He did not wish her to dance. She had to wait until he died before she started training.

She entered the Denishawn School in Los Angeles while attending the Cumnock School and came under the spell of Ruth St. Denis. Thereafter she never took any aspect of dancing flippantly. When she was graduated from high school, she joined the troupe as a student and performed tangos with Ted, japanese flower arrangements with Miss Ruth, and music visualizations to Doris Humphrey's choreography. I saw her during this period. I remember her hurtling through the room to Schubert, or sitting barelegged on the polished floor with smoldering watchfulness. The mask of her face was like porcelain over red-hot iron. One felt that the gathering force within might suddenly burst the gesture, the chiffon, the studio walls, the pretty groupings of graceful girls. The intensity she brought to bear on each composition was not comfortable to watch. She went with the troupe on a European tour. Ted Shawn built an Aztec ballet around her which gave her the opportunity to vent some of her ebullience. In this she had the chance, for instance, to gnaw on his leg. No one subsequently, they told me, ever did this so well.

It was during this tour that she came under the influence of Louis Horst, then Denishawn musical director. He urged her to try her own wings. So she up and left, and with great courage came to New York and started out on her own. Horst left the home fold shortly thereafter.

Denishawn viewed this double departure poorly. Girls did not rebel this way. Not since Miss Ruth herself dressed up as an Egyptian cigarette ad in 1906 and gave Oriental mysticism a new lease on life by undulating in a roof-garden restaurant had a young woman broken with tradition so flagrantly. For the last two decades dancing had been Russian, which was art; American, which was commercial (tap, acrobatic, ballroom, or musical comedy, the last a vague term applicable to anything successfully cute); Duncan, which while emotionally good for young girls was fast losing favor; or Denishawn, which combined the best features of all. Graham had the audacity to think that there might be still another way, stronger and more indigenous.

Martha put in a couple of seasons in the *Greenwich Village Follies.* Then, with a little money saved, she started serious experimenting. She taught at the Eastman School of Music, entering the project with great diffidence. But Horst believed she had genius.

He accepted, however, no easy revelations. He scolded and forced and chivied; the relationship was full of storm and protest.

"You're breaking me," she used to say. "You're destroying me."

"Something greater is coming," he promised, and drove her harder. "Every young artist," he explained once, "needs a wall to grow against like a vine. I am that wall."

Louis chivied me also about many things. He never stopped urging me to leave Mother, to take lovers, to give up comedy pantomime, open my own school, to read Nietzsche, to stop practicing ballet exercises, to get away from my family, to give up all thought of marriage.

Louis had paid the rent and bills of I don't know how many pupils, had paid for their pianos, given his services, held their heads, buried their dead and taught their young. But my indication of normal well-being revolted him — or so he said, particularly in relation to Martha. She, he believed, had been set aside for a special vocation. There was neither time nor opportunity for private life. She had elected the hardest of all professions for women, and she was a pioneer in that profession. She was, I am sure, although she has never said so except indirectly through her work, also convinced in heart that it must be for her either art or life. . . . She could not have a home in the ordinary sense if she wished to serve her talent. Through her a new art form was to be revealed.

Ballet has striven always to conceal effort; she on the contrary thought that effort was important since, in fact, effort was life. And because effort starts with the nerve centers, it follows that a technique developed from percussive impulses that flowed through the body and the length of the arms and legs, as motion is sent through a whip, would have enormous nervous vitality. These impulses she called "contractions." She also evolved suspensions and falls utilizing the thigh and knees as a hinge on which to raise and lower the body to the floor, thus incorporating, for the first time, the ground into the gesture proper. All this differs radically from ballet movement. It is different from Wigman's technique, and it is probably the greatest addition to dance vocabulary made this century, comparable to the rules of perspective in painting or the use of the thumb in keyboard playing. No dancer that I can name has expanded technique to a comparable degree. She has herself alone given us a new system of leverage, balance and dynamics. It has gone into the idiom.

This may not seem much to a non-dancer. But compare her findings with the achievements of other single historical figures. Camargo in her lifetime is supposed to have invented the *entrechat quatre*, or jumps with two crossed beatings of the legs, and to have shortened the classic skirt to ankle length. Heinel created the double pirouette. Vestris, the greatest male dancer of the eighteenth century, expanded the leg beatings (batterie) from four to eight and evolved pirouettes of five or six revolutions. The father of Maria Taglioni put her up on full point although others had been making tentative efforts in this line. Legnani exploited the *fouetté* pirouette — not her own invention. None of these altered the basic principles or positions of ballet technique. Anna Pavlova is credited by Svetlov, her biographer, with adding the trill on points. These are each minute advancements for a lifetime of experimenting.

It may be argued that Duncan created a new way of moving. But this is not strictly true. She refused, rather, to accept the old way and evolved a personal expression that was based on simple running, walking and leaping. She worked almost without dance technique. Her influence has been incalculable, but her method was too personal for transference.

In the twenty years prior to the last war in Germany, Rudolf von Laban and, after him, Mary Wigman developed a fresh approach with an enormous code of technique and, being German, correlated a philosophy and psychology to go with it. But they and their schools represent the achievement of an aggregate of workers and their style stems strongly from the Oriental. Strangely enough, Graham's style, for all its Denishawn background, does not. And in evaluating her work it must be remembered that Graham's technique was clarified before ever she saw a dancer from Central

Europe. The two great modern schools, German and American, evolved without interaction of any kind. It is bootless to discuss which, if either, is more influential. I am inclined to think Graham's contains more original invention.

It is noteworthy of Graham that in twenty years of composing she is still what she was at the beginning: the most unpredictable, the most searching, the most radical of all choreographers. She is one of the great costume designers of our time, as revolutionary in the use of material as Vionnet. In point of view and subject matter, in choice of music and scenery, she cuts across all tradition. And for each new phase, there was needed a whole new style. Her idiom has shown as great a variety as Picasso's.

In ideas she has always led the field. She was doing dances of revolt and protest to the posh days of 1929. She was searching religious ritual and American folkways when revolution became the young radicals' artistic line in 1931–1933. The Communists then suddenly discovered that they were Americans with grass roots down to the center of Moscow and put every pressure on Graham to make her their American standard-bearer. But she was nobody's tool. She was already through with folkways and making experiments in psychology, and while other concerts were padded with *American Suites* and *Dust Bowl Ballads*, Graham began to turn out her superb satires, *Every Soul Is a Circus* and *Punch and the Judy*, which foreshadowed some of Tudor's work and a very great deal of Robbins and de Mille. The dance world seethed with satire and Martha concerned herself with woman as artist and then woman as woman, inaugurating her poetic tragedies *Letter to the World, Deaths and Entrances* and *Salem Shore*, and developing the first use of the spoken word in relation to dance pattern. Everyone else began to do biographies; Graham delved deeper and deeper into anthropology — *Dark Meadow*. She began to search Greek mythology for the key to woman's present discomforts — *Labyrinth, Cave of the Heart, Night Journey*. Nowadays the doctors sit out front biting their nails and taking sharp note.

Her students plainly worshiped. She was followed by a coterie of idolaters. To the Philistines, and they included all the press except Martin of the *Times* and Watkins of the *Tribune*, she was a figure of mockery, "a dark soul," a freak. The public and critics were in turn outraged, exasperated, stimulated or adoring. No one was ever indifferent. This is the exact *status quo* today — twenty years later.

The center of all this turmoil one might have supposed was a virago, a wild-eyed harridan. Well, she could be. If she thought her prerogatives were questioned, she was a very bold woman to cross. I was told by her girls that Martha in a rage was like something on a Greek tripod.

Furthermore, she could be formidable when it takes great courage to be. In 1936 the Nazi government invited her to the Olympic Games — the only American artist so honored. This would have meant world-wide publicity and a whacking great sum she badly needed. Let anyone who so much as bought a German boat passage between 1931 and 1939 dare to look down his nose at the offer. Martha received the representatives courteously and replied, "But you see half my group is Jewish."

The Germans rose screaming in protest. Not one of them would be treated with incivility. Their status as American citizens and as her pupils would ensure their protection.

"But," said Martha, "I also am an American citizen and their friend and sponsor. And do you think I would enter a country where you treat your citizens and their people in such a manner?"

"It would be too bad," said the Germans, "if America were represented by any but the best."

"It would be too bad for you," said Martha, "because everybody would know exactly why."

Martha told me this herself and added cheerfully that she knew she was listed at the German consulate in New York for immediate attention when opportunity offered. No dancer from the United States went to Germany that year.

I saw her only once in one of her alerted moods. It was during the time she was working under the direction of Massine in his *Sacre de Printemps*. They achieved a really splendid clashing of wills. He accused her of stubbornly refusing to do anything he asked; she claimed he asked her to do what was outside her technical abilities. She had never in her life done anything she didn't believe in. He, on the other hand, was a king in the theater and used to instantaneous and terrified obedience. Stokowski rode herd. She had resigned twice before they got the curtain up. I saw her sitting on her bed in Philadelphia with a cup of cocoa in her hands.

"I wouldn't have got out for anything in the world," she said pleasantly, her eyes bright as a vixen's in the brush. "There is no power that could have made me give up. I think he hoped I would. But I won't. But of course I've had to resign repeatedly. Oh, but I was angry today. I strode up and down and lashed my tail."

Strangely enough, the impression she has always made is essentially feminine. She is small — five feet three inches. On the stage, she seems tall, gaunt and powerful. She looks starved, but her body is deceptively sturdy. She has probably the strongest back and thighs in the world. She has an instep under which you could run water, a clublike square-toed foot with a heel and arch of such flexibility and strength that she seems to use it like a pogo stick. Her feet have an animal-like strength and suppleness that makes you feel she could, if she chose, bend her knees and clear the traffic. She is able actually to do things with her feet in an inching snake-like undulation that no one else has even approximated. She has a split kick, straight up, 180 degrees.

She is well-turned-out, almost to the degree of being crotch-sprung. (I am not now speaking sartorially. She is that as well.) It was on her own body that she built her technique.

Her arms are long and inclined to be both brawny and scrawny; the hands are heartbreaking, contorted, work-worn, the hands of a washerwoman. All the drudgery and bitterness of her life have gone into her hands. These are the extremities, roped with veins and knotted in the joints, that seem to stream light when she lifts them in dance.

But all of this is statistical chatter. It is the face one sees first and last, the eyes and voice that hold one. I mentioned the other characteristics because once she starts talking, there is no time for remarking them. The shape of the face is Mongoloid with skin drawn taut over the bones. The cheeks are hollows. In the eye sockets, the great doelike orbs glow and blaze and darken as she speaks. Her eyes are golden yellow flecked with brown and on occasion of high emotional tension seem slightly to project from the lids while the iris glows like a cat's. The little nose is straight and delicate. The mouth is mobile, large, and generally half-opened in a kind of dreamy receptivity. The skin of her glistening teeth, the skin of her lips, the skin of her cheeks and nose is all exposed and waiting with sensitive delight like the skin of an animal's face, or the surface of a plant as it bends toward light; every bit of surface breathing, listening, experiencing. The posture is just this, a delighted forward thrust that exposes the mouth. In more than one way she resembles Nefertiti, the long passionate neck, the queenly head, the bending, accepting, listening posture.

Her laughter is girlish and light — quite frequently a giggle. She has a sly wit that reminds one in its incisive perception of Jane Austen, or of Emily Dickinson whom she so greatly reveres. She loves pretty female things although she lives stripped to the wheels, and she manages to dress with great chic on an imperceptible budget, having the happy faculty of always appearing right for any occasion. Her hair is black and straight as a horse's tail. Her voice is low, dark and rusky, clear and bodyless like most dancers'. Her speech — who shall describe Martha's speech? The breathless, halting search for the releasing word as she instructs a student, the miracle word she has always found. The gentle "you see it should be like this," as her body contracts with lightning, plummets to the earth and strikes stars out of the floor. "Now you try it. *You* can do it." Thus Diana to the rat catchers.

No one can remember exactly what she says, the words escape because they are elliptical. She talks beyond logic. She leaps from one flame point to another. People leave her dazed, bewitched. Young men fall in love with her after every lunch date. Young women become votive vestals, and this can get tedious. They tend to clutter up the hallways clamoring for Martha's wisdom like sparrows for crumbs.

Everyone who could has always gone to her for advice. God knows how many she has heartened through the years. She has talked vocation problems with anyone — even nondancers. She has laid a steadying hand on the back of all young men starting on the black and uncharted path of the male dancer. Having something of the quality of a nun or a nurse, she has always given one the sense of boundless strength, the reassurance that although circumstances might be tragic or dismaying, they were not outside nature. No one could say she was the healthy out-of-doors type. On the contrary, she was a thoroughly neurotic woman leading a most unusual life, but she had faith, faith in the integrity of work and in the rightness of spirit. This she has always been able to communicate. To every boy and girl who entered her studio she has said something that has illumined the theater, so that it could never grow shabby or lusterless again.

I very soon took to going to her for advice, for reaffirmation and for critical help. Although she never admitted to the role, although we worked in alien styles, she became a kind of mentor. After every concert I rushed to her for analyses. Three times she said the word that has picked me up, dusted me off and sent me marching, the word that has kept me from quitting.

Why could one believe her? Was it the sense of obsession in the face, or the sheer integrity of her life? One faced a woman who for better or worse never compromised, who, although she had known prolonged and bitter poverty, could not be bought or pushed or cajoled into toying with her principles. She was a brave and gallant creature. There are few such in the world, almost none in the theater. One stood abashed, and listened. If her words sounded arbitrary, there was the seal of her life upon them and the weight of her enormous achievement. One could not turn aside lightly. In the most evanescent of all professions she is now regarded, and I believe rightly, as an immortal. Dancers for untold generations will dance differently because of her labors. The individual creations may be lost but the body of her discoveries is impressed into the vocabulary of inherited movement. Boys and girls who have never seen her will use and borrow, decades hence, her scale of movement. Technically speaking, hers is the single largest contribution in the history of Western dancing.

In 1931 she produced *Primitive Mysteries* based on the Catholic Amerindian concept of the Virgin, and with this composition our native dance theater reached a new level. Thenceforth Martha was recognized as a notable in the field of American creative art. For a new work she was granted half a Guggenheim Fellowship. (Being a dancer, although the greatest, she was naturally not entitled to the usual grant awarded a painter, or writer, or scientist.) She went to Mexico.

The following winter I had occasion to visit her in her studio on 9th Street. She said to come late, see the end of rehearsal — about eleven o'clock. (She had to work at night. Most of her girls had jobs during the day.) I came late. This was the first time I had actually seen her in the throes. At the conclusion of rehearsal, the girls were dismissed and Martha went into her little sleeping cell and didn't come out. Louis Horst said I was to wait, that Martha was out of sorts. I waited the better part of an hour. Then Louis suggested, in a dispirited way, that I might as well go in as not.

Martha's room was about five feet broad as I recall it, and it contained a bed, a chest of drawers and an armchair. Louis more than filled the armchair. I took a box. In the center of the bed was a tiny huddle buried in a dressing gown. The only visible piece of Martha was a snake of black hair. Every so often the bundle shivered. Otherwise there was no sound from that quarter.

Louis droned on through his nose, "Now, Martha, you've got to pull yourself together."

There was a great deal of wheezing and huffing as he spoke. That was because he had four chests and all his mechanics seemed to get muffled down. "You can't do this. I've seen you do this before every concert. You're a big enough artist to indulge yourself this way, to fall apart the week before and still deliver on the night.

But the girls are not experienced enough. You destroy their morale. You tear them down. They're not fit to perform."

He was right. She not only rehearsed the girls and herself to the point of utter exhaustion, changing and re-creating whole sections until the very eve of performance, she always ripped up her costumes and spent the entire night before and all day when she was not lighting in the theater in a fever of sewing. Incidentally, she cut and stitched her costumes herself with the aid of a sewing woman. Apparently she had to do this as a nervous catharsis. Contrary to all rules governing athletes she never slept for two nights before an appearance.

The girls worked for nothing, of course. The box office barely paid the advertising and rental, never any of the rehearsal costs. Martha taught the year around to pay these and her living. To meet their expenses, some of her pupils waited on table. None of them were adequately fed or housed.

These girls are not to be thought of as the usual illiterate dance student who fills the ballet schools. They were all adults; many held degrees of one sort or another and had deliberately chosen this form of dancing as opposed to the traditional for serious and lasting reasons. Among their ranks they have numbered great soloists, Jane Dudley, Sophie Maslow, May O'Donnell, Dorothy Bird, Anita Alvarez, Anna Sokolov, Yuriko, Pearl Lang. No other choreographer has had a concert group of superior caliber.

These girls had a style of appearance which became widely known long before their work was understood. We always said then they looked Villagy — but the term is misleading. They may have been unorthodox in many ways, but they embraced every possible sacrifice in order to serve their work, and lived like ascetics. They took the stage with the ardor of novitiates and the group performance was incandescent.

Their leader worked them without mercy and I am told used to grow almost desperate. She worked them until midnight every night except Sundays and holidays, when she worked them all day as well. The abandoned husbands formed a club, "The Husbands of Martha Graham's Group," to amuse one another while they waited. One New Year's Eve the men turned ugly and things eased up a bit after that.

"You cannot work your girls this hard and then depress them. They will not be able to perform," said Louis to Martha on the sad night.

Without showing her face or moving, Martha whimpered. "The winter is lost. The whole winter's work is lost. I've destroyed my year. This work is no good."

"It is good, Martha," said Louis persuasively.

"It is not good. I know whether it's good or not. It is not good."

"It may not be so successful as *Mysteries*" — whimpers and thrashings — "but it has its own merits."

"I've lost the year. I've thrown away my Guggenheim Fellowship."

"One cannot always create on the same level. The Sixth Symphony followed the Fifth, but without the Sixth we could not have had the Seventh." (This was sound thinking and I stored it away in my own breast for future comfort.) "One cannot know what one is leading into. Transitions are as important as achievements."

"Oh, please, please, leave me alone," begged the little voice. I ventured a very timid ministration. I felt like Elizabeth Arden approaching the Cross.

"Martha, dear. Dearest Martha, I thought it was beautiful." There was the sound of a ladylike gorge rising.

Louis got stern. He rose; he loomed, not over — that was impossible because of bulk — but near her. "Martha, now you listen to me. You haven't eaten all day. Get your clothes on and come out for some food."

Martha tossed the blanket a bit. The snake whisked from one side to the other.

Louis got his ulster. Louis got his cap, a flat one with a visor which sat on the top of his white hair. Louis put the coat on Max, his dackel, and leaned to pat Martha's Maedel. Louis progressed down the street displacing the winter before him. Low in the

Horst umbrage cast by street lamps the dachshund wagged on the end of a string. Louis wheezed out his disapproval in a cloud of warm breath. "It's not worth it. Every concert the same. It's not worth it. She's put us all through the wringer. She destroys us."

"But, Louis," I said, pattering after and peering up and around his coat, "she is a genius." He snorted. "Would you consider working with anyone else?"

At this he stopped. He slumped down layers of himself to a thickened halt. "That's the trouble. When you get down to it, there is no other dancer."

The date of this conversation was 1932. Up till 1949 he still played for her classes, conducted her orchestra, comforted her girls. He still stood beside her, hand in hand, to take the bows at those times more frequent in her life than in most when the power and the glory are present and spectators and performers are wrapped in mantles of bright communication.

I begged Martha to let me study with her but this she refused. I had genuine need of her help. I had need of her encouragement. Doubt, like a mold, had begun to film over my hopes. It wasn't just that I was afraid I wouldn't succeed. There was also the growing belief that whatever I did, however expert I became, I would never be more than a glorified parlor entertainer, could not be for the very nature of the medium I had chosen. Martha moved; I grimaced. One gesture of true dance opened doors that were to be for me forever closed. I had therefore obviously to learn to move. I was not a good dancer and no choreographer whatever, but following the promptings of a persistent instinct, I turned my back on all I had done and faced the dark.

During the next five years I taught myself to choreograph, and I took a hostile press right in the teeth for that period of time. Five years is a long period in any girl's life; in a dancer's, it is usually one third of her career.

I was trying to learn to compose dances, not pantomimes, nor dramatic stories, nor character studies, but planned sequences of sustained movement which would be original and compelling. I did not know how to begin. Everything I attempted seemed to develop either into trite balletic derivations or misconceptions of Graham. I tried to learn form and style through studies of English and American folk dances and through reconstructions (necessarily largely guessed) of preclassic (1450–1700) European court patterns. It was slow work and it was bloodless. One does not think out movement. One moves. One thinks out pattern. One moves well if one is used to moving and originally if one has developed through exercise a spontaneous idiom of expression. But I had nowhere to dance, and no company to work with.

Out of the top of my head, from fined-down nerve points, I tried by friction of will to generate ideas. Creation is not teased this way. Creation is an opening up, a submission to the dear, unwilled forces of human life. But how was I to know this, or knowing it to respond, I who was shut away from all the good, natural happiness of the world?

I used to try not to wake in the morning, and when awake, wonder what I could do all day. When I left a rumpled room for class, I was late. My exhaustion in class prevented any progress. I ate alone. I struggled with undancing all afternoon. I resisted the temptation to run to Mother for dinner. I ate dinner alone at a restaurant. The evenings were dreadful. I couldn't work. I couldn't play. I withered, unwillingly, inch by inch, with mounting terror, and the lifeblood grew black in my heart, and I could think of no good dances.

Every creative worker goes through bad periods, but today he usually manages to keep performing. If one can but just keep moving, the creative log jam breaks. Through muscles, through the racing of the blood, the running of feet, rhythms are set up that generate below fear and one is away on a new pace before one has given it a thought. But if one does not keep dancing or if there is no reason for dancing . . . I would stand in my studio two or three hours and not know whether to start north or south, whether to lift an arm or let it alone.

Mother didn't understand what I was doing, and she didn't like it. But she never withheld her savings or refused any possible effort to help. She followed in blind loyalty, although her heart was oppressed.

Why all this fancy experimentation when I could be funny, genuinely funny? Friends expostulated. My family wailed. And I fought the mists.

These were the days when Martha Graham moved like an angel in the night. Just to know she was there finding paths where my feet trod vapor, with the strength in her spirit to leap out where I stood dumb, was companionship. "We all go through this," said Martha. "You are being tempered. You are a sword in the fire. Be glad. There is achievement ahead."

"But, practically, Martha, what do I do tomorrow between waking and sleeping?"

"You make yourself a program of activity, and you do not stop once for five minutes to consider what you are doing. You do not permit yourself to reflect or to sit down. You keep going. That is your only responsibility."

"But if someone would only give me a job."

"That is beside the point. Whether they do or they don't, we keep going."

"Martha, let me work with you."

"Certainly not. Find your own way. I won't let you lean on me."

"Martha, you have genius. You know where you're going."

"I don't know where I'm going. None of us knows that. And someday I'm going to give you a good smack."

"Martha," I said one day, beating my breast over a sundae, "I have no technique and I have no time or energy to acquire any — that is, not sufficient."

"Technique!" Her voice rang with scorn. "Technique! I can see technique at Radio City. From you I ask something greater than that. From you I ask what cannot be learned in any class. Reaffirmation. Your '49, your American studies, have given me courage."

Martha Graham said this to me.

CHAPTER 16

Flying Colors

MY MICAWBER LUCK held. Nothing promising turned up, and Warren, who was dependent on a job for eating, grew desperate. It looked as though we would have to abandon our repertoire and plans for dancing together while he got work, any work, anywhere. As a final shot in the dark, we called together eight volunteers, among them Anna Sokolov, and set a couple of routines to audition for a Broadway show by Howard Dietz and Arthur Schwartz. In order to save money, I myself accompanied. After the tryout they brought in their producer, Max Gordon, and the three of them went into a huddle.

"All right," said Dietz. "You can have the show. The whole show. I put it in your hands. I may be a fool."

So we had a Broadway job at last. A job? The dances and musical numbers for a whole show. And I who up till now had never passed a single audition was to sit out front in judgment of all the boys and girls. I had no idea how these affairs were organized. But the machinery began to turn anyway.

Girls were picked for appearance by Dietz and Schwartz. I asked to see them dance. For the most part they weren't dancers at all. "Do a *tour jeté*," I called from my place in the third row to a long-limbed creature that looked as though she belonged in a Petty calendar. The girl placed a well-shod foot on the stage coping, relaxing the knee to show the lengthy and very beautiful line of her inadequately muscled leg, and pushed back a lock of honey-colored hair with her jeweled hand. "I don't know what you're talking about."

"You are obviously not a ballet dancer," I commented. But I was the one who was flustered — not the babe.

"I was good enough for Madame Rasch," said the girl.

"I am not Madame Rasch. Show her," I said to one of the ballet girls.

The long blonde regarded, shrugged her shoulders and left, to be seen shortly in close converse with Arthur Schwartz. He advised me to accept her: she had been with Madame Rasch several years; she was dazzling from the front; she needed the job desperately. I didn't believe the last, but I didn't choose to call either of them liars. So I said yes and hung a millstone around my neck. I repeated this process eight times. Clifton Webb and Tamara Geva were also present and they had a good deal to say about the dancers. In fact, it turned out that the only person not well-suited was to be I. In addition we hired sixteen colored girls (the title of the show was *Flying Colors*) but they were enigmas; no known tests applied to them.

We started rehearsals. There were lots and lots of dances to be composed. Most of the preparation I had done was daydreaming as I quickly discovered. I did not know, for instance, how dancers would look when moving, and in my trade that is basic ignorance. I attempted to find out on the stage in the presence of twelve glassy-eyed bitches, four dancers and whoever wandered into the theater to observe. The difference between an effect vaguely desired and a complete visual image counted out in sequence is the difference on which strong theater reputations are based. I can now project in my head as many as five groups moving simultaneously. At that time I could not.

The mornings went by and nothing got done. Geva appeared for her numbers, looked concerned and took over. Geva was experienced and gifted. She had been a member of the Diaghilev company and Balanchine's first wife. She never seemed at a loss. She always appeared chic and carried a bottle of the finest eau de cologne. I had no intention of competing with her. But handing her numbers over to her did not rid me of her. She used to sit and watch me at work, which made me very nervous. I had not the gall to tell her to leave, nor the courage to continue. Finally, one day, at the end of a half-hour nerve paralysis, and only after Warren threatened to handle the matter himself, I suggested she go away. It took me more than a decade of effort before I could say "Clear the hall." Had I had the guts then to say what comes so easily years later, my story might have been happier. I wish the girl of 1932, drawn, white and quivering and sweating cold, could see me ready the decks for action now. "If you don't want us here, just tell us to get the hell out," said Arthur Schwartz, bringing up a chair and planting it beside me in the very middle of the stage.

I sweated quite a lot those days, the cold, inner sweat of fear. I knew I was failing. I bit my nails to the quick in front of their blatant stare. I fussed and picked and changed, while Warren, dancing with apprehension at the back of the house, shouted objections to everything I attempted and the poor girls, not really interested, smoked and muttered and grew daily more bewildered and insolent. I used to pray that something would hit the taxi that carried me to rehearsal so that the day's horror would be postponed even half an hour.

We took on the colored girls at night. But this proved to be an entirely different business. They did not stare at us with supercilious scorn — they looked at us wide-eyed with the bland regard of children and either thought we were nuts or took fire and began to move in wonderful, compelling ways. For them, I began to have ideas. No one bothered us at night. We were quite alone and when after a week we showed Howard Dietz what we had done, a dance about reefer smoking, he decided not to fire us as he was being urged on all sides to do. So we got on with this number and took courage from it.

There were conferences about costumes and scenery. These should have given me great pleasure — affording me my first unlimited opportunities of working with materials, colors and sets. But we were proceeding on the old-fashioned premise — costumes and scenery first; dance steps later, that would not interfere with the dress designs. The costumes for several numbers held heads, arms, and even legs immobile.

Norman Bel Geddes designed the scenery. He is a small man, but forceful. He can solve anything and no matter what idea he is propagandizing, he treats it like the girl he is going to marry. Any discussion turns out to be a breach of taste. He explained the sets to all of us, and they were complex feats of engineering. "I don't need all that," I cried, "and I want all my dancers, all the parts of them visible at once, not separate hands and legs. I've got used to seeing whole dancers." He looked at me with stupefaction. Then the humor of the situation struck him. "Well," he blurted, "if you haven't imagination or wit to use a set . . . " "You haven't seen what she's done," said Dietz. "She's got something good." "Hah!" said Bel Geddes and turned his back to discuss another set.

Since we were hesitant and slow, since we disputed between ourselves and could come to no easy terms with the company, the experts began to take over and get their own numbers done. Clifton Webb and Tamara Geva were not the people to stand by idly wringing their hands. Their reputation was at stake and we were proving ourselves quite unreliable. We were pushed out steadily, dance by dance. As our responsibilities diminished it would seem there might have been less need for frenzy, but we slaved. The cast was now in open disobedience. If they didn't like what they were asked to do, and they didn't like Warren's brusque rehearsal manners, they stood still and stared or walked off stage and complained to Dietz.

We came to the run-through before leaving town. It was August and dreadfully hot. Warren and I sat on the fire escape in the theater alley waiting for the ordeal to begin. Bel Geddes, in a white linen suit, breezed by. "Well, children, what are you doing here?" he asked heartily.

"Praying to die!" we answered.

"Oh, come now. It's not as bad as that. When you've been

through as many rehearsal periods as I have, you won't mind this a bit. You come to me if you need help. If anyone at all gets rough with you, you come right to me. Mind now," and he put his expensive cigar in his mouth and bounced in through the stage entrance.

We got through the show, not all of which was finished. But when we got to the reefer number, the cast applauded and cheered and the bosses beamed. It was damned effective. Dietz patted my hand. Bel Geddes was right at me, his cigar in our faces. "That's fine, but think how it would look on a shelf twelve feet in the air."

"Different and not so good," I said.

"Come with me," he roared and grabbing me by the arm, pulled me up on the stage. Warren followed, lean, keen, and angry. "Think if this back line of girls were up in the air."

"It would spoil the design," I protested, "I don't want that great set." (The truth was that Bel Geddes had convinced Dietz and the set was already in work.)

"It's damn dangerous," said Warren, "lurching and jerking like this, twelve feet up with a light in one's face — they'll all get vertigo and fall and twelve feet is no joke." The colored girls had turned gray during this conversation. I had made no mention to them of any shelves or heights.

"They have a three-inch lip to tell them where the edge is," doggedly persisted Bel Geddes.

"That will be a hell of a help as they set out in space," said Warren. "I'm a trained acrobat and I've done nearly everything, but I wouldn't do this." Bel Geddes's voice suddenly came from the middle of his forehead. There was no warning of the change. He was on the instant beyond himself with anger. Warren plunged. Three men caught him. Bel Geddes departed with haste up the center aisle and buried himself in blueprints and apprentices for the rest of the evening.

"Get him back here, get him where I can reach him," said Warren, pawing up the footlights and waving his arms.

"Have a drink," said Schwartz kindly.

"I never drink," said I.

"Well, then, pull yourself together. We've got to get on with rehearsal."

Meanwhile, across the city the set was being built — a shelf — three feet wide, twelve feet in the air, with a three-inch lip on the edge, to be covered with black velvet and lit only by a floor spot in front of each dancer so intense that if a girl so much as touched it, she would burn.

There came a day when Dietz took me into the carpenter shop to inspect it. It had everything but hot and cold running water and for our purposes it was very, very dangerous. They set it up on an empty stage and I introduced the cast to it. They sat silent without moving and stared. I called for volunteers and Warren ran up and down the ledge and laughed and jumped and made with casualness. No one moved. Finally, I suggested that they just walk out and he would go before and I behind, or better still creep on all fours, which is what we did until we got over any fear of dizziness. Then we sat with our feet hanging over the edge cracking jokes with those down below who had suddenly grown remarkably gay until the feeling of formality induced by stark terror had relaxed a bit. Then we all walked slowly around and waved our arms a little. That was enough for that day.

On the way to Philadelphia, Warren and I tried to figure out just exactly what we could ask them to do that would look like dancing and not involve serious risk. The carpenters had taken over our theater, so we were given an abandoned stage somewhere and on a row of chairs, girls walked back and forth for four hours, pretending they were doped with marijuana and twelve feet in the air. In the middle of these interesting processions, word came that we were to proceed directly to the other theater as dress rehearsal was about to begin, that the platform had broken, and until fixed it would not hold the weight of one human being. The dance was to be done flat as I'd always requested.

Dress rehearsal began immediately we had crossed the street. It went on for thirty-six hours. But there were a lot of unexpected interesting episodes to keep us from being bored. One colored girl, finding herself in her robot dress, bound like a trussed pig, masked and stifled, grew hysterical and fell over senseless. It was discovered, on cutting her loose from her costume, that the metal bands which bound her arms had bitten half an inch into the flesh on her back. None of my numbers came off. Tap dances had to be performed on thick carpets, exits were found blocked by electricians and those special spotlights that were capable of such quick combustion. There were miscalculations about scenery and costumes.

"The number's no good," said Bel Geddes blandly. "Take it out."

"God in Heaven," wailed Schwartz, "we've got to postpone."

"Don't be an old woman," ordered Dietz. "Agnes, make up a new ending."

As the dress rehearsal lengthened, Schwartz grew distraught. Dietz with the aid of a Thermos flask just kept his nerve. Max Gordon had been ill and was in a hospital. Only Bel Geddes was serene and jovial.

At last Dietz said, "Now we will have the reefer dance." It was four o'clock in the morning. Drunk with fatigue and desperation, the girls improvised an ending on the spot. They gave me a finish that was very moving and we all felt cheered.

Next night, after five hours' sleep, we opened. It was a difficult evening. The reefer number went as planned and the girls danced brilliantly, but it turned out the audience didn't have the faintest idea what it was about, which, of course, weakened its effect. The introductory song concerned marijuana smoking; the dance was about voodoo ritual — the one having nothing to do with the other. How this disparity could have escaped my attention for the whole of the rehearsal period, I cannot say. It was an important point to have overlooked.

The day after the opening, Dietz sent for me. Due to my lapses and chaos in many departments, whole numbers had to be restaged. "Look," he said, "we've got to have five new dances in five days. Can you do this?"

"You know I can't. I'm worn-out. Also, I've lost my nerve."

"That's what I thought," he said. "Whom shall I call in?"

"The best," I answered, "Albertina Rasch."

"All right," he answered, "I'll send for her."

He did not express himself altogether accurately: he had sent for her. She had been in town quietly for several days — working hard.

"I'm very sorry," he said.

"You've done everything you could," I replied.

And he had. Most everyone connected with the show had wanted me thrown out from the first week.

Dietz promised me two things — that my name would be on the reefer number and that not one gesture would be changed without my written permission. He gave me his solemn word for this. We parted friends. Schwartz grabbed me backstage. "You're not licked, girl. You're not licked. There are still night clubs and moving-picture houses."

During the drive back to New York, I reviewed my past in an effort to understand what had led to this failure. A little of everything, I figured, beginning with my relations with Father. Every time I had said yes when I meant no, I had paved the way for Bel Geddes. Every time I'd worn the hat of Mother's choice, I had made it impossible to throw the bloody costume designs back in the dressmaker's teeth. I was geared for failure; I decided to alter. This self-examination took place between Trenton and New York, while Warren guided the car through a submarine maze of lights and blurred vision and the September rain streamed and washed away. Warren led me to the door of Mother's empty apartment (she was in Hollywood with Margaret), kissed me tenderly and ran for it. During this rigorous bout of thinking, I had sobbed steadily and audibly, I learned. I must have been a dandy road companion. He was feeling none too chipper himself; his bread and butter had gone by. The year was 1932, he had no savings, and we were heading straight into the darkest period of the depression.

Four weeks later, *Flying Colors* opened in New York. I was sent seats and I invited Dug to escort me. I wished to show him that his faith had not been misplaced. We dressed up and he pinned an orchid on me. It was not until we were seated and I opened the program that I discovered that my name had been totally deleted. There was nothing of my work left but twisted remnants and no credit. Dietz was sorry and said so, but he felt helpless. Madame Rasch wished things this way! It was, he said, her price for saving the show.

Paris — Brussels — London

IN THE SPRING before *Flying Colors* when I had waved off
Madame Argentina, she had said to me, "American and Spanish
dancing have one characteristic in common — rhythm. You must
find the American rhythm and develop it as I have developed the
Spanish rhythm." She repeated this suggestion to Martha Graham
and several others. It was a good, quotable slogan.

Arnold Meckel, Argentina's manager, urged me to allow him to
present me in Paris since concerts there cost one fifth as much
as New York appearances. "You realize, I have no money?" I said.
"There isn't any moving-picture money behind me." But Meckel
hastened to protest. He was not interested in money. He was interested only in my future, which he assured me was something he
believed in strongly.

This was the autumn of 1932. Mother's income had dwindled to
half, what with the depression and mismanagement by the trustees
of her fund. There was indeed no money behind me; I was speaking the truth. Although I was getting a small allowance from Pop,
it was totally inadequate to finance theatrical ventures. No one ever
spontaneously suspected that the de Mille resources were not buying me a professional footing and protecting me every step of the
way. My confreres were wary and only very slowly grew to recognize our common plight. I, therefore, could make use of none of
the dodges and cuts of other professionals and I was charged

double for everything. Living within the aura of wealth and yet so powerless I came to find extremely galling.

Mother managed the concert costs by giving up all luxuries, thenceforth, for life, taxis, lower berths, good theater tickets, good restaurants, everything but the cheapest clothes.

My brother-in-law, Bernard Fineman, lent me the thousand dollars for my share of the trip and Mother, having sublet her apartment, took the gamble.

The exact circumstances of our departure, tourist class on the *Ile de France,* were quite typical of all such expeditions. I quote from Mother's diary:

. . . From midnight until 5:30 A.M. — and again at 7:00 — I labored at moving my Lares and Penates out of accustomed places into one closet, and then — a sip of tea; a last visit to the bank; back to get hand luggage and Mildred (our maid) who'd never seen a big boat and who in the excitement promptly shut her thumb in a door, I dashing back for a bandage; a last anguished look at my unbelievably messed-up home — and off in a taxi to Pier 57 — bandaging Mildred en route, worrying about Agnes who had taken the L to Gimbel's to pick up her new hat; remembering a hundred previously forgotten chores and arriving at last in the tourist end of the *Ile de France,* a few minutes before the "all ashore" signal; the safe arrival of Agnes later; the scrambled meeting and missing of friends; last injunctions; the discovery that I had only a minute in which to send a wire to Margaret; my race to *première Classe* and the nice officer who dashed down the last gangplank with my telegram and $2.00; my race back to watch our friends become specks on the dock as the great ship skillfully and swiftly swung her way out into midstream and carried us down the Bay.

. . . Then part of the first course of lunch and the sudden realization that I'd left half my jewelry in the top drawer of my chiffonier; a leap for the bird's-eye maple and purple velvet salon where *Touristes* write; two scribbled notes to Mildred, peppered with stamps for special delivery; a leap out into the companionway where not a brass button of any size or shape was to be seen, down a passage that led me into the bird's-eye maple and purple plush again — out and around the deck where, with great difficulty, I disengaged two stewards from their interesting conversation, who leisurely told me I was too late; another flight downstairs — and into the purple plush place; a flight down further and wild yelps in French from two gents who, cleaning the floor with what I am sure was cold cream, seized me by the elbows with such vigor as to all but dislocate both shoulders and shoved me into the *ascenseur* where a small youth shot me out into the bird's-eye maple; another dash and at last a "Buttons," small and static, to whom I yelled at the top of my lungs so he'd understand, "Where's the pilot?" Galvanizing into life, "Ah, the toilet!" and pointed a semaphorelike arm. Fleeing again and waving my two letters wildly I dashed on — and ran into the sub-purser. "Too late, madame," he said coldly. And that was that.

. . . There has been so much to do I haven't had time to read *The Epic of America*, as I meant.

❧

It was raining the night we arrived. Meckel did not meet the train, being engaged elsewhere on Madame Argentina's concerns. His secretary came with a wilted bunch of flowers and took me to the office which she unlocked (it being then near midnight) to cheer me up with a display of the advertising material. As the 15,000 folders were a dingy printing job and contained incorrect dates, the effect on me was disappointing.

The theater selected was a small one, the Théâtre de l'Avénue at the Rond-Point, run by the Pitoëffs. It was a charming little household affair. The head scene shifter and his wife, who ran the box office, locked the doors every noon for two hours and lunched on a checked tablecloth in the front lobby.

Meckel was planning to paper the entire house. We told him to stop. He thereupon stopped all managerial activities of any sort

including publicity. Mother, undaunted, went to work on Paris
with her letters of introduction. Geraldine Farrar had written out
about fifteen by longhand; she brought them to me herself in New
York. Mother began slowly working her way through the chocolate
cake and tea of the faubourgs.

There was then in Paris an ardent and brilliant Single-Taxer, Sam
Meyer. A true liberal and a Jew, Monsieur Meyer was taken to
Auschwitz during the Occupation and destroyed. But at the time of
our visit, he had a beautiful house in Suresnes and a wide circle
of influential and sophisticated friends. He and his wife put their
entire weight behind my debut. I have never heard of a business-
man giving up so much time and effort to help someone he barely
knew. This he did out of deference to my grandfather and, of
course, to my mother. He and his wife and Farrar's friends turned
the first concert from a dirty little swindle into a legitimate performance.

For it was a swindle. Meckel did nothing. The advertising and
publicity were negligible. The stage was covered with a thick rug
up to the morning of the concert. The piano had not been tuned,
the cyclorama not cleaned. Whenever I lodged a complaint, the
secretary found she could understand neither English nor my
French. Meckel had another American girl giving dance recitals at
the time. The uncle of this one was a director of General Motors.
Meckel evidently figured he had tapped two American gold mines.
In the meantime, he was busy with Madame Argentina.

There was an audience — a paying audience. Meckel admitted
himself stupefied, but grateful. The rug did come off the floor because Mother wept on the phone to Madame Meckel, and
Madame Meckel personally attended to many matters, coming
backstage to help with the costume changes.

Mother wrote in her diary:

Paris, Sunday, Oct. 30, 1932

Well it's over — the first one, thank goodness!
The floor of the stage which had so worried A. had been

covered with linoleum — and the dirty little theater looked quite clean, which it really wasn't. The black velvet curtains on the stage had been swept and garnished, and looked very nice too. I stayed in the lobby till the last bell rang for the curtain . . . then took a stance at the door. The usher tried to wave me into seats here and there but I was deaf — stone deaf and she ultimately pulled down a tiny shelf in the door-way — where I perched. The curtains parted and A. made her entrance in *Stagefright* — her orange and yellow tutu re-made and fresh from the hands of the woman who makes the tarlatan skirts of the Opéra ballet, Barbara Karinska. There was a dead silence — not *one hand*. Not a trace of welcome. I froze for I knew she had not been prepared for this custom any more than I had. She started her dance — and did well but drew not one ripple such as she had *from every other audience*. Suddenly she slipped and fell — the new linoleum — not the fake fall that comes later — but a real fall that left a black mark on her silken leg. I died. . . . I flew around to Meckel, pulled him out of Argentina's box and told him to get rosin for the stage floor.

Next came '49 (*"Danse des plaines de l'ouest"*) and they certainly didn't understand that.

Next came the *Gigue* of Bach. As the curtain parted and Agnes stood there in her brocades and white wig, looking very beautiful — the audience came to — and applauded and sat on the edge and at the end called "Bravo" and clapped for I forget how many curtains. Her technique was never so good. From then on I could begin to relax.

At first, the French didn't think I was a bit funny or even intel-ligible. It was Kurt Jooss who broke the horrible stalemate halfway through the first half by jumping to his feet after the Bach *Gigue* and shouting "Bravo" repeatedly. He also did spadework in the lobbies between halves. As his *Green Table* had just taken every prize on the Continent and was playing nightly to packed audiences in Paris, he was someone to listen to.

Startled into attention by Jooss and others, Meckel made a shade more effort on the second concert. For this we had nearly a full house. Since the Parisians were slow, he explained, fifteen more concerts would certainly do the trick. Fifteen! I gasped, for my money was running low. I'd received no gate receipts whatever. And, by the way, where was the money that had been taken in at the box office?

Meckel grew vague and bothered. There were so many taxes, so many, many government taxes. He would have to go and figure it all out. This conversation took place in the cellar dressing room with me stark naked, in a bath towel, running make-up and sweat.

Sam Meyer said he would inquire about my accounts. He could talk French — the secretary could not pretend not to comprehend him. Monsieur Meyer phoned every day for the next two weeks in the morning and in the afternoon, but Monsieur Meckel was never in.

ॐ

My next engagement was a Brussels date Meckel had arranged, and one morning Mother, Warren and I boarded a train and rode through the magnificent October woods to Belgium. We arrived late in the afternoon and phoned friends who had promised to lay the city at our feet. They were dismayed. Not having seen a line in the press, they concluded, not unreasonably, that the engagement was canceled. I telephoned the manager but he had gone home for the day and left no message. So we spent that night in something akin to apprehension. The Belgians were perfectly right; inquiry failed to disclose any publicity whatever.

The next morning early Madame Gottschalk, a friend of Sam Meyer, took me to the Palais des Beaux-Arts and we faced the situation. It was not promising.

"*Mais, si,*" the manager had inserted an ad in the paper. He exhibited two lines of printing in want-ad type.

Gladys De Nil of the Hollywood De Nils will
dance tonight at the Palais des Beaux-Arts.

"This is unpretentious, certainly," I said. "Also inaccurate. How many seats has this sold?"

"Not one, Mademoiselle."

"How many seats in the auditorium?"

"Fourteen hundred."

"Have you papered?"

"No. We had no instructions to do this. And besides, this takes time, and costs money for secretaries, and we thought the Paramount people would take care of tickets."

"What Paramount people?"

"The Paramount people — your father's company."

"Who is my father?"

"Cecil B. de Mille, the head of Paramount."

"Did Meckel tell you what kind of dancing I did?"

He shook his head.

"Did Meckel send you any press or photographs or instructions?"

"No."

"Why then did you agree to manage me?"

"As a favor to Meckel. We owe him much. He sends us Madame Argentina. He asked us to let you dance in the theater. We did not expect to spend any money on this. He said that you would take care of all costs, that the Paramount people were behind you."

"Sit down," said Mother to me. "Let me think."

"I will cancel," I said. "I will not dance before three or four people. I cannot stand this."

I probably looked very ill because Madame Gottschalk put her arms around me and launched into rapid and angry French. I was too disturbed to note what she was saying but it must have been effective. I believe she invoked the name of several cabinet ministers. Her family, it seems, was extremely influential. She flew at that blasé, indifferent young executive like a hen partridge. His manner changed. He turned to me with something like kindness. "You understand, Mademoiselle, nothing was made clear to us. We will do what we can."

Then Annie rose to her feet. Of course, she hadn't far to go. But she had a way of gathering herself up and lifting her head that produced the effect of drums and flags. "You'll dance, Agnes, and before an audience. We've paid for this trip and we'll have this performance. I'm going to the American Embassy. You do the lighting." And with that she left.

I went out on stage where Warren was already trying to cope with sullen stagehands who spoke only a kind of catarrh. Three hours later when we had set the cues for the last dances Mother phoned. "It's all right," she called cheerily. "I'm at the American Consulate. There are five secretaries working under my direction. There will be an audience. No money, but an audience. The Consul-general is coming with his entire family which is very large — that will take up twelve seats. And they will all wear full evening dress. The press is coming and the Consul has invited you to tea as soon as you're finished."

The kind Consul, Walter Sholes, and his wife and daughters were waiting around a fire with tea and chocolate cake and consolation. He could not speak openly because of his position, but he was angry. I was not the first young American artist to come to Europe and be rooked.

There were four hundred people in the audience — four hundred summoned by phone between noon and six o'clock. Any theatrical secretary who has tried to do papering knows what this means. Did you ever try to give away theater tickets — even so few as four — the afternoon of a performance?

The management provided no dresser. The management did not even clean the dressing rooms. Mother swept them and laid down newspapers on every surface floor and table while I warmed up. Then Mother pressed the dresses while I did my face. When it was time to begin the manager knocked on the door, and I began. I went through every dance as programmed without sufficient applause to take a bow. Not a laugh. Not a sound. It was like a two-hour-long audition before hostile agents. Paper audiences are traditional. So is the Belgian temperament. I left the stage sobbing for breath and crying tears of vexation and shame. At the end I took Warren by the hand and said, "God damn them. We'll take a bow. And we'll be leisurely." But we were brisk. The sound of diminishing applause sets off a train of automatic reactions no performer can withstand.

The manager was in the wings as I made my final exit. He seemed pleased. "Mademoiselle, you are a success."

I lowered my eyes in anger.

"On my honor, Mademoiselle. The press did not leave. It will be very enthusiastic. I congratulate you."

And strangely enough, the press was just that, very intelligent, very discerning and very enthusiastic.

The Consul was in the wings, sure enough, as Mother said, in white tie, with his lady in fur and velvet, and, oh, the comfort of home accents and home approval! The quiet, tall, Southern gentleman saying I had done well, and that they were proud. The audience, he added, was highly pleased also, but they were not accustomed to showing it.

Mother and I started to pick up the costumes. Everyone had gone home, the manager first of all. We collected and packed unaided. Warren went out to search a taxi, rare in that part of town. Mother and I pulled and tugged the great trunks and sacks down the lengthy hallways to the door where two hulking Belgian brutes shouted at us to hurry, hurry, did we think they were going to stand there all night? If we didn't get on with it, they'd lock us in.

I was hungry so we had supper in our hotel bedroom. Mother had providentially thought to lay in a stock of cheese, milk and crackers.

⌯⌲⌯

We didn't get any box office from Meckel until the night before we left for England. It amounted to forty-eight dollars — not net, of course, gross intake. We had paid all the bills as they came in with our cash. The accounting followed ten months later.

Mother and I were very pleased to leave Paris. Our last impression of the Parisians was of the Gare du Nord porters screaming and howling for larger tips. Mother crept whipped into our compartment and promptly had a heart attack, her first, which was very frightening to me. I did not realize exactly what the trouble was, nor did she. By the time we got to England, the blue mark had gone from around her mouth and characteristically she did not trouble to see a doctor.

London was kind to us. This time we managed all our business and with the help of Romney Brent, an actor and a devoted friend of the family, we did well.

Romney turned London inside out for me. He was playing at that time with enormous success in a Noel Coward revue and had become the darling of the drawing rooms. For three weeks before my concert at the Arts Theatre Club, he took me with him to Lady Sybil Colfax's, the Raymond Masseys', Noel Coward's, Dame May Whitty's. "This," he would proclaim to their polite astonishment, "is the greatest pantomimic artist in the world." And because of his charm and his own undoubted gifts, they all came to see. The house was sold out; the house was warm — there was even a little cheering.

Arnold Haskell rushed back to congratulate me. "Come back," he said. "Make your home here and dance often. Whatever you want me to do I will do. I believe in you absolutely. I want to help."

Marie Rambert was nearly as enthusiastic but in her own way. "I can teach you much. Stay and study with me."

Financially we had broken exactly even; that is, the recitals paid for themselves. The press was fine. On the heels of the success came an invitation from Ashley Dukes, the playwright, and his wife, Marie Rambert, to give a series of concerts at the Mercury Theatre. I accepted and the arrangement was made that I give one recital a week and study with her in between times — all at my own expense. No great profits were possible but at least the plan guaranteed steady performing without undue loss. Mother and Warren went home, and for the first time in my life I embarked on a project absolutely alone. As Rambert led me into the practice hall for our first business conference, we stepped across flats spread out on the floor. Two young men in sailor pants were bent over painting scenery. They straightened up and regarded me in the fading afternoon light.

"You know Antony Tudor and Hugh Laing, of course," said Rambert. We shook hands.

Marie Rambert

THE BALLET CLUB — or as it is now called the Ballet Rambert —
and Mercury Theatre were twin organizations housed in the same
building and drawing their inspiration from Marie Rambert and
Ashley Dukes. She took care of the dance department, he the
dramatic, producing such plays for the first time as *The Ascent of
F6* by W. H. Auden, and *Murder in the Cathedral* by T. S. Eliot,
directly after the Canterbury *première*.

The theater was run on a shoestring, the house being scaled to
£25 maximum. I have always believed that Madame's ballet school
paid most of the bills. Rambert was chief teacher, assisted by a
young friendly drudge named Antony Tudor. Tudor also served
when need arose as secretary, accompanist, stage manager, and
janitor, for a fixed salary of £2 a week, room and tuition thrown in.
Some of the better pupils also helped out with the teaching now
and then, but the school and theater were run on a strictly professional basis: dancers got 5/6 a performance, choreographers lump
sums and a royalty. Tudor, for instance, was paid £10 for his
Jardin aux Lilas, 2/6 a performance royalty. We all, except Tudor,
paid Madame for our classes.

Mim's parsimony never failed as a stimulus to dressing-room
conversation. She was relentless about pennies, ha'pence even. The
one thing she did not think worth saving was energy, hers or anyone's. Costumes were let out, material redyed, coats turned, scenery

painted over rather than squander an extra pound and start afresh. In this, she was like my mother and I had a sympathy for the point of view.

She had to do this; it was carry on this way or quit. She had no endowment that I know of beyond Ashley's personal income. They turned everything they earned back into their theater and its many experimental productions; they lived very quietly without even permitting themselves a car — they considered the Mercury their only luxury. She gave a performance nearly every Sunday night throughout the year and mounted fresh pieces regularly. She furnished her pupils and apprentices with a place to learn and practice their trade. She did not also expect to pay them. Coming from America where there was opportunity of no sort and where one paid overtime for whatever paltry chance, I considered myself lucky to have found such a berth.

The Ballet Club functioned in what had been the vestry house of a small odd-shaped church situated in an apex of land on the Notting Hill Gate bus routes. Outside it looked like just what it originally was; inside it was a geometric conglomeration of boxes, hallways, levels, closets, tiny auditoriums, and stairways. I think I loved it from the start because it reminded me of the castle I had constructed in our garage. All larger divisions were lit by long ecclesiastical windows which gave an air of sanction to everything that went on inside, even the quarreling. One entered a vestibule hardly big enough for five people to stand in together, warmed one's hands at a coal grate exactly like a Cruikshank hearth, bought a ticket at a cardboard wicket and walked into an auditorium that seated one hundred and fifty people. The stage was by actual measurement eighteen feet square. The whole place had the air of a tiny eighteenth-century princeling's court theater. And it was in this shoebox, this Punch and Judy show, that the renaissance of English dance occurred. Frederick Ashton proved himself here. Antony Tudor matured into a finished choreographer, the greatest in Europe. Alicia Markova was a regular performer in the days when no one else would give her footroom.

Pop and I

Pop in Hollywood with Margaret and me

Agnes, Mother and Margaret

Aged fifteen in Mother's garden

Ruth St. Denis

Geraldine Farrar

Ballet Class
after Degas

(Photo by Soichi Sunami, New York)

Civil War

(Photo by Soichi Sunami, New York)

May Day
with Warren Leonard

(*Photo by Soichi Sunami, New York*)

The Parvenues

(*Photo by Maurice Goldburg, New York*)

Uncle Cecil with his adopted daughter Katherine (made up for
a Mae West picture) and me on his *Cleopatra* set

(*From* Martha Graham *by Barbara Morgan, published by Duell, Sloan and Pearce.*)

Martha Graham in *Letter to the World,* her dance-drama based
on the life and poems of Emily Dickinson

Antony Tudor

Marie Rambert

Elizabethan Suite —

London, 1938

(*Photo by Angus McBean, London,*

Anna George de Mille

(*Photo by Bradford Bachrach, Boston*)

(Photo by Carl Van Vechten, New York)

Venus in *The Judgment of Paris*

(Photo by Soichi Sunami, New York)

Gala Farewell

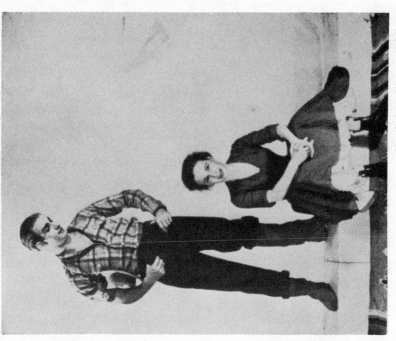

(Photo by Louis Mélançon, New York)

With Frederick Franklin the night before the *Rodeo* opening. These are faked costumes, the real ones were not finished.

(Photo by Maurice Seymour, Chicago)

Rodeo, 1942

(Photo by Gjon Mili, by permission of Vogue)

The school revolved around the practice hall which lay alongside the auditorium on a lower level. One went down precipitous steps at the back and entered a large oak-beamed room with a typical ecclesiastical vaulted ceiling. The windows were high up in the clerestory and admitted a pale reflected light because this part of the building was surrounded by Notting Hill dwellings. Voices and music sounded unnaturally loud as in all empty high-studded rooms. The floor was of oak polished to the shine of a dining table and literally worn into the grain by human flesh. I can still feel the knots, nailheads and joinings under the balls of my feet, the bruising crack under my heel. Down the length of the walls ran *de rigueur* the barre. At one end of the room hung a large old mirror, at the other, encased in iron railing, stood a potbellied stove which grew rosy when prodded by the janitor, and gave off mustiness but no heat. The pianist with blue fingers sat at her upright, her back to comfort, in two sweaters, a shawl, a coat, an old felt hat. Whenever a dancer passed close to the stove, she steamed slightly. The whole room smelled of damp black woolens. The walls sweated. The gray damp of English winter streamed and thickened on the pale windows. Visitors sat fully coated and hatted without dreaming of undoing a button. The dancers dressed in lumber rooms and storage closets filled with old scenery and costume trunks. The practice clothes hung three deep on hooks all around the walls and they did not dry of body sweat from one day to the next. On arrival a girl would rigorously pull off her woolen dress and standing in her woolen undershirt hold her damp black tights over the oil stove while her pale flesh quivered at the exposure. I never put on my pants without looking for mushrooms in the seams. The dank contact made my skin jump.

The English girls took it all quite naturally. Those astonishing English girls! Modest, shy, dogged, and indestructible, with plain bodies, all large-boned and rheumatic. They were virginal, flower-skinned, their cheeks already veined with the raw damp, their knuckles red, their joints and backs punished with incipient arthritis. Their bodies had not the resilience or nerve of American bodies. By comparison, they seemed slow. American speed in learning, American brilliance in turns, American bounce and recoil were bywords on the Continent. "Every race," said Karsavina to me, "has its time for growth, flowering, and decline. Racially your bodies are young; ours are old." The English dancers learned their trade doggedly. How so many of them became great artists is the miracle. But this is an English faculty: the achievement of glory through daily plodding.

The English girls stood long and slender in their black woolen tights and long-sleeved black jumpers at the barre. Their names were Andrée Howard, Diana Gould (Mrs. Yehudi Menuhin), Elizabeth Ruxton (Lisa Serova of the Ballet Russe), Betty Cuff (Nelidova of the Ballet Russe), Pearl Argyle with a face like an anemone, Elizabeth Schooling, Prudence Hyman, Mona Inglesby, and Mim's daughters Lulu and Angela Dukes (Lulu later danced the comedy lead in the English *Oklahoma!*). Beside them were the boys. Their names were Frederick Ashton, Antony Tudor, Hugh Laing, Frank Staff, Walter Gore, William Chappell.

In the center of the room darted Mim, Madame Wasp, queen hornet, vixen mother, the lady boss of Notting Hill. Knobby, knotted with passion, her little legs in wrinkled black tights, her child's tough body in a shapeless baby-pink garment ruffled at the hips, a veil around her little dark head, she scrabbled from side to side in the room, pulling, pushing, poking, screaming and imploring. Now and then she would stamp her foot and literally howl with distaste. Her hands were not kind. "Long the arms," she would say, pulling an arm almost out of its shoulder socket, "Eggie" (that would be me). "Long the arms and the hands long to be in line," and she molded the fingers roughly into a pointed clump. "Now, relax!" And she sharply rapped the extended wrist bone. "Down the shoulders" — a blow on the collarbone. "Up the head!" A jerk behind the ears. "Frrrrreddie, pull in your great bottom. You flaunt your bottom like a banner. Schooling, how dare you be late. With your woolly legs? I give all my time and strength to making something we have not to be ashamed of and you bring

your woolly legs to class late without a *plié*." Schooling's face goes
like custard and she quietly walks out of the room. "Eggie! Relax!"
Diana murmurs between exercises, "I saw you-know-who at the
Ballet Russe last night. He'd grown a new mustache, and he did
look too Madonna!"

"Deeanna," shouts Mim. "Do not make jokes! I am tired of
your humor. I am tired of your wit. I would prefer one good arabesque to six jokes." Diana's face hardens. "Sue, you use your leg
like a mop. Down the eyebrows, Eggie, down the eyebrows. No,
not that music, Norah, how stupid!"

All this time the pumping goes on around the room without
surcease, the heavy breathing, the lifting and falling of legs, the
striking and stroking of feet on the floor. Mim, hanging on to the
barre around the stove, practices along with the class. Hugh Laing
suddenly leaves his place and goes and sits in a corner by the stove
brooding. Schooling, with pink eyes, returns. "Andrée, you will
never dance if you persist in this ugliness. You have been losing
ground steadily for the last six months." Andrée's gray eyes fill.
Mim believes in Andrée's choreographic gifts, and feels sorry for
her because she has heart trouble. From here on Andrée weeps
silently until the end of class. Antony potters along neither very
good nor very bad, biding his time. Ashley Dukes, that "tawny
man," as Diana calls him, wanders in from a conference with W. H.
Auden, and stands in the door beaming in a kind of effulgent dis-
like. "I must say I do hate all forms of dancing," he remarks as he
leaves. "Antony," calls Mim, "they need an accompanist in the
basement. Go do it, please." Antony docilely leaves and goes down
to the children's class which contains three little girls closely related
to nobility. Hugh is sitting with glazed eyes fixed to a crack and
apparently sees nothing. Mona Inglesby demonstrates an adagio.
Mona is subject to headaches, and a mother. She has lots and lots
of money. Mim gives her a great deal of attention and she is becoming an unusually fine dancer. "Deeanna, I hope you watched
this. That is what I call real feeling. No comments, please." A
new mother is led into the room. She has two daughters of the

proper age for ballet training. Mim suddenly turns girlish and frisky. There is a complete reshuffling of the class. Pearl is brought to the front as well as the rebuked but defiant Diana. I am hidden at the rear. Class is reorientated to what used to be called in court dancing "The Presence."

It ends at last. Mim does three cartwheels and stands on her head. She shouts, "Frrrrreddie, catch me!" and jumps into the arms of the blushing Ashton. The mother is surprised. Mim cackles like a banshee, invites the visitor for lunch and goes off to change.

At the back of the room we discover Alicia Markova who has been there quite some time waiting for Ashton's rehearsal to begin. She sits upright, her long slender legs in their hand-wrought tights crossed like two knitting needles. Beside her sits Hugh, unmoving. The pianist, Norah, has spread a coat over his bare legs and is talking in a low motherly way, and although he hasn't stirred he is obviously softening up inside. The damp has become almost visible. Antony has promised to bring him some hot tea and a sandwich so he won't have to leave off his interesting occupation. We pass through the auditorium. Markova is doing finger-turns on Ashton's hand, six, eight, ten turns like a piano stool, round and round, and then smooths out as easy as butter at the end.

Mim goes to family lunch in her home on Campden Hill around the corner. The children and Reine, Miss Dukes, chatter like squirrels in the technical jargon that is comprehensible only to ballet students and more particularly to Cecchetti ballet students. Mim nibbles and sips, taking her spoon from her mouth, to contradict Ashley when he becomes too grandiloquent. Ashley doesn't hear the children, doesn't mind Mim, sits like the last of the Georgians, ruddy with satisfactory food, making finely balanced pronouncements. Buttressed by the august tradition of English letters he heaps scorn on the arduous labors of his womenfolk. One would gather from his remarks that they were indulging in some sort of time-killer like Victorian needlework or acrostics. The continual mockery of her lord and master can have been of no comfort to Mim but she apparently turns it all aside with gaiety. She nibbles a bit of biscuit, demolishes with one phrase the latest West End play, works out mentally the cost of a set of costumes at 4/6 each; analyzes Angie's pirouettes *dehors et dedans*, hums a little Prokofieff and sounds out the mother sharply on the likelihood of her daughters' starting lessons soon. I cannot answer for the mother. She probably loves it, as I always did. What she cannot understand she must recognize as robust, salty and explosively vital. The chances are the daughters will be enrolled before cheese.

We, the pupils, eat at Sally's Tea Room in Church Street. Elizabeth Schooling has found her tongue at last. Schooling is a true English beauty, all pink and white and powdered gold. She has a pink pout for a mouth and her voice sounds like Miss Muffet out of sorts. Diana, deep in a sultana pudding, sums Mim up in terms that would have done Wilde no discredit. But Andrée only sits, tears still streaming down her cheeks. I eat. I'm hungry. And besides I have a three-hour rehearsal ahead of me in the afternoon, in a basement where there is no heat whatsoever.

It is difficult to give a just appraisal of Rambert. At the very mention of her name dancers sometimes lose all self-control. Sometimes their eyes fill. Sometimes they grow pale. However, after they have spent their exasperation, they usually add, "But you know, she could be wonderfully sweet. And after all she did do a lot for English dancing."

By God, she did! Had she had an organization behind her comparable to the Sadler's Wells, Rambert, like Ninette de Valois, might have turned her theater into a national institution. More, because of her daring, her catholicity of interest, her infallible taste and her enormous flair for new talent, and this was her great flair beyond anyone else's, she might have headed the first lyric theater of Europe. De Valois was a great organizer; Mim a poor one. She drove people nuts. They left. This is no small tragedy.

As a pupil of Dalcroze she had been hired by Diaghilev to help Nijinsky count out the *Sacre* music. It was while at work on this project that she learned ballet technique under Cecchetti. She married Ashley Dukes during World War I and immediately started her classes.

She was very small with jet-black hair, smoldering dark eyes set in a little sharp face, a fine forehead and a mobile, vulnerable mouth that was held in a tension of artificial politeness against the world. When she was not laughing too shrilly or talking too quickly she looked as though she were about to scream. Sometimes she did scream. She has been known to roll on the floor, throw chairs and cry out with the intolerable anguish of her balked hopes. And when the agony had passed she looked as though she had made a truce with God that might rupture at any moment.

Her true genius lay in perception and stimulus. Somehow most unhappily she mismanaged matters. She had not the iron traplike intention to force success. There were confusions. There were distractions of rage or love. There were quarrels. Matters never marched straight ahead. Every so often she would remember in the middle of a class or a conversation some cruel bottomless disappointment and she would reach out and break whomever she was with. Antony, being possessed of the inner durability of genius, learned quietly to step aside in a kind of mental jujitsu and let her fall against her own fury. Ashton escaped. The rest were cowed on odd days, recalcitrant on even. But Hugh shouted back, not always with reason. Being young and male and without scruples when angry, he usually did her down. These bouts were not pretty to hear, but Hugh would emerge from them as from a Turkish bath, refreshed and exhilarated. "That wicked woman" — Mim could be heard scuttling and muttering back of the partitions as she made her way to a cup of tea and Ashley. "That dreadful, dreadful wicked woman," he would say with shining eyes as though each phrase were oxygen to his fainting lungs. All she had done was give him a sound beginning in dance technique and prepared him to be the instrument for great choreography. "How can you talk to a woman like that?" I exclaimed. "Don't you ever talk to me like that or you'll be sorry."

Sometimes, Mim merited a scolding. She behaved on occasion

outrageously. She has been known to walk down the theater aisle and say to paid customers, "I would like to sit next to Lady Oxford, do you mind moving to the back row?" And she moved them to their astonishment although they had held their tickets for weeks. She has turned cartwheels in Piccadilly Circus in broad daylight and right down Notting Hill High Street after a performance. She could, of course, at will conduct herself with distinction and elegance. She was a wit. If in any of the above I have suggested that Madame could not command English grammar, I shall not have been exact. She spoke brilliantly in several languages and her English was vivid. Many a columnist has made copy of her talk. But she had learned dancing in the Russo-Parisian dialect that was the studio jargon of all the Diaghilev generation, and the idiom stuck.

Above all, she was warmhearted. She could be motherly-kind, if one were in trouble, darling, wise and loving. Her woman-to-woman talks were tender with experience. It was just one's good fortune she could not bear. That is, not every day, under her nose, in her own theater, not if one achieved it independently, against her advice, free from control. Rambert, like most women, wanted to feel indispensable.

Mim has at last received some part of her due. The Ballet Rambert is known throughout the British Isles, on the Continent — even as far as Australia. The Queen attended her Gala. She is recognized as a cultural force.

Her hair is now white; her daughters are grown; she has seen many a boy and many a girl through dreadful times. When my husband, an officer in the American Army, went to call on her she was enchantingly gracious. But the old fires still burn. At the end of the war in '45 while I was at work on a picture in London, she shrieked denunciation over the phone for ruining her life's work. (I had engaged one of her principal male dancers for two weeks during his vacation and thereby worn him out and altered his perspective on money matters, she claimed.) "Mim," I yelled. "Stop shouting and listen to me. I am going to have a baby."

"That's fine, Eggie. Splendid! But how could you do this to me?

How could you as a woman knowing my lifelong struggle against incrrrredible odds?" So we parted. But there was a cable at the birth of my son, and when later my ballet, *Fall River Legend,* was performed at the 1950 Edinburgh Festival, Rambert, I am told, threw herself weeping into Nora Kaye's arms. She said lavish things about the work and she wrote me long and poignantly. "Forgive me, Aggie, dear, if I didn't think you had it in you — but I didn't."

She seemed a touch wistful about the unprecedented triumphs currently achieved by the Sadler's Wells and Ninette de Valois. "I also like beautiful legs and feet, but the Wells has the entire world to select from. I only get the rejects. But I remind myself that among the rejects were Frederick Ashton, Antony Tudor, Andrée Howard, and, I dare say, Aggie de Mille."

So we were indeed. It is to Rambert we owe our deepest bows. We make them with love.

Antony Tudor and Hugh Laing

Over the next six years Antony Tudor and Hugh Laing became my close friends. At the time I met them they were living in a mews off Campden Hill. Their flat consisted of six rooms, but they lived mostly in two — Antony's was gray (silver oilcloth curtains), Hugh's was biscuit (bronze oilcloth curtains). On some days Hugh lay and shouted in the biscuit room and other days he lay and roared in the gray. He was a high-strung artist of twenty-two. His progress at the school was somewhat retarded by his days at home.

Antony was better disciplined. Weather or temperament, he showed up when he was supposed to.

Hugh Laing Skinner had been born in Barbados and was probably the most beautiful young man I ever saw in my life. Black-haired, golden-skinned and slender with the long skull of Egyptian sculpture, he suggested a transplanted native. On good behavior he was bonny and merry; on bad days, he was a tiger.

He had come from his island in 1931 to the Grosvenor School of Modern Art to study painting, for which he showed ability, and while there had attended a performance at the Ballet Club and decided he would prefer to dance. So he changed his career without apparently a day's hesitation.

A year after I met him I asked Hugh to partner me in a concert at the Mercury Theatre, and he revealed himself suddenly as an actor. His personal and wonderful style of dramatic dancing developed thenceforth. The following year, Antony created *Jardin aux Lilas* and they both came into their own. From 1934 Hugh partnered me in every concert I gave in England until the war drove me home.

Everyone acquainted with ballet knows of Hugh's gifts as an actor-dancer. They are unique, but his role in the creation of works is known only to the companies who have performed them. His taste is impeccable and his instincts extraordinarily right for each problem. He works with fervor and invention and has been throughout an enormous sustaining help to Tudor — as indeed, to all choreographers with whom he has dealt, far more help, I should say, than is usual with even the very fine solo performer. Of course, he can be equally destructive whenever he chooses.

His gift for costume design is enormous, and if he should wish to retire from the arena, he will be able to make a good living in this other way. He designed all the dresses for *Judgment of Paris* and was crucially influential in the designing of *Pillar of Fire* and *Shadow of the Wind* — but American union rulings prevent his getting credit.

Antony Tudor was British, fine-boned, quiet and thoughtful with characteristically wicked British humor. At the beginning he seemed self-effacing, endlessly patient, very slow to anger, gentle even. I got to learn that his temper when roused was something to fear. Hugh prodded and kicked and teased him to show more spirit and finally unlidded a volcano, which surprised all, even Tudor. Hugh also worried him toward more ambition, but he need not have troubled himself on this score. Here he was dealing with one of the natural forces of our time. When Tudor finally got ready, oceans moved. Mim called them both "bone lazy" but she could not have been more mistaken. They worked by fits and starts, they wasted strength in quarreling, they mooned and dreamed, but she had no clear idea of the welter of crossed emotion that rocked and paralyzed a heart like Tudor's. Here was a gigantic talent, and the way to organizing its forces was not easy for him or comfortable for his associates.

Tudor had worked as a clerk in Smithfield Meat Market until

one evening he passed the Opera House, saw the Diaghilev Ballet advertised, bought a ticket and went in. That did it. On inquiring he found that lessons could be had from Marie Rambert. He offered his secretarial service in exchange. She exploited him in every possible way, but she gave him his entire training, and it was a good one, and she gave him a company on which to learn choreography.

I don't know how much formal education he had. He knew everything he needed to know for his work. He could read in French and German. He could play the piano excellently and often accompanied rehearsals. His understanding of music has set a new style in choreography. He always expressed himself articulately and could address an audience when need arose with wit and aplomb. In short, he is a man of parts, and he was when I met him.

At that time he had produced *Cross-gartered, Adam and Eve, Lysistrata,* and *Atalanta,* and was considered a minor, gifted figure in English dancing, capable of original movement but little else, not for instance to be reckoned in a class with Frederick Ashton. This attitude persisted in influential circles until 1946 when Tudor returned from New York with Ballet Theatre at Covent Garden and the British connoisseurs realized with considerable shock what up to that point they had ignored. It is to Marie Rambert's credit that she always had a very sound idea of his caliber. In 1933 when I got to know him, his tastes were definitely eclectic. He had no very clear notion of what interested him as subject matter, or what he wanted to say. I urged him to do something English, to explore his own history and background, not realizing his native land was a point of view, an atmosphere, and not a place of birth.

I have said that Antony's humor was sardonic; it was occasionally diabolic. He teased for teasing's sake. He also said just what he thought, always a shocking experience. But he retained the unqualified admiration of his pupils. Even as a sloppy, penniless, out-of-work young man dreaming around London, he commanded the total unquestioning respect of his dancers and their very great love.

Antony's disorganized methods of work, however, exasperated everyone closely associated with him, for he never under any circumstances started composing until the last possible moment. Once under way he could work longer and at higher pitch than most and has for instance been known to compose a whole suite of dances in one afternoon. But at first he is slow, torturingly so. Maude Lloyd, on whom he composed *Jardin* and *The Descent of Hebe*, said the rehearsals were a two- and three-hour agony for a single posture or jump.

To this day he procrastinates and delays until the zero hour, and only when time is running out does he begin to work with quick inspiration. At this hellish moment he does his best work, literally his best, but the wear and tear on the company and manager are frightful, beyond what is easily imagined by the layman. *Premières* used to be postponed two days, then five days, then a week, until managements just got too outraged and held him to an appointed time, but that did not change his methods. The final heartbreaking movement of *Dark Elegies* (*Kindertotenlieder*) was composed on stage the night of the opening with the company in full make-up and dressing gowns. *Romeo and Juliet* was not finished by opening night and three quarters of the way through, the great gold curtain of the Metropolitan came down and stayed down. Antony stepped through the folds and addressed a few courteous but terminal sentences. The next morning he calmly set about finishing it. Forty-eight hours before the opening of *Shadow of the Wind* there remained forty-eight minutes of choreography to be composed, a residue longer than most full-length ballets. He finished in time for curtain rise but everyone worked without sleep. However, I am years ahead of the story.

In 1933, he was slow, gentle, diffident, humorous, courteous and much abused. He taught and composed for almost nothing, watched everything with remembering eyes and drank his tea quietly wrapped in his dreams of world ambition. He was a kind of hibernating carnivore.

We did a great deal of talking, up and down the streets of London, sometimes at night, along the banks of the Thames. We walked on and off for six years, chattering and joking, leaning against the tawny brick walls as we laughed. We explored Whitechapel, the docks, and when the boys moved out to Chiswick to a lane called with happy appropriateness "British Grove," we explored Hammersmith, the eighteenth-century country mansions, Chiswick Lodge, Walpole's "Strawberry Hill," the church where Hogarth lies buried, Becky Sharp's school and any pub that would give us tea, bread and butter and jam.

Hugh, with the help of the Caledonian Market and an unerring eye, had made a delightful home of the studio, which was largely glass like a greenhouse. Upstairs there was a practice room and here Antony taught and rehearsed. The house reeked of urine because the dogs were not housebroken and showed no inclination to become so. None of us minded too much. We kept them off the tables and out of the beds, but other people were not so casual and when they began using the piano for unworthy purposes, the accompanist, Norah, who was an impeccable housekeeper and besides loved music, got up in a rage and left. She came back, of course, the next day, first looking gingerly through the Dutch door to be sure the dogs were secured before she lifted herself up the perilous iron steps to the studio.

We worked upstairs very hard. Someone put the kettle on downstairs so that tea would be ready when rehearsals were finished.

They asked me to make my home with them, but Chiswick was too far out from the center of town for my comfort. The arrangement also struck me as a trifle unconventional, but this excuse seemed so bizarre to them that I stressed the first only.

Every period of life seems to have its own atmosphere and climate and the climate of my time with the boys was the blue June skies of a London summer, brilliant with clouds and the white gay brilliance of church spires in Wren's city. The memories of the hummed accompaniment of Antony's teaching are mingled with bell tones, dissolving in sunny air. I hear his counting, I hear his quips, and see again the polished brass of the neat and hospitable doorsteps, the prams sunning in the old elegant squares, starched curtains blowing into the morning, the towering magnificence of late lilac. Footsteps and cartwheels sound along the street in the strange, un-American quiet, a voice is discernible two blocks away, an impossibility in my own country, and I sense in gratitude once more the promise behind every vine-covered wall and tidy door of good living, of interested people, of courtesy and participation. The skies stretch blue over British Grove and the May trees shake down their petals from high walls. The sun lances off the glass of the studio roof as I wait at the Dutch door with a bottle of wine in my hand while Hugh tries to keep Tobias from knocking me down, and the rich and grateful odors from Antony's kitchen come teasing to welcome me. I am not alone in this alien land. I have folks.

In the summer of '33 Edward James organized *Les Ballets 1933* with Balanchine as choreographer and James's wife, Tilly Losch, and a thirteen-year-old child named Tamara Toumanova as stars. Their season was brilliant but short-lived and they were followed within weeks by the first season of the Ballet Russe de Monte Carlo organized by Colonel de Basil with Diaghilev's great star, Leonide Massine, as choreographer and chief character dancer. Besides a repertoire of brand-new ballets, including the first symphonic work (Tchaikovsky's Fifth), the company boasted an incredible galaxy of young unknown virtuosi, the children of Russian *émigrés* born and reared in Paris and trained by the exiled ballerinas of the Imperial Theatre. They really were young and they really were impressive. André Eglevsky, aged fifteen, with his phenomenal turns and the "soft great jumps of a lion cub," as Mim said, David Lichine, Igor Youskevitch, Nina Verchinina, Morosova, Eugenia Delarova, Tamara Toumanova, Irina Baronova, Tatiana Riabouchinska and from the Diaghilev troupe, to add authority and experience, Alexandra Danilova and Anton Dolin. London was knocked into a heap. Nothing so fresh and hopeful in ballet had happened since the war. The Alhambra lobby, the dancing schools and the salons buzzed.

Toumanova had the kind of beauty that made one understand all about Helen of Troy. Her features were classically perfect, her bearing noble. Dark great eyes flashed beneath childishly long lashes, black as her raven hair. Her skin was the color of old ivory. And to this chiseled beauty, proud, tender and provocative, were added virtuoso technique and a brilliance of delivery that stunned. Her assurance and the maturity of her personality made one question her thirteen years, but when one stood beside her, it was quite apparent. She was vulnerable. There were the moist and untouched eyelids of a real child, the fragile shadow around the lips, the bloom on the skin, the shy, quick fluttering of lashes. She was young, and enchanted, tender, girlish, adorable. How the jaded art world of Europe loved her! Receptions were given in her honor to which she went in an inexpensive and touchingly unbecoming party dress. (This was no affectation. She did not have any money.) Arnold Haskell, the critic, gave her an autographed letter of Taglioni and grew apoplectic in the press. And right behind her, pacing her step by step, was a similar creature, blond and blue-eyed, named Irina Baronova — Snow White and Rose Red. They were the stuff of legends.

But the furor evoked by the baby ballerinas and the love commanded by Danilova were not in a class with the adulation accorded the master of all, Leonide Massine. Seeing a Massine ballet had become one of the erotic pleasures of the London season. The expensive spectators in the stalls contented themselves with "Bravos" and gush. The devotees upstairs gave themselves unrestrainedly to screaming, jumping up and down, beating the railing, hugging one another, slathering at the mouth. If one stood quietly among them, critical, attentive and undemonstrative, with, I dare say, an occasional low mutter, the cult turned as on unbelievers. Antony and I were all but ousted on two occasions, simply because we did not join in the screaming.

At the formal run-through rehearsal of *Chorearteum* (Brahms IV) held on Covent Garden stage at midnight after the performance to an invited audience, Sir Osbert Sitwell introduced the proceedings by remarking that Massine was without peer in the entire world. The audience of artists and patrons cheered for minutes. Massine was a man of no small achievement but I thought of Graham and Humphrey and Balanchine and dissented. Yes, I even thought of Tudor who all unrecognized and lonely and frustrated was working out new ways at Notting Hill Gate. But to question Massine's pre-eminence in the 'thirties in London was heresy. Mim, for one, burned incense at mention of his name.

The Russians by nature are self-assured. Due to the sort of encouragement they received that summer, they developed an arrogance that was Romanov in its perfection. After their initial trip to New York (where I might add they ran into their first adverse criticism), I met the young Toumanova, now fourteen, at a party. I had thought of the New York dancers along with Wigman as the vanguard in the field and I was eager to know their effect on this brilliant child. "Did you see any of our dancers?"

"There is no dancing in America," she drawled. "Outside, of course, of Harlem."

"Martha Graham?"

"Grahhm," she said, "has a great technique, but no ideas. She has absolutely nothing to say. Someone else should do her choreography."

"You fascinate me," I replied in awe. "Pray continue." But we were separated by two adoring young men who came to escort her to the supper table.

Aside from her feeling about herself, and her mother, who has throughout her life been literally inseparable from her, Toumanova, I imagine, regarded with deference just two objects in the world, Massine's will and Baronova's legs. And Toumanova's mama took into account Tamara's legs and the rival's mama. The mothers used to sit in the wings, naturally, when their own children danced, but also during the more difficult stint of the rival and, fixing their concentrated dark gaze somewhere between the metatarsal and the thigh, wait for the icons to work.

Massine rarely committed himself on any subject. His silence in public was imperial. He was not gracious; neither was he unpleasant. He was totally, unattainably withdrawn from casual contact and you could place on his attitude any interpretation you chose. He was Massine and a very impressive figure, the most powerful in the dance world. He was also a great performer, of his kind, character dancing, the greatest.

Tudor and I admired much he did but we can be pardoned for standing aside with hungry eyes, muttering. This adoration was Roman and we were barbarians with other gods. The new bright young things are even now muttering in our galleries. If they only knew how fully aware we are of the weaknesses they discover with such ebullience. Indeed we ourselves could blueprint them. And I now, having grown kinder for a little success, believe Massine knew his.

I have been told by friends who were his intimates that he lived and worked in absolute terror and that his haughtiness was due to unbroken malaise. When he traveled he never mingled with the company, but slept and ate apart.

Historically, the most stimulating works of the season proved to be the Balanchine ballets — *Cotillon, Concurrence, Mozartiana,* and *Errante.* Why these extraordinary pieces, not to mention his *Apollon* and *Prodigal Son* which I had seen five years previously, did not influence me deeply is hard for me to explain. Perhaps because at the time I considered myself a soloist and had no thought of doing ballets, I did not study his work with the intensity given anything that might have personal application. In the twenty years that have since passed, Balanchine has developed into the greatest craftsman in the profession, and in many ways the most poetic and evocative. His invention, always within a classic frame, seems endless, and his list of enduring masterpieces lengthens each year. But in the time that has intervened since I first sat, dull and unreceptive, before *Apollon,* I have developed the means of understanding his technique. I am, on the whole, glad I responded so late and that, although aware of his daring and skill, I remained unmoved in the face of what seemed at the time precious, decadent, even arbitrarily perverse. I think I may have been lucky. His effect through the years on young admirers has proved so over-whelming that not one among them has been able to develop an independent style, with the single possible exception of Eugene Loring.

The Sadler's Wells company at this point was merely a troupe of students located way out to hell and gone, herded and driven by the implacable Ninette de Valois, who had vision and an iron nerve and took the brunt of long years of slogging. Margot Fonteyn and Moira Shearer were still in the classroom. The company's soloists were by no means first-rate until de Valois enticed Markova away from the music halls and Ballet Club, and until she commissioned Frederick Ashton to compose works for her. Ashton had been de-veloped by Rambert; de Valois gave him a full-sized company and an adequate stage. He began devising his matchless comedies and caprices, *Wedding Bouquet* and *Patineurs,* and his handsome lyric piece, *Nocturne.* De Valois herself composed with growing strength *Rake's Progress, Haunted Ballroom.* Little by gradual little, most of the good dancers and choreographers in London with the notable exception of Tudor and Laing were absorbed into the developing group and the children in the Sadler's Wells school began to grow up and step out. Suddenly Markova danced a full-length *Giselle* and it was a performance to compare with the greatest. Suddenly a dark adolescent named Fonteyn danced a lead. But during my London stay, I seldom went to see them. They were so inconveniently located and the personnel and reper-toire of the early years did not compel me. No one at that time guessed to what heights the company would one day reach, except its architect, Ninette de Valois. I rather fancy she knew.

The times I have recorded sound very much as though we were all on a prolonged vacation. Actually we were working very hard. I gave three recitals my first spring at the Mercury. They were nicely successful and the London papers each accorded me a para-graph of praise. Jacob Epstein, moreover, said my Degas studies were "tragic and tender and beautiful." The *New English Weekly* printed a sonnet acrostic in my honor and Haskell went out on a limb in large type with "Thank you, America, for de Mille." I was taken to lunch with Bernard Shaw and I danced at a Charity Bazaar before the Prince of Wales. I also had lunch with Margot Asquith, Lady Oxford. She ate three string beans, half a carrot, and two bites of lean chop. "Is the good lady ill?" I asked the mutual friend who had arranged the séance. "She will starve."

"Not at all," I was assured. "She eats a hearty lunch before dining with someone she thinks will bore her. In this way she doesn't have to stop talking for a minute. I must say, my dear, you got more remarks in than any other young person I've heard try."

And I had lunch with Tamara Karsavina, the great Diaghilev star. Beautiful, serene and gentle, she sat at her table in a hat with grace as became a diplomat's wife and reminisced in the voice of dark metallic vibrancy peculiar to many Russian women.

"You can't think," I said, "what this means to me. A young poet might feel this way about sharing cold chicken with Shelley. How does it feel to be part of an immortal tradition?" She turned her extraordinarily noble little head, balanced like a deer's; she opened her enormous, heavy dark eyes, limpid with sadness and patience, burning with somber glory. She spoke matter-of-factly. "We were all part of it together," she said, "all of us. We were the last flowering of the old regime. That time has gone forever. A new time is coming. You may be part of that."

Two women who transformed London for me opened their homes and kept a weather eye on my welfare — Rebecca West and Elizabeth Bowen. They could not help professionally, but they made a considerable difference in my delight in living.

I took a lesson every day, sometimes private ones from Tudor. (It was Mim, of course, who got paid but, as she explained, spent the money on his next ballet.) He was the first teacher to help me to understand the principles behind the technique. He was a fine teacher.

I lived at the English-Speaking Union on Charles Street off Berkeley Square in the cheapest room they had — a half-timbered attic room called John Bunyan, sparsely furnished, but with wonderful Jacobean chests and chairs, and I was happy as a clam.

The concerts were successful — that is, I didn't lose or make a shilling one way or another — but they were hard on me. The dressers used to be alarmed at the coldness of my body, covered with sweat but clammy cold, this being the effect of pure exhaustion. I have known the black weakness engulf me in center stage, the knees, the thighs, the stomach, the head grow light and hazy, the breath belt across my ribs like a whip, while I measured in feet the space I would have to cover before I could pause, and the weakness took me in full flight like a flood. More than once Tudor has picked me up in his arms and carried me to succor, chuckling wickedly. This is the exhaustion runners know. And afterwards sitting in overcoats, covered with rugs, I would drink an entire quart of milk, sometimes two, before I could stop shivering. It took me a week to recover sufficiently to do a repeat performance.

There was no avoiding this. At the very first, before I'd asked Hugh, I had no partner. I danced twelve or thirteen dances in succession. There were thirteen costume changes, tights, toe shoes, hair arrangements, make-up to be made in two-minute intervals. I never spoke between dances. I briefed the dresser before performance and merely pointed.

The lighting and stage-managing devolved on me, although in England Tudor managed every concert I ever gave except the last, which was six years after the first, managed them beautifully and without remuneration, out of pure friendship. When he learned my program he spared me the lighting rehearsal. No one ever spared me the business or financial responsibilities. If I looked strained when I entered the stage, it was because I was ready to drop before ever I'd taken a step and because of my nagging worry that I should lose more of Mother's savings. I was earning nothing toward my keep and lived in perpetual debt.

One day Rambert explained to me why I did not give the appearance of beauty and ease which, she added, was the basis of all attraction. Standing me before the great studio mirror (this interview was mercifully held in private), she arranged my face as she had so often arranged my members, pulling the eyebrows long, folding down the lids to look languid (the Sylphide expression — the expression of detached absorption which, Rebecca West once said, always reminded her of light constipation), twirling up the corners of my mouth. When she had done she said, "There, that is my idea of relaxed serenity." I raised the drooping lids and peeked without altering the tilt of my head. Stark amazement and shock stared back. It was the arranged face of a corpse. And somewhere I seemed to see another tense woman curling the same head and placing a party wreath atop.

"Don't you think you look better?" she asked with the urgent concern of a saleswoman adjusting a hat.

"Mim," I said, "let's be sensible. If I had more help, if there was any chance to rest before a concert, I'd look considerably different."

"Not necessary! Not necessary!" She waved it away. "Of course, we'd all like assistance. Do you know what I do every day? Do you know what I do the day of an opening? Do you think I also would not like a secretary and a lady's maid and a proper wardrobe mistress and some kindness and consideration, Eggie, from my pupils? Some kindness? Do you think they are grateful for what I do for them? Not they! Who else would take the time, the infinite trouble, who else has the taste? But that's how it is, I do what I can and what is the reward? Now, take Hugh, for example — "

Somehow the point of the conversation seemed to have gotten out of hand. But I knew that no matter how flighty she seemed, the next time I went on stage, her X-ray eyes would be trained on the corners of my mouth to see if they curled with the desired relaxed serenity.

CHAPTER 20

American Dancer in London

IT WAS ROMNEY BRENT who helped me get my first paying job in England in a new musical produced by Charles Cochran of London. The show was *Nymph Errant* by James Laver, with music and lyrics by Cole Porter, and Gertrude Lawrence in the lead. Romney himself directed. This time I was joining the Big League.

Mr. Cochran was very charming as we discussed terms in his half-timbered office in Old Bond Street. The walls were covered with signed photographs of the theater's great, the really great — Duse, Bernhardt, Coquelin *père*, Isadora Duncan. He was courtly and we settled the business details to my disadvantage with grace and dispatch. I was to get a weekly fee, modest, but no royalties he explained. He then complimented me on my dress. I had dropped in on the way to a garden party and was in white organdy, a Watteau hat and blue satin shoes. This was before my feet went to pot and I was wearing size two. As his eyes fell to my slippers, he smiled enchantingly. Incredible man, he had flattered me on the one vanity I dared believe in! I left the office, minding the contract only a little.

This was my introduction to the theater in the grand manner, the theater about which I had read. He asked me out to his country home. A Rolls-Royce, with a silver cockerel on the hood, fetched me. There were salutations and courtesies the day I started rehearsing, roses in the train, roses again in the Manchester hotel room, and on opening night, the works. And every female member of the staff was treated with like royal consideration. After rehearsals, there were midnight suppers at Rule's, with Cocky reminiscing over good wine. I liked all this very much indeed. It was quite different from my treatment in New York.

The night after the first showing of the dances, we repaired to Rule's and Cocky raised his glass to me.

"My dear," he said in mellow, meticulous syllables, "I will give you, if you like, two concerts in London. I have presented only one other solo dancer — Argentina. You have earned this, at the very least, from me."

Romney put his arms about me and kissed me.

Nymph Errant opened in Manchester and after the usual shuffling and changing shook down into form. The odd thing about this job was that I didn't get fired and that two of my dances stopped the performance every night. One was a Greek Bacchanale with a wonderful score composed by Cole Porter in 6/4 time, the other a Turkish solo danced on a satin pillow.

The play was in reality a vehicle for Gertrude Lawrence and Gertie was herself, which is to say a smash hit. She has always seemed to me an eighteenth-century figure, reminiscent of George Ann Bellamy or Lavinia Fenton. She had the wit, the grace of a historic charmer. Her taste was a touchstone. People watched to see how she knotted a handkerchief or clasped a necklace, and that was the style for the next winter. She lived prodigally, lavishly, keeping open house every night after the theater. At least one earl had offered his hand, and there were rumors of attentions from higher spheres. Nearly everyone was in love with Gertie. Admirers followed one another in and out of the doors of her dressing room as in a French farce. She always had champagne cooling there and held a sort of levee after the show every evening. Her room was so thick with men in black and white and women in diamonds and velvet that the maid could barely press through them to take down Gertie's new Molyneux evening gown from its hanger.

The theater was in very truth her playhouse. She showed up for rehearsal exquisitely garbed and had a fine six hours until it was time to put on a better dress and go out to supper somewhere. I do not mean to imply that she fooled around or wasted time. She is one of the greatest technicians in the business, but she seemed to accomplish everything without strain. Her flair for improvisation being phenomenal, each performance, each rehearsal became in the great tradition a direct, fresh experience between her and the audience. She repeated nothing, including sometimes the author's lines, but remade new magic afresh each time out of her enormous zest. This can be trying. The other members of the cast did not always know what was going to happen. In fact, they could be pretty sure they wouldn't know. Rehearsal with her proved a new kind of experience for me — the work flowed so fast that I lost track each hour of what we had done. She had no need of me. When the curtain was up, she strolled across the stage in the famous Lawrence lanky parade, grabbed the proscenium arch with both hands and kicked the back of her head. The house was enchanted. I was not — that is, not at first seeing. But what did it matter? She could have done anything at all. She was having fun — so was the audience, and to me who managed to turn almost every experience in the theater into agony — working as I did on some notion that if one enjoyed the job or if it was easy it couldn't be good — Gertie was a dazzling and impressive lesson to the contrary. It followed as a corollary that she was never fatigued — her energy was as boundless and spontaneous as her wit.

Her presents to all the cast and staff on opening night were princely and she herself received gifts fit for a royal birthday. It took five men to lift down one basket of flowers from an admirer — £50 worth. I gazed at it in awe the second night, when there was enough space in her room to look around. I had never seen so large a basket of flowers in my life. It was over six feet high and the top roses brushed the ceiling. She glanced up at the mountainous jungle of bloom and said dryly:

"Well, thank God it's white, darling."

I was eager to get on with my concerts and in order to do so turned down an offer from the New York Theatre Guild to perform in the Molière-Langner *School for Husbands.* I also canceled my winter's teaching at the Neighborhood Playhouse. Cochran of London was going to make my fortune. I felt so sure I summoned Mother, and she set sail.

In the middle of rehearsals came a call from Mrs. Cochran. I went to see her at teatime, among all the Sickerts. The plans for the theater, she explained, had somehow gone awry and under the circumstances Mr. Cochran did not feel he could continue with the project. I turned on her, and refused to be put off. Cocky was in Paris and she went on, very polite and sympathetic in her efforts to erase me quietly over a teapot. I wasn't having it. On his return we held a council. Since the original plans couldn't be carried out; since it would be necessary to rent another theater and in view of the expense, he hoped I would be willing to share the costs, half and half, and the profits. I warned him there would be no profits. He chuckled in agreement — he had never realized more than £50 on any soloist except Argentina, he said. We had sherry and parted, as always after these perilous contracts, in a pleasant glow.

Then he forgot about me. He was engaged at the time in bringing Elisabeth Bergner to London in *Escape Me Never* and, not unnaturally, gave that venture his entire attention. My concerts became an office nuisance and I was passed down from subordinate to subordinate. There was no publicity. The throw-aways were not printed. There were delays here and fumblings there. I could have done far better alone.

I finally wrote my own publicity, and signed Charles Cochran's name. "It is with the greatest pleasure that I am able to present Miss Agnes de Mille . . . who in her personal appearances brings to the London Theatre a new form of dancing at once fresh, individual and provocative." When I complained of the lack of advertisement he thrust this paragraph into my hands as proof of his unflagging attention and the length to which he and his staff were willing to commit themselves.

Mr. Cochran was also busy presenting Constance Collier and

gave a great press party at his house in her honor ten days before my first concert. But no newspaperman had been informed of my appearances. They simply had not been told. As one of Cocky's projects I had expected to share in this publicity and when ignored I tore out of the house in something akin to hysteria. I remember clinging to the iron railings of his areaway in the streaming November fog and sobbing that I would not go on, that I would not, that I'd been humiliated enough, that it was a repetition of Paris and Brussels all over again. Mother stood dim and compact in the fog beside me and stamped her little foot on the resounding pavement.

"Pull yourself together, Agnes," she said, fiercely. "Control yourself. Why do you do this to me? I have to go off to a Single-Tax dinner. I cannot stand here while you weep." But I refused to control myself. My brand-new hat, bought on Berkeley Street especially for the press party, fell into the wet. My brand-new gloves were ruined with the marks of the soaking iron.

"I can't bear it. I can't bear it any longer," I wailed.

"I cannot be late," said Mother, "I have to make a speech. Why do you do this just before I make a speech?"

A bobby strolled by and looked us over with considerable care — two well-dressed women, cursing, sobbing and muttering in the fog, clinging to the railings of the house where the big party was.

Well, Annie went off to make her speech and I went back to John Bunyan and an evening of bottomless dismay.

But suddenly the phone rang, and a fresh voice, full of vigor and hope, said, "I'm Douglas Fairbanks, Jr. Your mother has just phoned me. She says I'm to save your life. I'm coming over."

Between collecting her wits for her speech and receiving and giving all the salutations and amenities of a Georgist gathering, Annie had thought of the one person who could help and had gotten a message to him. She hadn't spoken to him in the twelve years since he had dumped a pitcher of cold water on her best hat (a black velvet tricorne with ostrich feathers) when we were singing Christmas carols under his mother's windows, but now, in our hour of need, she turned quite simply to him, and in the name of our common childhood and the long friendship between the parents, asked him to put a brotherly arm about me. He did. When he learned that I had undertaken to pay half the expenses, he rolled his eyes and groaned. "Oh lamb to the slaughter! I'll get Gertie to help!"

Why should she? But of course she would. Gertie sold over one hundred tickets personally — put them in her rich friends' hands and pulled the money out of their pockets.

We got to the day of performance. The cyclorama was dirty, there were no lights (see Paris and Brussels), nothing was in order. Danny, Noel Coward's stage manager, was astounded and perplexed. "This is not like the old man," he said, "I have never known this to happen before." Not having worked with the boss before, I couldn't say. I certainly had a poor way with managers.

Cochran was out of town with Bergner. He did not even send a wire. Mrs. Cochran came and was astonished; she plainly had not expected me to be any good. It was rather embarrassing for her. The audience was enthusiastic; the press exuberant. On the repeat performance came the following cryptic wire from the boss: SORRY I CANNOT BE WITH YOU AGAIN.

Then followed the reckoning. My share of the costs cleaned me. A lawyer advised me that I could have sued, but it seemed unwise to sue Charles Cochran for one hundred and fifty pounds.

The financial situation was, in truth, serious. Mother's money had dwindled and she was at the moment engaged in suing the bank that administered her trust fund. And now, my Pop, who had worked all his life brilliantly and so tirelessly, found himself the victim of a series of business reverses which made it impossible for him to continue supporting me. Hospitality, advice, and love he never withheld, and many a time I was to creep to his home and lay a tired head in the room he always kept ready for me — but he could no longer offer a personal allowance. Indeed, he had paid me one at grave inconvenience for some time past. I had been mighty egotistic in my troubles; it never occurred to me that in the depression other people were being as badly or worse hit. The news that I was on my own came with startling surprise. The concerts had taken all the money I had earned choreographing *Nymph Errant* and since I drew no royalties, I was broke. The picnic was over. Now I faced life like other dancers.

Mother sailed home in some trepidation. I moved from my heated room to a shilling-in-the-meter attic in Glebe Place, Chelsea, and for the first time in my life knew real cold.

On Christmas Eve, I went to Danny, the stage manager, where he stood backstage running *Nymph Errant*, which was selling out but which, of course, furnished me no cash. I kissed him.

"Danny," I said, "I cannot even give you a box of cigars." And that very kind gentleman put his arms around me and replied, "A favor is not a favor, if you expect something for it."

Cochran, years later, after he'd been knighted, wrote me a note of deep regret. It is, perhaps, ungallant of me to have told this story, for he was preoccupied and not aware, I am certain, of what was happening. The results, however, altered my whole approach to the business. Right at that point I stopped being a dilettante.

I lived sparsely in the months that followed. It was a full year later before I contrived with luck and the assistance of a friendly staff to give a series of recitals at the Mercury which almost paid for themselves. Mother assumed the year round rehearsal costs and my living. The woman who made my costumes inexpensively with consummate taste, Grace M. Kelley, also dressed me and in short order learned beforehand what to get ready. The whole afternoon of a performance need not any longer be given over to instructions concerning the costume changes. Antony had got the stage-managing down to a fine point; Hugh partnered me. Peggy Laing (no relation to Hugh), who had become a firm friend in the Cochran debacle, took care of my excellent publicity, and the beautiful Elizabeth Hewitt, business manager of the Mercury, supervised my financial concerns with all the love of her heart. The refugee architect, Margot Wittkower, designed my printing. The same pianist, Norman Franklin, always accompanied; the same pianist, Norah Stevenson, assisted at performances and always rehearsed.

Of all the people who assist in the building of a choreographer's career the rehearsal accompanist is in many ways the truest collaborator. She sits in the room for the duration. She must know the music of course, but a good one knows the dance as soon as there is one established gesture and remembers all. A great accompanist will understand the dance before it is visible, and help from the start, arranging and adjusting at the moment of composition, slipping a rhythm in front of the dancers to catch their footfall. A good one can count with the dancers, which is on the phrase and with the music, which is on the bar — quite a different matter. Pit musicians go absolutely mad when they hear dancers racing around mumbling and muttering to themselves in counts that have nothing to do with the bar divisions. There was, for instance, one passage in my latest ballet, *Fall River Legend,* where Diana Adams counted eleven three times and then sixty-seven before she hit a landmark. The musicians in the pit began to laugh and would have looked up to see what in God's name was going on if they had not been considerably occupied themselves.

The accompanist keeps track of all cuts. And if you think this is simple just try to read a page of rehearsal music. The accompanist quiets and comforts the choreographer. She listens to the grousings of the dancers. She is disciplined and steady. She never tires. She is above all unobtrusive. She must sit passive for twenty or thirty minutes on a stretch while brains are worried. Repetition is her atmosphere, hope her function. If she gets bored, a blight settles over all. No composer that I know of can fill this role; he either turns aggressive or desperate.

An elderly woman of considerable bulk and boundless wit, Norah Stevenson showed an intuition during performance that was unmatched, and a patience and sustaining sympathy throughout the rehearsal period that made possible the composing of new works under prolonged difficult circumstances. She used to accompany me with her face to the wall because she knew it was torture for me to be watched. She knew from my breathing when I had stopped, when I was ready to repeat, and the split second when to put her fingers on the keys. Only once did she balk. She quietly took her hands off the keyboard and said in a subdued English voice, "That will do. You have been on seventeen bars for three hours, and I cannot play it even once more. I never told you, but I don't fancy this music anyway." Such a show of resistance was unusual for she rarely criticized except gently and at the proper times.

Norah Stevenson widened her service to include a cup of tea after every tiring bout, also nursing if I felt ill, or soothing if I felt desperate. She tided me over. She was a great artist in collaboration. Her fee for playing was 3/6 an hour; the motherhood and nursing were thrown in free.

I keep referring to the rehearsal accompanist as a woman because, although there are extraordinary men, the greater majority are women. The job calls for a kind of patience that is peculiarly female. All the choreographers depend on them. In New York now we call on Geraldine Schuster, Helen Lanfer, and Trudi Rittmann and Genevieve Pitot, who are also composers, and one brilliant, patient man, Arthur Kleiner of the Museum of Modern Art.

Across the footlights one night at the Mercury came a great sheaf of jasmine. "To a pioneer," said the note, "in memory of Russian Christmases in California — from Vera Fredova." She had grown gray at the temples, but she still stood straight. She still dressed exquisitely and moved like a goddess. But, alas for all of us, she no longer danced; neither did she teach. Summoned to England by her father's death, she had made the bitter decision to live there and, having just turned forty, she saw realistically enough that it was now too late to start her career over, so she stopped dancing and became the assistant of an entomologist. She had never had the ballet career that had been promised her. She lived alone in one room and every morning, on rising, did a thumping hard barre before going quietly off to classify bugs.

I begged her to take me on, coach me, groom me, discipline me, order my affairs and my life for concert appearances. She refused quickly and finally. She had turned her back on the theater and to enter it in any capacity she said would be to tear open every wound in her heart. My pleadings were fruitless.

We went together to the Sadler's Wells. "Ah," she sighed as she watched the young Margot Fonteyn. "There's a girl I would like to take charge of." When I left London she was signing up for Air Raid duty, and all inquiries during the war failed to discover her. But in the summer of 1950 when I was in England for the London production of *Carousel*, I saw her in the lobby and threw myself into her arms. White-haired now and one of the heads of faculty of the Sadler's Wells Ballet School, she has become again Miss Winifred Edwards as she had been when her father first took her, a long-legged girl, to interview Anna Pavlova. I think with envy of the children she instructs.

The English were always chiefly responsive to my Americanism — whatever that might in their eyes appear to be — the American folk dance idiom and jazz style, the energy and verve (Mim said I was Dionysian), my peculiar technique (Mim always had me show off my turns at the end of class, and she said that the touch of my feet on the floor was like the best pianist's touch on a keyboard), but chiefly to my comedy, dramatic style of composition and point of view. *'49*, which began with a slow walk on the stage and a salute to the sunbonnet, was considered the absolute essence of the Southwest, while *Blues* and *Strip Tease* were said, by Rebecca West for one, to be a good evaluation of New York.

My approach toward folk dancing gradually became over the years less realistic and ethnological. I have however always aimed to preserve above all the attitude and culture behind the dance gesture. There are certain liberties that can be taken in stylizing and expanding folk forms that will not rupture the basic meaning. There are certain liberties that cannot. The artist ought to discriminate, for the audience will. No pioneer man, for instance, would, in a courting or social dance, turn a woman upside down — a slut, possibly, but not one of his own women who were valuable and to be treated with courtesy and gentleness. Nor would the women squat on the ground and jump around like frogs. Yet I have seen these tricks used in American folk reconstructions, together with Central European and Slavic idioms. If the young choreographer should ask if there is a basic difference and does it matter, I reply that there is and it does — a basic difference. I don't like to see grim and angry girls in bare bruised feet romping and slapping and crawling through court dances. I feel something essential has been overlooked, possibly elegance. Of course, Martha Graham once stood on her head in a court saraband and became thereupon the embodiment of high protocol. She also did things in *Frontier* no other woman would risk west of the Hudson. What applies to Graham does not necessarily pertain to her followers; few students have her faculty for reaching the bones of life. Indeed no generalization can be applied to the true creator. He will give me the lie with his next fresh idea. But as for myself, in attempting to express my point of view, I had to search through to what spoke simply of the way of life behind the dance. When I was setting *Oklahoma!* I asked May Gadd, the head of the American Country Dance Society, to spend a day instructing my boys in how to offer their hands to the women, to bow to them, to pass them in and out of the groups, courteously, gallantly, as if they cared about them, a point of view in which many of the boys could afford to take instruction.

I made several pilgrimages to Haslemere to study preclassic dance forms with Arnold Dolmetsch. I studied carefully Charles Darwin's *Expression of the Emotions in Man and Animals* and medical reports of the compulsive gestures of the insane. I worked in the British Museum. I went to Cornwall to see the Padstow May Festival. From all these researches I began to abstract a style. Rambert said that in the *Agincourt Song* I moved for the first time with originality and power.

I had developed a passable ballet technique and I had learned to run off concerts without accident or collapse. I had also learned what is virtually the most difficult thing in the concert business: how to build a program. I had learned to organize and execute projects without family participation. I was beginning belatedly at last to live on my own strength.

That is, I had succeeded in doing so in one tiny protected corner of a foreign city. Could I maintain the same professionalism and independence among the tumults and ferments of my mother's household, in the hostile and expensive conditions of my own country? But in America was the advance guard work, and I panted like any exile to hear the shop news of my colleagues, to learn what Martha, Doris and Charles Weidman were up to, for what Paris was to all artists in the 'twenties, New York was to dancers in the 'thirties. If one could please in that unpredictable town: jackpot!

American Dancer Comes Home

THIS trip home I made alone and without assistance, a minor achievement. First, there were the costumes to pack, twenty-four of them
with shoes, wigs, make-up and accessories. The finer tarlatans,
gauzes and satins were attached to the trunk with surgical adhesive
tape to prevent wrinkling, a system I devised myself. A complete
typewritten list of the various trunks' contents had to be prepared
for the customs at both ends and when I left the home-port affi-
davits filed. All my press material, photographs and music went in
two great briefcases. Lacking a secretary I sorted this without help.
My personal wardrobe was extra. I gave this no thought but it
occupied another trunk and two suitcases. Since all the packing
was undertaken in the last twelve hours, I wearily crawled on the
boat too tired to fight seasickness. That I wasn't more uncomfortable was due to the kindness of Monsieur Villar, *commissaire* of the
Ile de France, who arranged for me to travel in off seasons for $125
round-trip tourist, in the comfort of a private cabin first class.

Warren met me at Pier 57 with a Christmas kiss and the un-
welcome announcement that inasmuch as he had decided I
was too dominating an influence in his art life he intended
to try his fortunes alone — a very manly decision but ill-timed, I
felt, since our Guild concert was scheduled four weeks later. I
have never at any point urged a dancer to continue working five
minutes beyond inclination, so I gave Warren my dismayed

blessing and set about the almost hopeless task of replacing him. The brilliant and highly trained young men who abound today were not around in '35. I had to settle for two partners, one a muscle-bound, overgrown athlete who could move to a small degree and the other a nimble member of the Group Theatre who could act. The latter was Robert Lewis, who has since become a director of distinction. He was chosen at this point for his pantomimic abilities, but he footed a Galliarda with friskiness and aplomb.

We approached the performance with the usual disorganization, frenzy and exhaustion. Alas for my British staff! All my New York friends, however, turned to loyally and helped. The mailing list which was usually done by professionals for one hundred dollars was done in our parlor by whoever dropped in. I addressed through meals, phone calls, conversations, rests. Mother never got up from her writing table except to pick up her needle. That saved a hundred dollars. A friend did the boxoffice supervising free which saved another hundred. We couldn't save on stamps; the postal service has fixed rules. This time, the last, we were able to pay Louis Horst. The tension mounted.

Mother's diary reveals the atmosphere in which this homecoming was attempted — true chaos, which had through the years become a sickening constant.

Feb. 1, 1935 . . . A rehearsal with Louis Horst. I made collar — and started on Elizabethan ruff and cuffs and took them with me to luncheon at Inez Irwin's at 1. But couldn't work. 12 women. Home at 4. Worked till midnight on Queen Eliz. costume. Got A.'s and my dinner. She off to light rehearsal — expecting to be home about 10 — instead home at 12 — exhausted.

Feb. 2, 1935 . . . A. to Ballet School. Then I with A. and some costumes to Guild. She rehearsed. I saw some of new dances. When A. got back I gave her hot milk and put her to bed.

Feb. 3, 1935 . . . After breakfast, A. to Guild. Mildred with her, with costumes. I worked furiously at phone — asking

people to recital and trying to finish wrist cuffs. Sent Mildred
back with electric iron, etc. She home again. I over to Guild.
A. rehearsing. Brought her home about 3 for lunch. She took
nap. She had supper and over to Guild Theatre by 6:30. I
still worked on wrist ruff but could not finish. Dressed.
Edward Johnson called for me at 8:25 and taxied me to Guild.
Went behind to see A. Full balcony and mostly full down.
Many friends. William and Clara in front. A. *excellent.* A
superb performance. 12 dances — 6 new. After to Mary
Hunter's to supper party. Margaret and Bernie phoned from
Hollywood about 3 A.M.

Up to this point in my career, John Martin had been a stanch
supporter, softening his sterner tastes whenever I did anything
uncouth or maladroit, but on this Monday he loosed the irritations
of years and an impatience augmented by the fact that I had
stayed away from my native land too long. The *Times* was blistering. I was distraught. I threw myself despairing into Martha
Graham's arms. "They never raised a statue to a critic," she said
cheerily.

It must be abundantly clear to the reader as to me now why I
was not getting on. Long since my relatives, all except Mother,
had given up hope of a brilliant career for me. They were
kind and they were patient, but the protracted financial strain and
the total lack of joy and effectiveness pulled on their nerves. I had
become a family problem. I sensed something or other basically
wrong, but could not understand what. It did seem odd, however,
considering what a gay and successful childhood I'd had. No
problem then had been too much. I'd licked each one with verve.
I couldn't be given tough enough ones. Now in the full bloom
of my youth, healthy, presumably alert, hard-working and dedicated, I was a bust, or very nearly. What was the matter?

Only some few choreographers have mastered the technique of
success, and among these the most reliable and adaptable are not
necessarily the most creative. It has always seemed to me they are
more exposed than other artists to betrayal by their problems than,

let us say, writers or painters or composers. But the lack of time, publicity of effort, dependence on other bodies and temperaments which prove such difficult hazards, cannot be held accountable for the prevalence of failure. In plain fact most of the great creative personalities in the dance world contain in themselves tragically the seeds of destruction for the very gift they support. The great exceptions are George Balanchine, who has achieved during twenty-five years an unparalleled amount with no nerve storms whatever nor any great variation of caliber beyond the steady and gradual growth of the maturing genius, and has held throughout the adoring respect of his companies, and Frederick Ashton, who has also, and for only a slightly shorter period, functioned with happy effect wherever he has chosen to work. All the others I have known, even the ones I have loved and respected the most, are partially suicidal. And of all choreographers, good or bad, it seems to me I was the most disorganized.

I could only rely on my instincts, which might be faulty, and on the advice of trusted professional friends, and on the reports of critics. Can one rely on critics?

The trouble in the 'thirties with American dance criticism was that it had remained for so long almost exclusively in the hands of two, the critics of the *New York Times* and the *New York Herald Tribune*. That is not a body of opinion. That is two men with unnatural influence. All the other papers were in the hands of music critics who knew nothing whatever about dancing. Furthermore, out-of-town writers took to quoting the *Times* as a reliable model over their own signatures, so that one could travel across the continent and receive the same notice in the same language from coast to coast. John Martin has been on the *Times* for twenty-five years. His power was so great at first that his word alone would sell or break an artist on tour. Many times managers have sought vainly to oust him, but the man was writing, quite properly, only what he believed. The dancers naturally all quivered at his slightest dictum. Most of us knew him personally. He was charming, kind, friendly, intelligent and participating. He has done more to explain and propagandize dancing than any other writer in our time. Yes, and to encourage the practitioners. His taste is catholic. But he was independent, unpredictable and tough.

Martin frequently took us out to lunch after a stern rebuke and had long, fatherly talks, but the punishment had been administered. The situation has since been somewhat corrected. There are some fourteen knowledgeable critics now writing in the United States and the music critics have at last, through exposure, become more sensitive to this other branch of the theater.

But for fifteen years Martin held the fort alone, and he still remains the most powerful and, in the long run, the most perceptive of all. We know he is human; we know he has foibles; we shake in our boots. All of us do.

I had lunch with John Martin after my return concert. He bade me be of good cheer and pay attention to no one, including himself. He did not, however, say this in print.

My predicament was further compounded by the scorn which was heaped on all ballet dancers by the militant moderns. I found myself suddenly, to my dumfoundment, in a stylistic backwater. In London I had been considered slightly uncouth because not an able classicist. In New York I found if one were not MODERN, one was decadent and/or Tory. Influenced technically by Graham and Wigman and theoretically by well-organized left-wing groups the critical pressure within the dance world was brutal. Today's problems demanded nonballetic expressions, it was said. (Lincoln Kirstein said otherwise but at the moment nobody paid very much heed to him. He was just starting and his first venture, the initial American Ballet season with a program entirely choreographed by Balanchine, got a terrible slating from the press.)

In 1935, Hurok imported de Basil's Ballet Russe de Monte Carlo and the craze began that was to endure seventeen years and sweep everything else to the corners. The audiences, which have thronged to see ballet since, have not troubled themselves with these theories. They just liked ballet. But for a long time they accepted the impresario's conviction that only Europeans could devise or perform it. England, which at that moment was extending its "Buy British" program into the realm of art, was both forcing and supporting its young artists. When, however, even the very good Britishers were taken into the Ballet Russe, they Russianized their names. They were all put back overnight as patriotism mounted during the war.

The tendency within this country in the 'thirties to scorn ballet dancing as the expression of defunct economic and cultural systems was as superficial as it was biased. The eighteenth-century village Maypole dance and the gavottes and minuets of the court are basically the same and basically different from the dances of another culture. We took over much of the European language, etiquette and social customs; we inherited their art expressions; we were quite prepared to inherit their theatrical entertainment. And to argue that the style is alien and nonrepresentative because Harry Truman governs by parliamentary discussion and Louis XIV did not is nonsense. Let us try to do a pueblo corn dance and see how far we get. Most ballet dancers think they can. It demands no muscles they haven't got. But the Indians can make the rains come.

We were pinched for cash but we all went West once more. Warren had begged back, freedom having proved neither comfortable nor remunerative. Margaret was living in Bel Air and she offered shelter, food, and her help.

But although I tried all the agents and producers again, not one offer was made, not one of any kind, albeit the studios were busy filming musicals.

Mother and Margaret kept telling me that the reason I didn't get on was because I didn't dress better or look well-groomed. But I had no time, and small funds. Anyhow, I didn't believe them. I looked all right on the stage and who cared how I looked off?

But I shall never forget Uncle Cecil's amazement as he saw me climbing into a rabbit-skin under-jacket which I had purchased in Selfridge's basement to make my summer coat do through a New York winter. "Good heavens, baby, what is that? Don't you make any money at all? Are you in this for your health?"

I looked at him in surprise. I was of course. I thought he knew.

Mother rustled up a proposition for a ballet performance at the Hollywood Bowl which I was to compose, organize and mount myself; fee two thousand dollars paid by the Bowl management, for a wonder. That sounded enormous, but on consultation with Fanchon and Marco I began to realize it was not munificent. Fanchon had staged all the dances and entertainments in the Bowl up to that point and had made ends meet only by road-showing the ballets in her cross-country chain of movie theaters. "Why do you want to do this?" she asked after adding a few figures. "You'll lose money."

"It's an opportunity to compose works I've always longed to do."

She shook her carefully marceled head. "Thank God I'm not an artist!"

I chose Percy Grainger's "Molly on the Shore," the Finale of Gershwin's Piano Concerto in F, and a collection of Smetana's *Bartered Bride* and Moldau suites. The undertaking was enormous, my cast swelled to eighty and they all had to be costumed. Robert Lee of U.C.L.A. offered his services as a designer and the making of the costumes became a summer project for the university art students. With incomparable kindness, the director, Mitchell Leisen, once my uncle's costume designer, edited and advised. Many of the Czechs (I called on the national clubs) had their own native dress, which helped.

The Bowl can seat about nineteen thousand people. The distance from the rear rows to the stage was so great that a gesture was perceptible a beat ahead of the sound. The Bowl stage was then in front of the orchestra shell and stretched to one hundred and four feet in width. The arc of radiation being acres wide, there seemed to be no center and no sides. Where most stages fronted three sections of seats, this monster faced twelve. One's head moved one hundred and eighty degrees to take in the front row. All patterns flattened right out unaccented and unfocused like a panoramic photograph. Everything subtle or delicate disappeared. The solo figure did not exist. It was quite a challenge to a soloist who in

London had worked on a twelve-foot stage and made a name for delicate facial expression.

But the back-breaking work was the rehearsing and composing. The wage I paid was a sliding one from one dollar to fifteen. But as there were eighty performers, even these paltry fees began to add. It did not include rehearsal time which was to be considered, I explained to the dancers, under the heading of experience, and to the Czech singers as a demonstration of national feeling. The dancers understandably had to eat during the two months of rehearsal so they took whatever paying jobs offered. I was never to have the same company for two days' rehearsal. There were gaps in every group, girls substituted for boys, dancers came and went as through a training camp. An hour of every rehearsal period was wasted in catching up the absentees on lost work. My spirits failed me again and again. It was Penelope's work, over and over and over the same faltering patterns with new recruits. Four lieutenants stood fast, Warren, of course, Mary Meyer, a beauty whose auburn hair fell below her knees, Bella Levitsky, the star of the Lester Horton group, and Paul Godkin. We got the work done in ten weeks. It should have taken three. The *Harvest Reel* was good. I hope to remount it. The costumes, all of them, were lovely.

Then we entered the Bowl for the final rehearsals. The orchestra rehearsed every morning. They offered me the lunch hour, but this, of course, was homicide.

We chose five o'clock when the great California afternoon turned slowly away behind the hills. In that muted time we straggled up the dusty road with dancing clothes under our arms and my puffed pianist, sweat runneling her powder, lugging the music case. The dancers threw themselves on the grass, or clustered under the bushes like bugs. I stood on the baking boards of the stage and surveyed my domain.

This was the Bowl cratering up into the ringing sky, my mother's Bowl. (Hadn't she and Artie Mason Carter, their hats askew, dashed home to say you could hear a fifty-cent piece drop in any quarter of it?) During the first summer's performances I sat four nights a week on a blanket in the sagebrush. The next summer there were wooden benches, but the spring rain had rotted them and they tilted back on their moorings so we sat with our feet in the air staring straight into the stars. In the mornings, the hot, expansive mornings, I had permission to attend rehearsals and listened to Papa Alfred Hertz put the boys through their paces. I was present when Galli-Curci rehearsed standing very tiny in a white silk coat and holding an adorable little flowered cretonne parasol over her face lest she faint. When she finished all the musicians beat their bows on the stands and I was so overcome I had to rush to buy an ice-cream soda to settle my feelings, but found I could not swallow it. The night before I entered the university Hertz played the Valhalla music and my heart nearly burst within me. So much of my inner life had transpired in musical experience, so much of that music had been first heard here!

In 1924 at the head of the long road we had just plodded up, there once stood a large papier-mâché bowl and Mother and the stars she commandeered, Wallace Reid, Milton Sills, Conrad Nagel, Thomas Meighan, called for pennies as the audience streamed out. "Give your pennies to buy the Bowl! Pay off the mortgage of the Bowl!" The mortgage was burned by Artie Carter on stage the last night of the first season. Mother had stood by that bowl every night until all the audience had left and then had taken her group home for hot chocolate and cookies.

I surveyed the cement tiers of seats. The tree was gone. The seats reached the very rim of the hills. A fence surrounded all. Gate crashers could no longer wander casually over the crest of the mountains and sit down free and comfortable in the brush.

I walked out to what had been Artie Carter's box and started rehearsal. The dancers couldn't always hear me, because the acoustics worked the other way, and they couldn't see me at all because the sun was in their eyes. Warren and I did five-hundred-yard dashes up and down sheer slopes trying to ascertain what our work looked like a quarter of a mile away and at an angle we never dreamed of. We worked out a series of semaphore signals with scarfs by way of communication. Once through each number was all the dancers could stand. They had to walk barefoot in the grass every five minutes and soak their feet in water to keep them from blistering. The heat in that cup of hills with the sky still aglow smashed them flat. The first time Warren raised me on his back and I stared up into the blue dazzle the heavens went black.

"Put me down," I croaked, "I'm going to faint."

"You damn well are not," said Warren. "We can do it. You've been putting us through this for days. We can go to the end, and you're going to."

I did.

The night of dress rehearsal the family attended, and Bernie helped, the first time a male member of my family had been on hand during the deathwatch. (Father was at this point making pictures in the East.) The ballets looked beautiful. The orchestra sounded fine. (The concert master conducted, not the maestro, who in accordance with tradition disdained to accompany dancing.) *Harvest Reel* was really first-class and we worked out splendid lighting. The air was cool at night. I stretched out my arms in the moonlight and flew. I raced and raced in the cool night expanse, on the largest stage in the world. Around me the mountains ribbed the sky. Under my feet lay the beat of a full symphony orchestra.

Unknown to me, hiding high up in the empty seats because she had not the price of a ticket was Carmalita Maracci with her gang. She saw a good rehearsal.

The next night the place was full. We danced our damnedest. But the electrician mistakenly did not turn up the lights beyond the first cue, which was just under visibility. One could not tell man from woman nor blue from red. There being no telephonic com- munication with his box on the side of the hill, Bernie ran up and down the aisle trying in vain to get to him and correct matters. But he could not get through. We had not been able to afford two expert stage managers, one to sit with the electrician, the other to marshal the hordes backstage in the peculiarly unprofessional shacks which served as dressing rooms, and now we were paying dearly for our economy. The electrician, by failing to press one master lever, undid three months' work. Bernie nearly went mad. Mother bit her fists. We kept dancing, hoping someone could see, and that something would happen. Nothing happened. Fifteen thousand people waited restlessly in the dark for just what they didn't know. The electrician remained passive, gazing into the deep dusk with serene complacency. For this service he charged $360, which was deducted from my check.

The other numbers were lit, but only the Smetana piece, which was suitable to the monstrous dimensions of the place, succeeded. The press was unfriendly. "De Mille girl fails," said one black heading. The other critics took an almost personal zest in pointing out that Fanchon and Marco had been more effective.

We lost a thousand dollars — one of Mother's last bonds.

Hooray for What

WHILE WAITING for something or other to happen I lived at Margaret's house and took classes from Theodore Kosloff and Carmalita Maracci.

I had heard about Maracci from many sources, but the first time I saw her was when I went to class at the Perry Studio on Highland Avenue. She was dressed in a little knitted bathing suit and she sat upright on the edge of her chair, her insteps, the most beautiful feet in the ballet world, crossed precisely before her. She was smoking. She had tiny hands with long, quick fingers, the nails extravagantly long for castanet playing. She was very small, doll-like, and compact. Her black hair was nailed, Spanish style, in a knot at the back of her head. I have said she was doll-like, but there was no hint of prettiness in the face. She had rather the head of a precocious monkey or a wicked marionette. Under the bald, hard, round forehead, the eyes opened large and were flecked with yellow lights reminiscent of Graham's. The large mouth, peeled back from strong teeth, was aggressive and mobile. It was an angry little head, proud, taut and passionate — the head of a Spanish gypsy. She always held it curbed in as though there were a bit in the mouth, the cords of her neck jutting out in strong, vertical lines. She looked under flickering lids as though she were about to bolt. Her voice rang out in flat Southwestern speech. (She had been born in Montevideo of Italian-German parentage, but she talked like a housewife in Bakersfield.) "Oh my goodness," she said, in washday Bakersfield impatience, "show some gumption! You look like limp lettuce leaves. What do you think you're doing?" And with this she threw her cigarette down and ground it out on the studio floor under the toe of her pink satin slipper. "Now, let's get going!" Up came the chest, the spine tautened. Her neck and head assumed the tension of accumulated force which is a dancer's preparation. The long arms moved to fourth position, her knees galvanized, and she was off on cold legs, without a *plié* or an excuse-me, in a series of the most astonishing *chaîné* pirouettes one could ask for, revolving as fast as the eye could follow, as smooth as silk unwinding from a spool. Her lungs were filled with smoke, her thighs relaxed from sitting down. She stopped in arabesque, erect like a T-square, the straight supporting leg planted on its delicate point, the structure of her body balanced and counterbalanced, sinew against bone against height against sinew hung in the air, tension counterbalanced on tension. And the lovely, tense foot was adequate to all, attaching itself to the bare floor and permitting the body to branch and flower above. She posed there on one point, in defiance of gravity, until her knee got tired, and then, and only then, she allowed her heel to touch ground. She had remained immobile, in full flight, for about twelve seconds.

"Glory be to God," I said.

"Well!" said Carmalita, with a throaty chuckle. "That was pretty good. I think I'll have another smoke on that one. Now, how about some of you trying?"

One day Anton Dolin, the English star, visited her class. Carmalita rose from her cigarette, winked at her girls and unleashed a series of *entrechats-six*, interspersed with *entrechats-huit*. She sat down, breathing a trifle hard, her nostrils flaring, and asked Dolin for a light. I dare say his hand shook a trifle as he tended it.

"Stretch your feet," she would yell suddenly, sitting on the floor at our ankles and taking the offending member in her strong,

surgical fingers. "Isn't that a good pain? I like to feel pain like
that. That kind of pain is accomplishment."

As we left at the end of an hour and a half, not too tired (her
classes were built for exhilaration, and she had the great peda-
gogic faculty of helping us each day to do one single thing we
had not done before), she would change her slippers and re-enter
the empty studio to practice herself, alone — something very few
ballet dancers will force themselves to. She also practiced two
hours of castanet and heel work daily, all of this in addition to
her composing.

She lived and worked in a cottage that had been built out of one
of the schoolrooms in the Hollywood School for Girls. It was
strange to walk up the familiar path with dancing clothes under
my arm instead of Caesar. She and her husband invited Warren
to make his home with them, and I tagged along whenever I
could arrange to. She never had doubts about her work. I found
out shortly why.

Up to this point, I had not seen her dance. I had heard rumors,
but these were so extravagant that I gave them little attention. The
night before she entrained for a San Francisco concert, she asked
me to watch a rehearsal. I sat in a studio where I had done a daily
practice for six months and where we had had our parties. The
place smelled of wood and floor wax; the trumpet vines tapped at
the windows. Carmalita walked on incredibly high heels to the
center of the room and sat down on a kitchen chair. She said to
the pianist in her plain dancing-class voice, "I'm ready, I guess."
And it began.

The dance she showed me was her *Cante Jondo* or *Deep Song*.
It was one of the greatest solos I ever saw in my life. This girl
worked with thunder. At the end I walked to her quietly and
put my arms around her.

"I'm glad you like it," she said, matter-of-factly. "I think it's
good myself."

It is no ordinary experience to discover one evening that an
intimate, a known, well-loved, daily companion has something

close to genius and stands outside of the standards we set for ourselves. The person speaks with the usual voice, laughs with the ordinary expression and then, without transition or warning, becomes a figure of magic. I have known this experience three times, with Carmalita, Antony Tudor and Sybil Shearer. It is a very humbling experience. It involves some of the fastest reorientation a person can be asked to make, and strong discretion because one is brought up sharp against the knowledge that the other fellow has known the score all along.

Carmi has remained a stanch friend and a great teacher. I have never seen her dance in concert that I was not deeply moved. She is brilliant, passionate and strong. She can also be delicate and impish. At once satirist and tragedienne, there are few of like caliber.

I continued taking classes with Carmalita through the autumn of '35. I even organized a class of my own and started experimenting with gesture and the teaching of pantomime at the Perry Studio. A lanky youth who answered the phone and kept the studio bookings used to wander in and watch. I forbade visitors, but he seemed so inconsequential that I permitted him to come and go at will. His name was Richard Pleasant, and he remarked once on leaving that he intended sometime in the future to have a big ballet company of his own and planned to give me a chance at real choreography with a proper big group.

I said "Yes, yes," and "Thank you" and no, I wouldn't go out to tea with him.

I was desperate for money. I organized an infant's class for rich moving-picture children. But I found I was not gifted with the young. Twenty minutes of my instruction would reduce the more sensitive ones to hysteria, sometimes with vomiting.

I lived, of course, with and off my sister. I lived presumably in luxury but I lacked the ten dollars' cash a starving friend once asked to borrow. I never had in my purse more than carfare.

The director, George Cukor, phoned one day offering me the

dances in the forthcoming Irving Thalberg production of *Romeo and Juliet*. Norma Shearer and Leslie Howard were to be the stars. I accepted with unbusinesslike alacrity.

I made my terms with Thalberg while he stood sipping a glass of milk for stomach ulcers, and the terms were splendid. He was a small and romantic man, as elegant as an Oriental prince. He made his decisions with the conviction and speed of absolute authority.

Terms settled I asked for a clarification of style; did he want a small party of, say, forty people in a realistic room of the period with sixteen dancers or so, or did he want a royal court ballet in the grand manner? He considered. Since the set was to be rather larger than the floor space of the Grand Central Station, and was to serve as background for five hundred people, ten greyhounds and a couple of chained leopards, we decided on a full-scale *quattrocento* entertainment and I planned to dish up something that would do no disparagement to the head of the Holy Roman Empire. My London pianist, Norman Franklin, was cabled to hunt music in the British Museum. Oliver Messel teamed reluctantly with Adrian and designed the fantastic and exquisite ballet costumes. A thirty-voice choir of small boys bearing golden apple trees and singing *a cappella* a fifteenth-century madrigal accompanied Juliet's entrance. It was a bit above the Capulets, I felt, but so was everything else in the picture. Thalberg was made acquainted with every step of our plans, and Cukor, who was an imaginative and encouraging director, paid daily visits to the rehearsal studio. But I did not actually see Thalberg again until he walked on the set the day of shooting.

Once hired, I was treated like a world-famous director. We had our own unit complete with assistant, prop boy, rehearsal studio, secretary and pianist. The beautiful auburn-haired Mary Meyer was my soloist and assistant. We worked unmolested on pay for four months.

To our surprise we were ready in three weeks, so in order to keep busy for the next thirteen weeks, we gave each other classes and studio performances of the dances for all kinds of guests, for everyone who was interested. Hardened business executives and studio managers grew quite soppy with enthusiasm; the toughest of the lot, the company accountant, dropped in often. It made him feel like a better man, he said. Only Thalberg did not come. He was too occupied. And the camera man — I begged the camera man to come. Every gesture was being carefully devised for a special camera angle. But he did not. He was too busy also.

Thalberg at last appeared four months later when we were on set in full costume. "What in God's name is this?" he said. "Stop the cameras. Shearer has not even made her entrance yet." The forty flaming torches carried by the forty boys were doused by the fifteen firemen and the girls and boys told to go and sit down. Thalberg was apparently taken completely by surprise and voiced his doubts at length to Cukor, but said not one word to me. That was Monday when we were supposed to film the first of the three dances.

Tuesday Thalberg walked on the set and said, "But this looks like a Hollywood spectacle."

"It does, doesn't it?" said Cukor, chuckling. "Let's improvise something different."

Having followed his exact instructions, however, and having achieved what was up to that point the best composition of my life, I refused to improvise. They shot the dance, which I had planned as a fugal arrangement of five groups of girls pivoting around the soloist (Shearer), but they shot it as a series of close-ups of Miss Shearer back-lit, and peeping around her hair. I wrung my hands. I shouted at the master camera man but he was out of hearing up in the air on a boom. "This was not devised for this angle," I called. "All you will get in eight counts is a row of rumps backing towards the lens." But they bade me be still and promised that it would look lovely anyhow, setting up their apparatus behind arches, under balustrades and around Italian youths, down flights of stairs and muttering about composition while they shuffled reproductions of Piero della Francesca, Simone Martini and

Ghirlandaio who certainly hadn't figured in my plans. They placed their machinery as fast as possible and got on with the shooting briskly since they didn't intend to use much of the dance anyway. That was Tuesday.

On Wednesday we did the next bit, another series of close-ups with no dancing figures visible. On Thursday, Thalberg had seen the rushes and his assistants told him they looked like Botticelli.

On Friday he was still afraid of the Hollywood connotations.

On Saturday he was undecided.

The following Monday we finished eight full shooting days on one dance sequence. (The balcony scene had taken six days to shoot, the potion speech four — for four days Norma Shearer wept and shrieked from nine in the morning until seven at night.) Thalberg came on set and thanked me gravely for the job I had done, which he said was of great excellence. I am told this praise was without precedent. He then invited me to do the dances in *Marie Antoinette,* which would have been a guarantee of further income and possibly greater opportunity. But three months later he tragically died.

When I saw a cut version of what actually had been filmed I went outside the projection room and lay down in the grass and was very, very sick.

Herbert Stothart, the head of M-G-M's music department, found me wandering around the studio late at night. He ushered me into his study and poured me a stiff drink. "Oh, my dear," he said, "this happens to everyone here. Every single artist that comes to this place. I have only one piece of advice: get it on film, somehow. Fight later."

I tried to get it on film to the point of nuisance. No go.

Stothart had his own troubles shortly. Having settled with Thalberg and Cukor to score the picture entirely in fifteenth- and sixteenth-century modes, he had arranged and orchestrated the major portion of the work and was happily in New York recording carillons and refined counterpoint by the best choirs and madrigal groups when Thalberg, by some unhappy miscalculation, heard a broadcast of Tchaikovsky's *Romeo and Juliet* overture. He was on the transcontinental telephone in ten minutes. "Why did nobody tell me about this?" he roared. Stothart was ordered to add the Russian tunes throughout. This he did, wretched man, counterpointing against the more lush passages fifteenth-century plain song — the whole poured like chocolate over the Elizabethan iambic pentameter.

The picture was a great success. It is still playing in Nicaragua. It was, notwithstanding its involved musical score, very moving — largely due to the acting of Shearer who turned in a superb potion and death scene. Shearer was no comedian, but she could reach tragic heights. She did again in *Marie Antoinette*. She enjoyed playing anguish; it exercised all her faculties. She could perform a scene over and over and over and over — pouring tears, her eyes like faucets. "Doesn't this tire you?" I asked. "Not at all," she replied. "I love it," and she began to pour afresh as she ran back under the hot lights and bathed her face in spouting salt with the vigor of a kill at the tennis net. She brought this athleticism to every activity.

Thirty or forty complete shootings were made of every important scene. But of my first dance — not one, and of the second dance only half of one and that mostly in close-up. The third involved forty people but was played as a love duet between actors.

The dances must have cost close to one hundred thousand dollars. This however, by my reckoning, was not the greatest waste. The dances were good.

❧

"Nothing succeeds like failure," said Rebecca West to me. And sure enough, on the strength of *Romeo* I was given another chance shortly — a stage show called *Hooray for What*, directed by Vincent Minelli, the scenery and costume designer, his first directorial assignment. It was written by Lindsay and Crouse with a score by Harold Arlen and lyrics by E. Y. Harburg. Ed Wynn was the star. Kay Thompson and Hannah Williams (Mrs. Jack Dempsey) were the leading ladies. This is a notable group of names and one would think they might insure a high degree of professionalism. It turned out not. The project began decently enough with a telegram from Vincent Minelli. The salary was small but adequate. I came gladly.

The Business Manager, since deceased, I did not care for. It is the custom to speak kindly of the dead, but having entertained nothing except loathing for him when alive, I see no reason now to veil my opinion. He it was who set the dancers' salaries. "Thirty-five dollars a week and a little loving on the side." Plain and frank like that. I insisted on having two girls I knew, Mary Meyer and Dorothy Bird. He thought they were hideous. Mary had done a part for Thalberg and Cukor and had modeled for Hoyningen-Huene and *Harper's Bazaar,* while Dorothy was one of Graham's chief soloists and looked like something off the Parthenon. But they were not the Business Manager's type and he didn't want them around. Fortunately, Arlen and Harburg and Crouse disagreed.

The Business Manager's type, or the type of the men who put up the money, or their henchmen's type, I was to learn well as time passed. They did not assemble all at once; they drifted in day by day as rehearsals progressed, faded, jaded, raddled with drink, hawk-eyed, hard-mouthed and insolent. And for every one of these, I had to let a trained dancer go. I had to take them, and I couldn't fire them, not if they fell down dead drunk at my feet, not if they were three hours late. They wore fine furs over their bathing suits, and diamonds, and platinum slave bracelets, and they talked about how they wished they were Barbara Hutton. Great limousines with liveried chauffeurs fetched them at the stage door. They didn't know their left knee from their hair dye. One astonishing girl, fresh back from Australia or South Africa, allowed as how she always got a job whenever she blew into town. It didn't matter how far along rehearsals were. They didn't dare not hire her. She didn't specify why. She thought I was nuts, but she liked me. They all thought I was nuts, but Girlie was the only one who liked me. I committed the indiscretion of making the girls bend their backs the first day. The next rehearsal none of them could walk and complained to the management. I was asked to be reasonable. I also haughtily refused to give the favorites special things to do, although I knew very well what powers stood behind them. I might have played ball just a little, but I scorned to and worked my own ruin and knew it but would not change.

Right off I got into trouble. The management wanted the girls exposed as much as possible, face front always, bosom bared, legs just visible to the waist. Minelli had all sorts of trick costumes planned, which almost totally concealed everything, gas masks on their faces, barbed wire wrapped around them (made of rubber, forty-five dollars a yard). He was stressing irony. Business Manager was more interested in sex. Neither gave way. I took my instructions from Minelli since he had hired me.

Rehearsals were a horror, and there was never ten minutes of privacy or quiet. When I sat on stage I knew that the bosses had sneaked in and were prowling the aisles whispering. I developed a tic from snapping my head to see who was spying behind me. When I sat out front, I knew by the sudden inattention and heightened chattering and giggling that you-know-who had entered through the stage door, and was sitting just out of sight teasing and snooping. I pleaded for privacy. I denounced. I warned. No use. The evening rehearsal was the after-dinner fun of all the bosses and their lawyers and their lawyers' guests, and all visiting bigwigs from Hollywood, and all backers, and backers' wives, and all my little adventuresses primped and giggled and studied the guests with experienced eyes and paid me not the slightest mind. Naturally, I was on the way out already. Only I didn't know it. The management had never wanted me. They didn't like what they saw. It was Minelli who had forced me on them along with his damned gas masks and rubber wire. They got along busily with their plans at the back of the orchestra while I sat on stage and tried to compose something good and tried to see who was walking back there and why. And very soon, the great dance director of musicals, Robert Alton, made his appearance and I was told that he would divide the work with me. I had no agent. I accepted this without a word, but I chilled to the last nerve. Thereafter, I got the troupe only now and then.

We went to Boston. The dress rehearsal lasted without break three days and two nights. We went into the theater on a Tuesday and came out Thursday noon. Minelli had altered the sets for his own reasons without telling and whereas I had been given to understand there would be four exits at the corners, I now found there was one, directly center. Also the stage was not square but pie-shaped. Dancers were given trains, hats and swords they had not counted on. Several numbers became disasters.

And now the henchmen arrived in a real body together with the backers and agents and walked up and down the aisles and selected what girls they wanted and gave advice indiscriminately to everyone about whom to fire and what to cut, a very handsome, upright group of men, as helpful in this time of stress as they were entertaining and refreshing.

The book wasn't going too well and we were all treated to the spectacle of our chiefs screaming and reviling one another across the theater. Harburg, who had just gotten out of a hospital, denouncing Minelli; Minelli, his eyes bulging from his head with fixed fury, turning on Wynn; Wynn taking his time. B. M. harassing and chivying Crouse and Lindsay. Hannah Williams in tears. Jack Dempsey wanting to poke someone but not rightly knowing whom, Kay Thompson grim-lipped and sardonic. The chorus boys began to fall over like ninepins. The girls, of course, were indestructible, but they were not happy. As for me, I knew I was licked. I hoped only to save something of my work.

We opened. Most of the show was lousy, some was good. That night after the performance my girls were called on the phone and ordered up to a party. Mary and Dorothy refused to go; Mary was fired at the first pretext later. Two of the singers they were rooming with did go and came back very soon weeping. The hospitality upstairs was of the real old-fashioned kind.

The next morning I was fired. The following day Hannah Williams and the leading man. Two days later Kay Thompson. B. M. fired me in the middle of the Touraine lobby. He forbade me to re-enter the theater or speak to my dancers. I did go to talk to Paul Haakon, who had been a most sympathetic worker, but B. M. came hurrying after, called him aside and Paul slunk away to the other side of the house. Minelli had taken to his bed and seemed unable to cope. The others were busy tearing one another's throats open. I went alone to the railroad station. Someone had given me some red roses and I said good-by debonairly at the theater, handing them out to whoever was still brave enough to risk a nod and smile. A few broke from duress and stole away to the station, Haakon among them, and just as the train left, her face streaming with tears, came my Mary. "They're tearing your work to pieces. Every lovely thing you did. I couldn't save one thing. It's all wasted and destroyed. They wouldn't wait until you got out of town." I said something terse and four-lettered, kissed them all and climbed aboard. I was free of it.

The next night my New York phone rang at 2:30 in the morning. It was Kay Thompson and she said, "I have good news for you. B. M. has just fallen off the stage and broken his back."

"This isn't true," I said. "You're just saying this to make me feel good."

But it was true. His back was broken all right. He had been scrabbling up over the footlights to tear the pretty dress I had allotted Dorothy Bird from her back and give it to one of his harpies, his face distorted with hate, his fingers clutching for the hooks, when his foot slipped. Not one person on the stage moved to help him for appreciable seconds. But even from the hospital, he wove his spell. Thompson was fired, just tapped on the shoulder and told as she went from the stage, "That will be your last performance, Miss T."

Equity has made most of these abuses impossible. I am sure a great deal of the reform stemmed directly from this unseemly and disreputable production. This was typical for its time. This is what the musical theater was like, full of glamour and things.

The only pleasant episode connected with this experience was a conversation I had with Robert Alton, my successor. One day, toward the end, he sat me down in the theater and told me what mistakes I had made. He was neither pompous nor boasting; he spoke out of friendly good will and a vast experience. I have profited by his remarks ever since and I remember him with gratitude for a gesture of what I consider true generosity. His rules for rehearsal are as follows; I repeat them for the benefit of all young choreographers:

1. Begin with something technical and definite.
2. Begin on time. Be prompt.
3. Do not let the chorus sit down.
4. Never let them make a mistake. Do not pass over a fault. Stop them in the middle of a bar if necessary and correct.
5. Polish as you go along.
6. Never seem in doubt.
7. Never let the bosses see anything unfinished. If you have only eight bars to show them, show them this much and no more. If you have not this much, get up yourself and demonstrate.

There is one alternate to this set of restrictions, to wit: work in private. The first four rules I still observe carefully, except sometimes number four. Alton was referring to chorus dancers. He did not often work with artists. The mistake of an artist may be a godsend. The last rule, number seven, applies to the old-style producer. It has no reference to people like Rodgers and Hammerstein, Langner and Helburn, who have understanding of the creative process and who have, moreover, a sense of courtesy, who have — let us put it this way — common sense.

As for never seeming in doubt, that's ridiculous. Every choreographer disembowels himself and every experienced dancer knows it and expects it. But Alton worked the other way — at a speed suggestive of a radio sports commentator, with a whistle between his teeth. The dancers adored him. No time was wasted in his rehearsals. Slick, finished and speedy, the work went together. There were no great moments of dramatic revelation, but each routine was solidly built and effective.

This was my last brush with Broadway until *Oklahoma!*. *Oklahoma!*, I believe, was the first musical show where every dancer was hired for just one reason — that he or she was the best available performer for the role. I stand on the record that this system, although prissy, worked.

One last word about *Hooray* and I have done. I am pleased to be able to close on an exhilarating note. After I had gone back to England my incredible mother assembled these same chorus girls for a class in Single Tax. They came not once but often.

Hollywood had refused to film my group choreography and for various external reasons New York had dropped my dances from the show. So it seemed natural to go back to London where I had friends and where I had scored before, and I was eager to continue studies with a group. A friend in London loaned me his town house which had been closed. I prevailed on twelve girls to give me their time and energies, and for three hours every day we immured ourselves among the sheeted furniture and worked in dust and, since there was no piano, in silence. Six months later when we came out into a proper studio, we had the makings of a suite of American dances, one of which was called *Rodeo*.

This study contained every bit of gesture that was later used in the ballet *Rodeo*, and this is exactly how the movement was developed. The dances were performed publicly in London in April 1938. One year later I saw the first New York performance of Eugene Loring's *Billy the Kid*. There have been several statements in print by misinformed critics that I borrowed my western style from Loring. The exact chronology of performance is herewith stated. But I would like to add my view that the whole argument is bad-natured and specious. All contemporaries influence one another although the thefts are usually unconscious. In the hands of a master, all material, no matter whence derived, becomes a new act of creation; in the hands of a fool, the original is not even approached. It would be odd if contemporaries working as they often do under the same roof did not handle similar problems in a manner reminiscent. The more astonishing fact is that using the same dancers and rubbing elbows one with the other hour after hour they preserve their own styles to such a marked degree.

Peggy van Praagh, who is now director and head of the Sadler's Wells Theatre Company, was my principal dancer. I chose as protégée a girl to whom I paid a small weekly retainer and taught her to act comedy, and I promised her concerts in New York if she would return with me later.

While experimenting with group choreography, I gave a series of solo concerts at the Mercury with Hugh Laing as partner. These were run off in real professional style to sold-out houses. Each concert, as always in England, just broke even; there was perhaps a difference of four or five shillings one way or the other, so I lived on my Hollywood savings. The press was uniformly good.

Tudor was working hard on a new ballet called *Dark Elegies* for Rambert's West End season, to Mahler's *Kindertotenlieder*. He insisted that I dance the fourth solo and in the face of Mim's extreme and expressed doubt forced me into her company for this one work. I refused to let her watch rehearsals which further infuriated her. Antony practiced with me at night and on Sundays, but always shut away. He was kindness itself, and I cost him something in patience. I frequently came late. I was not quick or adroit, and his approach to music proved baffling. He never, for instance, counted.

This was the first time in my life I had ever worked under anyone's direction. We were both nervous. Mim prowled outside the closed door, baffled and furious. Whenever she entered the room I stopped, and we glared at each other like two hostile dogs.

I saw very little of the group rehearsals because I was doing the choreography for the film *I, Claudius* and had to spend all my days in an armory at the other side of London. In this film, I was engaged to do an enormous ballet with music by Arthur Bliss. We had not been in rehearsal more than a week when the star, Merle Oberon, put her face through the glass window of a taxi; the director, Josef von Sternberg, fell ill of an intestinal obstruction, and the film company went bankrupt. The episode was not important. I got most of my money. In remembering it I have, in fact, only one sadness. Merle Oberon phoned me at seven one morning to say she had spent the night deciding to play Messalina as a virgin. I rather regret the loss of that characterization. The important enterprise of the moment for all of us was Antony's ballet.

The first time I saw it assembled, which was the afternoon of the opening, I recognized it plainly as a masterwork but equally clearly as unfinished. I don't mean unpolished — I mean the last five minutes had not been set. The final song was completed at eight o'clock in full make-up and dressing gowns while the curtain was held and Mahler's publisher sat in the wings to see that the ballet met his official approval. The ending Tudor contrived in twenty minutes is very beautiful and a great many of the audience were in tears at the conclusion. Musicians, painters and writers went out of the theater raving and sat up at their telephones all next day spreading the news.

The season wound up in the usual battery of quarrels. Rambert was so deprecating about my dancing that the day after the last performance I walked into the Ballet Club, packed my practice clothes and left forever. I never again returned as a pupil. Hugh and Antony also left her theater, something they'd been hankering to do for a long time.

Having by this maneuver left ourselves with precisely nothing at all we decided to pool our wits and make our own ballet company. Hugh contributed his entire patrimony and I borrowed fifty pounds from Romney Brent (paid back with *One Touch of*

Venus). We bought scenery and costumes for Tudor's *Descent of Hebe* (Bloch), *Jardin aux Lilas, Dark Elegies* and a new work, *Gallant Assembly,* set to music by Tartini. I threw in all my costumes and the best of my repertoire. The Tartini ballet was an unfinished romp containing some splendid movement but on the whole formless and anticlimactic. It did boast, however, superb *décor* by Hugh Stevenson and a seduction scene for Tudor and me which I believe is the most obscene bit of nonsense in the literature of ballet and one of the funniest. We got ready (the Tartini uncompleted of course) and went up to Oxford where we were to perform a week at the Players' Theatre, only to discover on arrival that the reason for giving us the theater during examination week was the unlikelihood of any audience. And sure enough, as foreseen by the theater owners, we did very badly. In fact, we lost our shirts. The company was excellent and danced beautifully. All the costumes were new. The repertoire consisted of the absolute best of our work — two of Tudor's masterpieces. And in the cradle of British Culture all we could pull in was between two and three pounds a night. But Tudor didn't seem to mind. He delivered a gallant and graceful farewell address from stage on closing night to the handful of spectators, some of whom had come faithfully every performance, and we went out to a party which we gave ourselves.

The week's kitty was divided equally among all members of the company — £3 apiece. We at least owned the scenery although the boys left it lying in their garden in rain all the rest of the summer months.

One of the interested paying customers was Marie Rambert, who came all the way up to Oxford opening night to sit in the middle of the front row. She found, no one was surprised to learn, that Antony and I canceled one another. "A very wasteful clashing of styles," she said. She also found wasteful and extravagant the fact that our tights were of real silk.

No job offered all the next winter. Tudor, who had cut himself off finally from Rambert, made a pittance teaching at his studio in British Grove. What those long months of hopeless idleness and neglect cost a man of his tornado ambitions I hate to think. Hugh held his hands up all this time as also did the devoted girls who believed in him and who gave him everything including their loyalty and time. But there must have been hours of despairing horror; London was for him a city of no opportunity. He simply was not recognized; the people in power in both the commercial and ballet worlds who had seen his work did not particularly like it. So he sat down hard on his strong young bones and sharpened his feelings all through the foggy winter months. There was no help or promise. There was not even regularly enough food. And he had proved to a number of discerning people that he was the greatest lyric choreographer in Europe.

I was without employment also but I could always give concerts and I still had some Thalberg money and a bit left over from *Hooray*. Hugh had his own periods of grave despondency. Antony might not be publicly recognized as yet but those who knew him hoped for a brave future, whereas nobody foretold very much for Hugh. He all but beat his head on the bricks of British Grove. I never blamed him. I wanted to join in. I practiced dully. Hugh alternately raged and consoled. Antony waited.

In time when my group dances were finished I hired a West End theater and gave my last English concert. It was sold out solid and the notices were the best I ever got in England. Hugh as always partnered me and out of this concert came an engagement at the Westminster Theatre, for which I commissioned from Antony *Judgment of Paris*.

That wound up the season — it also wound up our professional union because, although the work had been friendly and good, matters did not stand as before. The forces that were shaping all of us had wrenched us awry. Rival directors have never functioned happily under the same roof without a strong whip to keep them in their proper corners. All co-operative groups rupture for lack of that whip. The ballet troupes are used to a boss and expect their impresario to be imperious and powerful with the manners of a lion tamer. It is generally advisable for him to have control of the money. The creative worker does not exist who can table his passions and give head to the greater need of a rival. I think more important, however, was Antony's deepening conviction that our styles were really incompatible and that the same theater should not house us both. So when he came to me later with the news that he had found a sponsor and was to be presented with his own theater and company, I was not entirely astonished to learn he felt he could dispense with my services.

My protégée and soloist was promised bits by Antony for his new project and was accordingly reluctant to accompany me to New York, although I had trained her and paid her for a year with this precise goal in mind. The choice forced upon her was torturing.

And the Home Office in refusing to extend my working permit made my dim-out official. It was September 1938. England was readying the decks for war; aliens were being sent home that autumn by the thousands.

I packed and closed my lovely flat. I had lived and worked in England for six years, but the two that waved me off in the black November rain from Waterloo Station were new acquaintances, two refugee Germans. It was neither my partner nor my collaborator, nor yet another whom I had thought to marry, but a boy out of a concentration camp who put a bunch of threepenny violets in my hand and wished me Godspeed.

C H A P T E R   2 3

Second Start

I WAS NOW NEARLY THIRTY and I faced life as stripped as at nine-teen except that I had my costumes and my repertoire. But I also had a good-sized fatigue. On the boat home I had long hours to review my late achievements — my collaborator was alienated, my partner gone, my assistant deserted. The small staff and company I had built up over so many arduous years far away and scattered. I was also without cash, was unable to maintain a checking ac-count and was going to have to ask Mother constantly for small disbursements of ten, fifteen or twenty dollars.

The situation was so stringent as to have a kind of cleansing effect. There is something fearfully strengthening about cutting free even if the ties bandage the heart itself.

From England I had written Mother to get me a room. I was going to have to live on twenty-five dollars a week and I wanted privacy before all, a barre, a few feet of space, a mirror, bed and bureau. She led me from the boat to a studio on East 9th Street, two large white rooms with an open fireplace, the street wall entirely given to French windows. There was a tiny room for costumes and music, a tiny kitchen with kettle and cups. Great mirrors leaned against the floor, and there was a barre. A fire burned on the hearth, the rosy shadows moved over the all-white walls. Cousins had sent autumn flowers. My books were assembled. I stood with clasped hands and shining eyes.

It was, of course, too expensive, and I placed myself deeper in debt to Mother, who never ceased to urge my return to her own house for economic reasons, but I declined although with heavy conscience, believing that my integrity depended on privacy. I lived there for eight years and knew peace, met and courted the man of my choice and waited out the war for him. It was here that my mother lived after my baby was born, and here that she suffered her final fatal stroke. In those two rooms I composed whole programs of recital dances and *Rodeo, Oklahoma!, One Touch of Venus, Bloomer Girl, Carousel, Brigadoon,* and *Tally-Ho.* Each added bookshelf or dish was paid for by a new dance. But I could not afford a good chair until after *Venus,* four and one half years later — then and then only, after ten years of debts had been paid, I spent thirty dollars on my first comfortable chair — French provincial and very beautiful. I placed it in the middle of the bare floor and I sat in it whenever I grew depressed and put my hands on the arms. It was mine, my own household, bought with my own earned money. It gave me an enormous sense of achievement. I called it the "obedience" chair.

But for five years guests sat on an old chest, or the bed, or the piano bench or the floor. It never hurt the talk. We lit a fire and had tea. But nonprofessionals entering the rooms looked about in astonishment and said, "Moving?" My father came once and was somewhat taken aback. "How Bohemian!" he remarked. "No rugs!" Dear Pop, he simply couldn't face the fact that I lived flat broke, and that there was no fooling about this. It was his wife, Clara, who took one look and sent me a rug; she also sent me a winter coat.

The Y.M.H.A., which has been a sanctuary for so many, hired me to teach two classes a week. That was twenty dollars. I tried at every other school in the town and was turned down. I tried organizing my own classes, inviting a few professionals as guest pupils to dress the room, and met the hideous humiliation of being told they had not the time to waste. I took my main meals at Mother's; I wore my sister's cast-off clothes.

This was the time for beginning afresh, so for the first time I had my teeth straightened. The orthodontist took me on credit. He was foolhardy, I thought, but kind. I also began to dress neatly, and I started appearing places on time.

If for money reasons I could afford no further recitals and few lessons, no more could others. Eugene Loring, Michael Kidd, Paul Haakon and I rented a studio for five dollars a week and coached one another. We were very stern and we improved greatly. After the practice which lasted two hours every morning, Loring and I had coffee and I talked for an hour and a half. I seem to have done an inordinate amount of talking whenever I was out of work.

I talked a great deal to Martha Graham and to Mary Hunter, chiefly to Mary. Mary was married now and in New York broadcasting nightly as Marge in "Easy Aces." She also directed a group of volunteers called the American Actors' Company. Pots and pots and pots of tea Mary brewed for me while I paced the floor and pounded the table with my fists and cursed and questioned and she sat quietly reasoning, bringing to bear on all my blistering sores the cool healing of her just perceptions. She was a kind of human blotting paper. Hardly a contemporary artist in her wide sphere of friends but has sent for her secretly in some obscure and dreadful moment to implore her to succor his life. We went back and back because the house was quiet, the drinks good, and Mary's understanding without parallel. It was something like college life all over again, except that now what we got mad about was no longer just theory. There was a good deal more feeling and less thinking, which is the exact reverse of what the aging process is supposed to be. Mary is now a vigorous and effective director in the American theater. In my duress she was always ready to come, always put the kettle on, talked through the night, made plans and, when need arose, ran my stage.

I kept steadily rehearsing. Three years before in the bleakest of periods I had received a fan letter, not just an ordinary fan letter, but a glowing, intelligent corroboration. It was from a student who signed herself Sybil Shearer. She said I had moved and excited her as Anna Pavlova had done, and she begged to study with me.

At this juncture she showed up again. A soloist now in the Humphrey-Weidman group she wanted to dance with me also and she turned out unforeseeably to have a kind of comic genius. I straightway stopped grieving for my English protégée. Sybil proved no ordinary assistant. She had a point of view, passion and talent, although how enormous this was I had no idea at the time. I knew only that rehearsals with her were stimulating and fun. She never seemed to need any time to get warmed up or organized. On being told the problem she just stood up and began, and could keep inventing, speedily without letup, three or four hours on a stretch. When stopped, as she had to be forcibly, she would find she was on the point of collapse. Several times after rehearsals I have had to sit her in a tub of Epsom salts. I have often waked in the morning to find her cross-legged on my couch in a Yogi relaxation. She would open her eyes and then jump right away into difficult rehearsing while I humored myself with tea and scrambled eggs.

Physically she presented the asexual aspect of a Renaissance angel, sensitive but not girlish, her face too strong for prettiness, her manner unbroken with the noble ease of an animal or a spirit. She might have stepped from any Botticelli fresco. She had the enigmatic smile, the airy magnificence, the unsexed purity and vigor of his heavenly youths. She was long-waisted and slender, with angelic long arms, hands that played the air like an instrument and the strong printless foot of God's messengers. She was a visitor in my studio, a visitor in this world, and serene in dedication gave herself daily to the beloved work with the absorption and success of a fanatic. She was happy to be possessed entirely. Each dance became an act of faith. She wore her hair — it hung straight from the temples. It was never for any occasion arranged. She combed it, and that was enough. She scorned powder or make-up of course, later even on the stage. She usually walked about in riding boots — not that there was any imminence of a horse, the boots were left over from some past experience. They were good leather and comfortable — reasons enough for wearing them. She talked a lot, arguing eight or nine conflicting philosophies simultaneously and was very hopeful of the fourth dimension, urging me repeatedly to study this. But remembering my trouble with spherical trigonometry, I declined. Ray Bolger excepted, she was the greatest comedian I have ever seen dancing.

I also procured myself a new partner — not without considerable hunting. All promising boys were soldered solidly with the existing groups and not to be torn or borrowed out. The availables were not appetizing. I decided it would be easier to find a man and teach him to dance than to attempt to teach a dancer to look like a man.

A very handsome and able young actor, Joseph Anthony, was at hand, playing leads in Mary's Actors' Company. Failing any monetary inducements I had to rely on her sales talk about the opportunities of applying the Stanislavsky method to dancing. This was not my technique at all, but Joseph pricked up his ears and came briskly to the first interview, only to decide I was the haughtiest and vainest woman he'd ever met. I had that very day had two teeth extracted in the preliminary teeth-straightening process, and I marvel to think I gave an impression of vanity under those circumstances. But, although not charmed, Joseph was interested. He gradually learned I was only a little haughty, and he learned to enjoy the work. He was a very cheerful help to me at this period of reconstruction. He was steady, gay, talented and courteous, not given to tantrums and quite capable of considering other people's welfare. Exhausted as I was from scrapping the results of six years' labor, I looked for very little, the chance merely to build a substitute skeletal staff to replace what I had left behind, and I found myself, to my grateful surprise, presently flanked by two assistants, gifted certainly and possessing more loyalty and steadfastness than anything I had before known. Joseph learned in two months to dance well enough for concert performances — no mean achievement. The months passed in industry and healing quiet. Joe and I danced occasionally at benefits and private parties.

The summer of '39, a group of young theater people — Theatre

Arts Committee — banded together for the purpose of helping Loyalist Spain and organized concerts of light and humorous dances at the Y.M.H.A. Sybil and I panicked audience after audience. We had frequently to slow down our comedy because the audience was laughing so they could not take in the points at tempo. Lorenz Hart (of Rodgers and Hart) said to me, "My God, you're funnier than Fanny Brice. I'm going to write a musical around you." That's all there is to that episode.

Each time anyone suggested a concrete project I believed with all my heart that this time I would truly have my proper chance. For fourteen years I believed each professional who made any kind of suggestion at all and jumped like a hungry dog after meat.

However, the T.A.C. concerts continued and I was asked to dance on every one, and they cost me nothing. I even sometimes netted twenty-five dollars to put in the bank. And I could use them as auditions for important theatrical people.

Toward the end of the summer I received an extraordinary phone call — Richard Pleasant, the young man I had met at the Perry Dance Studio in Hollywood, was forming a gigantic international ballet company, he informed me, just as he always said he would. And he wanted me to choreograph. He asked me to lunch. I didn't believe him, but a lunch was a lunch. At table he handed me a sheet of paper and a pencil and asked me to list all the ballets I'd ever wanted to do. I still didn't believe him. He made only one stipulation. I was not to dance in any of them myself. I sure as hell didn't believe him.

He contended that I would never develop a true choreographic technique until I stopped using my own acting style as model. Then he invited me to meet Lucia Chase, the sponsor of the enterprise. I met her. I began to believe — all of it, including my not dancing.

Pleasant continued adamant on this score: I was not to go on composing vehicles for myself. I was to become a strong inventive and varied choreographer. He offered me for cast the choice of the company but he refused to allow me to think in terms of my own limited technique and special acting talents. "I am going to save you," he said flatly. "I will not permit you to cripple your talents." I fought desperately, I fought with my vanity, conviction, passion and ego, for me as a performer. I pointed out that I was the finest comedian in his troupe. Okay he said, then let the other choreographers make use of my humor. My God, how I resented him!

Lucia Chase was a young widow of great fortune who had embraced the dance first as a hobby to beguile her bereavement, then as a passion, and then as a cause. She was now prepared to spend a million dollars or more on the project of building right quick that autumn the best ballet company that ever existed.

The history of ballet contains many chronicles of great sums spent to frame the posturing of some theatrically speaking amateurish figure — none of whom lasted long. And although they commissioned the great to serve them, few of their efforts counted. (Ravel's *Bolero*, ordered by Ida Rubinstein in 1928, is probably the most noteworthy exception.) But Lucia Chase broke all precedent. Starting as an amateur with neither professional discipline nor professional standards, and spending a couple of millions of her own money to buy herself a theater in which to star, she finds herself after eleven years with one of the three best ballet companies in the world, an unexampled repertoire of modern works, and for herself a few small character parts which she plays exquisitely. I submit this progress is unique in the history of the theater, and bespeaks a disciplining of spirit and ego, a passion for what is first class above what is merely flattering, that is wholly admirable. No actor, manager, star-financier that I ever heard of quietly reduced himself in the ranks while pouring more and more energy and money into the larger project.

At the time of organization, Pleasant was ordering the choreographers by the gross; cables went to every quarter of the globe. One had only to say idly, "I once heard of a ballet about an omnibus" to have Richard note the choreographer's name and, if alive, his telephone number. Not that the choosing was indiscriminate

— all the lists were sieved out very carefully, but when the forces were assembled there were ten ballet choreographers on the staff — Fokine, Mordkin, Bolm, Nijinska, Dolin, Tudor, Loring, José Fernandez, Andrée Howard, de Mille. We lacked only Massine, Balanchine, Ashton, de Valois, and Lifar to be comprehensive. (Robbins, Kidd, and Helpmann had yet to do their first works, and Dollar was still a tentative beginner.) A similar array of designers worked for us. Our soloists were Patricia Bowman, Lucia Chase, Karen Conrad, Viola Essen, Miriam Golden, Andrée Howard, Annabelle Lyon, Agnes de Mille, Katharine Sergava, Nina Stroganova, Edward Caton, Leon Danielian, Vladimir Dokoudovsky, Anton Dolin, William Dollar, Kari Karnakoski, Hugh Laing, Eugene Loring, Dimitri Romanoff, Yurek Shabelevski, Antony Tudor, Leon Varkas.

Not since the Renaissance court ballets had such a display of costumes, music and performances been put into simultaneous work. Diaghilev may have established higher standards aristically, but our scope and verve were unmatched. If his soloists were incomparably greater, our *corps de ballet* was certainly more astonishing. In our ranks the first year were Nora Kaye and Maria Karnilov, to be joined the second season by Alicia Alonso, Jerome Robbins, Muriel Bentley, John Kriza, David Nillo and Ray Harrison. Carl van Vechten, who remembers well, has stated that there were dancers performing solos for Diaghilev that could not have passed our first chorus auditions. During the initial three-week season eighteen new works were mounted and presented. We had a *première* every night. It was royal.

Pleasant had hired the whole floor of a business building as studios and there in adjacent offices as many as five ballets rehearsed simultaneously. They rehearsed daily for four months, and trained together in daily classes. An air of hope and excitement replaced the usual quarreling and frenzy characteristic of ballet rehearsals. Since only a few of the works were composed fresh for the season, the choreographers could rehearse with relative composure. And there was enough time. There was enough —

Fokine was on hand to brush up his classics, *Sylphides* and *Carnaval*, and to talk to the dancers, and they were the last group to benefit by his personal advice.

Never shall I forget the *Sylphides* opening night, advancing to the foots in a floating line, seemingly two inches off the ground — not a girl touched earth — not an arm stirred out of breath, a single impulse propelled them. Through the green twilight they came forward like a tide. They breathed together, an organic and spiritual unity. They beat together. They suspended together. Fokine had rehearsed them. And then Conrad clove the air like a swallow in the highest jump of any living woman, again and again and again, on tireless young legs. Oh, it was fine!

Everyone was startled. The Russians shook their heads and said it was very athletic but not poetry, by which they meant it did not have the proper morbid atmosphere. But those not involved in professional rivalries — John Martin, for instance — said it was as good as the best — a latter-day miracle.

Dolin restaged a fine *Giselle* and *Swan Lake*. Loring composed a ballet (*The Great American Goof*) with words by Saroyan. Tudor came with three finished works, *Lilac Garden, Dark Elegies* and *Judgment of Paris,* and knocked the company off its feet. Immediately the younger members of the troupe realized they were working with the man of the future. He made the hit of the initial season and was recognized for the first time by a large public for his true worth.

And how did Tudor get here? Pleasant had thought to invite Frederick Ashton, but I persuaded him to swing his choice to the younger and less known artist. Tudor, unlike Ashton, was associated with no large company and would therefore be available to come and stay. He would also, I believed, because of the nature of his gifts, prove to be in this country the most useful and effective of any European choreographer.

With him came Hugh Laing and Andrée Howard, who staged for us her *Death and the Maiden* and *Lady Into Fox.* I had welcomed the boys and it was tacitly understood between us that we would start afresh, holding no grudges. My pride was given a severe wrench, however, when Tudor promptly handed Lucia Chase without a word of explanation the role I had created in *Dark Elegies*. I had rather counted on this as one of the few roles in the repertoire I would certainly play. I kept my dance in *Judgment* and that was all I was permitted to perform the first season.

Since I was not to be permitted to perform myself, I avoided comedy altogether in an impulse of stubborn negation and sought to do something as uncharacteristic and surprising as possible — an exotic work for Negroes using the *Création du Monde* score of Darius Milhaud. No Negroes had ever been employed in a comparable organization, and Richard Pleasant showed courage in helping me organize the project.

I was extremely nervous. The competition was shocking — Fokine, Nijinska, Tudor and Loring were working literally in adjacent rooms, and their dancers passed through my auditions on the way to practice and appraised my amateurs with unenthusiastic expression. My brief and frenzied flurries with commercial troupes of mixed prostitutes and chorus dancers had not helped me build a technique of composing and rehearsing nor raised my confidence to speak of. But now I was being given a real chance. I had as much time as I wanted, the best in music and costumes, everything I asked for — in fact if I failed now under these propitious circumstances it would only be because I did not know my trade. Furthermore this was the most sustained composition I had ever attempted, twenty-five minutes.

Greatly to my relief, we rehearsed separately in a studio at the bottom of Fifth Avenue. My company was made up of heterogeneous and for the most part untrained performers. This was before Katherine Dunham established her school, and Negroes did not train for serious dancing because there was literally no opportunity for them to practice. They were not only without dance technique; they were without rehearsal discipline of any kind. They came late; they absented themselves; they came so hungry they fainted. They couldn't remember; they caught every sickness conceivable. We kept them warm, we kept them fed; but I at last called them together and said that I was stopping the project, their persistent tardiness had defeated me. The next night they were all on time, and there was a large bouquet for me on the piano — the gift of starving girls. The following night they were late again. However, it was done.

At one point I thought to change the leading dancer who, although very beautiful, failed in projection and tragic feeling. Katherine Dunham had just come on from Chicago and was waiting around for her first New York concerts. She offered her services. She came as far as the door of the rehearsal hall several times, but in the end I decided to risk all on the girl I had. I have since reflected grimly on this choice. Dunham turned out to be one of the most brilliant personalities of her time and is currently and in exact truth the rage of Europe and South America. My soloist did not. I have learned surely since what I suspected then, that the two qualities one cannot teach are timing and projection, both of these depending on deep psychological involvements.

Douglass Montgomery did not make matters easier for me by appearing at a last run through rehearsal and urging me, imploring me, to disobey Pleasant and dance the lead myself. That this substitution would most certainly throw the whole work out of racial focus he thought of no consequence. "You want to dance," he said. My heart yearned in response. "Don't trust this amateur. Get out there and sell the work. You're a great performer." Strangely, although my vanity bled at every pore, I stood firm without a quiver. There was such a thing as taste and the inviolability of an idea and over the years with every failure I'd become more certain of this. Dug shook his head mournfully. "Oh, Ag, Ag, you're going to have another flop." Joe Anthony made me some tea fast. "You nearly listened — you actually nearly listened. My God, how you lust to get in front of the lights!" How I did indeed! How I hungered and thirsted to have the large stage and the orchestra, the dressers and crew I'd never had, how I wanted to step out before the assembled audience and take hold. And oh, but I could — by just lifting my head or turning a hand. And this hunger had to be killed every month, every week, little by little, for years, before my creative gifts really developed. The vanity had all to go — the insistence on their looking at me.

My soloist did not take hold — she did not project at all. The ballet, *Black Ritual*, hardly had a chance. It was danced at its *première* at a pace calculated to kill all excitement. At one point opening night I ran out of the auditorium and literally beat my head on a pillar. At the next showing tempi were corrected and with time and recasting all faults could have been put right, but there was no time. The schedule was stuffed with *premières;* we were allotted three performances only.

And the press was murderous.

As the Negro troupe performed in no other work, they were quite understandably considered an unwarranted luxury. After the three-week season (cut short by the theater's previous commitments) my girls were dispersed and the work has never since been performed.

It was a good work, I think, but unlike anything else I had ever done, and it jarred people. It was neither funny nor healthy, and ethnologically it was not factual. Directly Katherine Dunham came along with authentic material, and everyone forgot.

But Ballet Theatre itself was not doing too well. After an unparalleled initial season it found itself blocked by the two great booking monopolies. Hurok managed Ballet Russe and therefore N.B.C. would touch no other company, and the rival agency, Columbia, was not eager to shoulder the risk of competing with the Russian Ballet.

However eager Chase might be to hold the dancers together, with no dates at all it was virtually impossible. Expense and dreariness accumulated. In any case my relationship grew tenuous — no further works were asked of me. Pleasant reiterated again and again that he would not permit me to choreograph for myself. The two who knew my abilities well, Tudor and Loring, showed no inclination ever to wish me to set foot on their stage. This was understandable from Loring; from Tudor it was hard to take. I had been crowded out and had to face the bitter realization that the native ballet company for which I had waited the whole of my life had no place for me.

At this point Lucius Pryor of Council Bluffs, Iowa, one of the most successful independent booking managers in this country, came to New York shopping for a dance attraction. Pryor was a small elderly man with a limp. He had the instincts of a horse trader, but he was honest and he was responsible. And he was the first and only concert manager who thought I had sufficient talent to make a large financial guarantee. He booked me for my first national tour.

Armed with this contract I went to Hollywood to raise money. I raised seven hundred dollars from three friends, the first money I had ever asked for. The bulk of the sum was loaned by Mitchell Leisen, the director, who said, "I'll give you the balance of all you need. I've been poor too." I think that loan was the exact difference between my stopping and my going on. At this point my father's wife, Clara, was most particularly kind and generous as she had been often before, tactfully and quietly offering help — money, shrewd advice, and necessary items for my wardrobe, and always warm and sheltering hospitality. For the tour she financed a complete traveling outfit of great smartness.

With the seven hundred I costumed my whole company, paid for composing, rehearsing, publicity material, pictures, and press books, and got the troupe of five, Sybil Shearer, Katharine Litz, Joseph Anthony, Louis Horst and myself, to the first date, Kearney, Nebraska.

How did we do this? We did most of our own work, sewing, writing, copying music, shopping. I sat up over the paper work until two or three in the morning. I did every single bit of the office routine connected with a national tour myself unaided. And when a wire came from the Midwest in the middle of a Scarlatti rehearsal for "mats" I did not know whom to phone to find out what was wanted or meant. However, when all was finished, the costumes made out of bits and pieces and paper flowers were enchanting. I held two evening-long rehearsals on packing the trunks with a stop watch in my hand. We could afford neither stage manager nor dresser. These days the union would insist on our carrying both dresser and stage manager as well as company manager and press agent. I could not have lasted two years under the current union restrictions which make no allowance for the unendowed beginner. I could not begin to recompense my performers adequately, but they received a living wage; I did not always.

Joe was responsible for the lights; Louis Horst for cueing the curtain; the girls and I for the pressing and packing of costumes, wet off our own backs. I was, nevertheless, determined that nothing should mar the professional smoothness of our programs, and nothing did.

It was very hard work. Where I had to pay the fares we traveled stringently, sleeping flat at night but moving into coaches at eight every morning, bag and baggage. Pryor took us through his territory in autos. He and his son Philip escorted us the whole way and took fatherly care of all business matters, the first professional help of the kind, I'd ever received. We ranged from Texas to Chicago and covered everything in between. We usually arrived at a town about noon. Joe immediately went to the theater to investigate the lights. The theater equipment varied from the university stage at Austin, Texas, which is probably the best-equipped amateur stage in the world, to high school platforms with no lights at all and a floor surface that necessitated our going barefoot in order to avoid falling.

I rested for two hours at the local hotel while the girls unpacked and started pressing. At four-thirty I briefed a green dresser hired for the evening; at six we had sandwiches. We then made up, warmed up and did a program which for me consisted of thirteen dances, packed the production into trunks, costumes, props, music and lights, and went to bed. Next morning we set out at eight.

We gave six shows a week, a different town each night. I grew quite thin.

But I was learning something important. The people of America, the ordinary people, understood my work and liked it very much. It was just the managers who found me unsuitable for popular recognition.

But I used to look yearningly at the theaters in the big towns, Kansas City, Dallas, St. Louis, as we whizzed by in our caravan toward the outlying colleges and universities with their unpredictable equipment. Those doors, however, were open only to the Russians and the darlings of Community Concerts. But we played to audiences intelligent and well-informed and responsive, and this was all that really mattered. People sometimes motored three hundred miles through desert and mountain to see us.

At Kearney, Nebraska, the president of the college stood by the tracks as we entrained at midnight. He stood hat in hand and alone. "I came here personally," he said shaking my hand, "to thank you for treating us like adults."

It ended up in a triumph — in a series of nights at the Goodman Theater, Chicago, playing in direct competition with both Ballet Russe and Ballet Theatre. I am happy to write that we sold out every performance and that people were really struggling for seats for the last Saturday night. Leonarde Keeler, now one of the world's best known detectives, came with half the police brass of Chicago and beamed with pride.

We were all nearly dead; but we had justified ourselves. Everyone was paid up — and I had netted six hundred dollars.

I was scarcely back in New York when Pleasant summoned me to get my Lucas Cranach morality play *Three Virgins and a Devil* ready in two weeks and dance the lead. No explanations were offered for the change of mind but I didn't stop to quibble. I was in rehearsal two hours after the first phone call pulled me out of ballet class.

Ballet Theatre was now housed in the old mansion on 53rd Street, later to become the new home of the Theatre Guild, and was practicing hard among marble and tapestries. *Virgins* was composed in what was later to be Lawrence Langner's office, and the materialization of the "devil" took place exactly where his desk now stands. I created the part of the devil on Sybil Shearer, or rather she created it in spite of the laws of nature and contrary to all human experience. Sybil suggested an Hieronymus Bosch animal whirling and scrabbling over the floor. She gave the impression of flapping in midair shoulder height, banging up against the walls like some untidy bat. She could fall over flat, of a piece, like a felled tree, and all the time there was a preoccupation of business in the face, a confused craftiness as if all the wheels of the brain were out of cog and racing separately. She has always had the ability to maintain three or four rhythms in her separate members without regard to what her head was doing. Guests who came to visit us in our den went out stricken and speechless. Sybil could not get up on point which barred her automatically from the company. She was also, of course, not male and therefore perhaps not eligible for this role.

Hugh Laing and I tried to make her connection with Ballet Theatre formal, but it was no use. Sybil shortly afterwards informed me that she had decided to give a recital on her own. I tried to understand. I said I understood. I thought she'd surely break her neck, but each young artist must learn to evaluate. So I complacently waited for her return. She announced an initial concert at the Carnegie Chamber Hall. I asked to see her dances beforehand, with some sort of idea of editing, I suppose, some big-sister idea of dressing her for the party. She auditioned for me in the girls' club where she lived. The first two numbers were weak, I noted with no surprise, but then she suddenly let loose to something of Chopin, and all the pomposity and condescension left me with a rupturing of ego that was one of the quickest decrescendos I ever experienced. I knew she was a technician, but she was dancing as few in the world can. She was composing as few seldom do including, most certainly, me. It became suddenly clear that Sybil had enormous gifts. I sat staring, looking white and, I'm sure, small. And she stood looking at me, dirty-faced, sweaty, with pure love in her eyes. She'd known all along.

After the audition, Sybil walked up from the assembly room, past the mirror in the hall where she did all her composing in the face of stares and comments by passing roommates, to the cubicle where she slept. This little room contained a bed and chest of drawers — nothing else. She had to climb on the bed when she opened the drawers. I left her sitting tailor-fashion, her mouth full of bastings, the skirt for the Bach chorale spread over her knees. Every stitch of the costumes was her sewing. She was going to be alone up there all evening, sewing. In the morning, she would do her laundry (she had fainted away in the laundry the day before doing Yogi exercises in the steam) and then practice in the open hall all day alone without music and with no privacy. Daily courage is a touching thing. As I turned away, I felt my throat tighten.

After her first New York concert six months later every dancer in the city knew she was a name to conjure with. But no one outside of our small cast during the *Virgin* rehearsals paid much attention to her. She was the girl in bare feet who waited in a room for me to get ready to rehearse. The drawback with using her as a model was that no one else in the world could move like her. Eugene Loring, who danced the role, was an experienced performer, but he was nothing like what we'd had in rehearsal.

Lucia Chase played the Greedy Virgin with a pallid intensity that struck to the bone, Annabelle Lyon the Lustful Virgin, and a more entrancing bit of lewd silliness was never perpetrated. I danced the dominant one. It was the role of a fanatic; I was not the daughter of a reformer for nothing.

Virgins gave a young performer of merit his first solo bit, a thirty-two-bar stage cross which was greeted with cheers and shrieks. He has continued to do well for himself since, but this was his first solo and I taught it to him in the hall under a crystal chandelier. His name, of course, was Jerome Robbins.

I had no particular hopes for the work. We had fun doing it. We laughed a great deal, but without scenery and props (décor by

Motley of London) it looked improvised and formless. I forbade Mother to come but she sneaked into the theater. I saw her little tricorne at the very back of the orchestra seats. I wouldn't speak to her I was so embarrassed, but as always she phoned. "It's fine, dearie. It's delightful. I feel very hopeful."

I got through my supper whimpering. "This is the end of me," I whined.

"Oh, for God's sake, shut up," said Joe Anthony, "eat your eggs and get back to the theater."

We followed *Giselle*, danced by Nana Gollner and Anton Dolin. The house started laughing with Chase's first sour expression and continued shrieking to the end. I wouldn't have believed it possible if I hadn't been there. However, the ballet struck me as faulty and I stumped upstairs to my dressing room, slammed the door in distaste and sat down to enjoy melancholia. My brooding was interrupted by a beating on the door. And there was Martha Graham, no less, the first backstage. "Open up, Agnes. Open the door!" I hung my head sulkily. "In a small, in a tiny obscure way, this is a classic of its kind — this is a little masterpiece."

Even as she spoke, Tudor's *Gala Performance* was rolling up delight like thunder downstairs. But I learned to tolerate *Virgins*. Properly played it was fun.

"Don't read Martin tomorrow," said my friends. "Promise, now. Don't."

But the next morning Mother came into my room with a bland, Cheshire cat expression and the *New York Times* spread before her. "You may read," she said. "Lean back in your pillows while I get you breakfast. Martin's all right." She spoke a mouthful. The tide had turned. Martin was just plain dandy.

Virgins became a staple of the comedy repertoire until it was withdrawn at my own request. The ballet requires five star comedians and very few companies boast this many at one time.

Ballet Theatre's personnel and the quality of dancing were then and later splendid, though not always recognized by the general public for their worth. In the third season, for instance, the line-up in the *pas de sept* of Aurora's wedding was in point of performance and personality as fine as any ever assembled. Behind Baronova, second only to Fonteyn as Aurora, and Dolin, the best cavalier, stood Nora Kaye, Alicia Alonso, Sono Osato, Karen Conrad, Annabelle Lyon, Rosella Hightower, and Lucia Chase. You would have to strip the companies of the world to get those girls together again on one stage. The houses were always half empty. So much for popular perception.

Ballet Theatre reached its creative peak with the performance in April 1942 of Antony Tudor's *Pillar of Fire*. As we sat in the Met at the *première*, I think everyone was aware of the momentous importance of the night. This was poetic theater in the great sense. Tudor had produced a classic. This had seldom happened since the Elizabethans.

What had happened in a strictly balletic sense was a revolution. To the new order I heartily concurred, and so did Eugene Loring, and later Jerome Robbins and Michael Kidd. We were all in time to make changes. Tudor led the way.

If the last years had seemed uneventful in terms of success and money earned it was not so in terms of dancing done. Few of us could pay our rent but a new style had been evolved, clarified and accepted. It remained only to transfer it to a theater patronized by the large public. The creative study was largely ready, and while we had seemed not to move at all, lo, gathering up behind us was the work of hours and hours and years of hours in British Grove, Chelsea, Notting Hill, Hollywood, 57th and 9th Streets. There achievement had formed choral-like, blindly, with little hours of work. Our edifice was about to be unveiled. But I, for one, did not know it. Only Tudor had so far shown the crystalline beauty of his labors.

CHAPTER 24

Russian Ballet

At night in the little personal hours I did the dreadful arithmetic. Youth gone. No husband. No child. No achievement in work. I used to wake cold and consider the situation. Time was passing. My prospects had over a decade ago ceased to be bright. When I was asleep and defenseless, nightmare took over. There was no answer to reflections of this nature but the lonely breakfast and again barre beginning with *pliés,* as barre had begun for the last twenty years.

In the meantime the world rocked and convulsed with war. If my dynamics had slowed to an imperceptible pulse the temper of nations quickened. Joe was drafted and in the army and for the third time I lost a partner it had taken years to train. I packed up the costumes carefully. I have never unpacked them. Concert work was finished for the duration.

I scrutinized prospects. They were not bright. I could earn nothing teaching. Broadway was closed; Hollywood impervious. The Metropolitan as always sealed off, the ballet world cool. The scenario I sent to Ballet Theatre (Sevastianov had replaced my sponsor Pleasant as managing director) returned immediately with the routine letter : "perhaps at a later date . . ." I might have been a novice peddling my first idea. But I was no novice. At this juncture I had been in the business fourteen years.

I could not go on bleeding Mother white. She was aging and

had suffered a second and frightening heart attack which laid her up for months. She had driven herself to the breaking point and as always resisted doctors' help. It was in rushing to snatch the phone from my sister's hands and to declare she was perfectly fine that she fell senseless between us. And as we labored to carry her to her bed, she moaned and muttered, "Don't stop your work. Don't think of me. Go back to your dancing. I have Margaret's dress to finish." Small luxuries counted now. She must have help although she seemed bright enough and despite all medical warning was pacing herself as before.

I had been given a fair long chance to prove my mettle, and I seemed only to drain off her resources dollar by dollar. Plainly I hadn't made good. But I had done my utmost. I must rest on this and accept God's will. There was however one further thing I could do. I could quit.

I intended to go down to Macy's, where Mag, now divorced, had been learning merchandising, and get a job at a ribbon counter or wherever they'd take me and earn a stipulated weekly salary, no matter how small. I would not continue to wear my sister's cast-off clothes as I had done for the past eight years. I would budget myself and live on my own earnings. At the end of a year I would be able to hand in an income tax — something I had done only once in my life. Or — I had heard there was to be a women's branch of the army —

The new irresponsibility lifted the burden of self-consciousness and strain from my practice. I no longer stood tense and drawn wondering if the other dancers despised me for my imperfect technique. I thought for the first time not so much how I appeared to them as how I liked doing the exercises. With nothing to lose, I kicked — and the damned thing went over my head. There was no future in jumping so I didn't worry; I bounded and soared like a boy. Against all my better intentions and instincts, I had relaxed.

About this time I met a young man it seemed to me a good idea to marry. Martha Graham introduced us. He was a nice guy, although he'd never seen me dance. Consequently he didn't give a damn whether I kept on or stopped. And I could afford to love him because I was giving up my career in any case. Since he was a concert manager he suspected at first that I cared for professional reasons — but events were to prove my disinterestedness. A couple of days after our first tea he was drafted and sent to Biloxi, Mississippi. He couldn't budge, and I hadn't the cash for even the most perfunctory of visits. All summer he was in camp in the South, we corresponded at mounting length.

In the meantime, I practiced. From habit. I was going into Macy's all right, but I put it off for a couple of weeks. On the way up to class one day, I met Irving Deakin's wife. The Russian Ballet was to have a new work, she said, and Irving was trying to persuade them that it would be a novelty to have an American ballet by an American and not by Massine. Irving was pulling for me, and had I got a scenario? I said yes promptly. I hadn't. I went home and locked myself in for three days. I'd better use dance steps I was sure of. It would be horrible to get stuck with all those fancy Russians standing around so I decided to enlarge on the *Rodeo* studies and use sections of choreography already worked out. Draining great pots of tea, I wrote it all out, and then it seemed simply awful. But in a spirit of total despair I submitted it anyway and was summoned to my first interview with the boss of the Ballet Russe de Monte Carlo, Sergei Ivanovitch Denham.

The great tradition of the Imperial Russian Ballet has during this century undergone many changes. A selection of the greatest performers and repertoire had been brought in 1909 from Russia to Western Europe by Serge Diaghilev. His company made their home bases thereafter in Paris and Monte Carlo and gradually took on the stamp of the Parisian *avant-garde* art movement during the 'twenties, losing almost entirely the original native and traditional character. It was a showcase for arbitrary and precious experiments. Fokine had been replaced as choreographer in the 'twenties by Massine and the young Balanchine, and the ballets produced at this time did not compare with the early Fokine masterpieces. Only a few works survive: *Boutique Fantasque, Tricorne, Fils Prodigue,*

Apollon. But the Diaghilev hallmark of perfection of performance, detail and daring innovation persisted. He has left a name unparalleled in theater history. On his death in 1929, the company fell apart and the collaborators and performers scattered. Balanchine formed his own company with the help of Edward James in 1933 and was subsequently imported to the United States by Lincoln Kirstein and Edward M. M. Warburg to choreograph for the newly formed American Ballet. Massine, after a stint at Roxy's in New York and several Cochran musical shows in London, became choreographer-in-chief, ballet master, star performer and czar of a company organized by Colonel de Basil, a Cossack with an *Arabian Nights* biography, and named the Ballet Russe de Monte Carlo after its patron, the Prince of Monaco. The repertoire included the very best of the old and the new dazzling symphonic ballets, and *Beau Danube, Scuola di Ballo, Gaité Parisienne, St. Francis.* They burst like fireworks over Paris in '33, came to London with equal effect and in the autumn of '34 were brought to America by Sol Hurok who toured them from coast to coast.

The beginning here was rocky and the press stiff. The *Times* and *Tribune* rather resented the foreign invasion. Nevertheless the next year they began to cash in. America had yet to learn the habit of ballet-going; this was the first big-time ballet company we had seen. (The Diaghilev troupe, greatly curtailed and minus some of its stars, had played only a skeleton tour in 1916. The box office then had proved disastrous and they were saved only by the personal generosity of Otto Kahn.)

The new Monte Carlo company was large, beautifully costumed, very young and exuberant. They became a box-office smash and have toured for seventeen straight years, returning until the war every summer to Europe. Alas for the quality of performances! There simply was not time enough to rehearse and the habit of improvisation and slipshod makeshift, which became a Ballet Russe characteristic, developed a deterioration Diaghilev would never have tolerated. New works were put on in shining condition, but old works were not kept up and AGMA, the dancers' union, by demanding a living wage and rehearsal pay, cut down the number of personnel, so there were fewer understudies and a minimum of rehearsals. Replacements went on frequently with only a verbal briefing. Massine was overworked: no creative artist could hope to do all he attempted, and his new ballets were not always up to his standard. A general air of preciosity, sterility and exhaustion pervaded the troupe. But the audience sat out front shouting anyway, so only a few of the more sensitive knew there was anything missing. The heads of the company either spurned or avoided our native dancers' work. They lived in a vacuum while the performers, never having a night off, failed also to educate themselves. They inherited the protocol, pride and artistic snobbery of a troupe they were too young to have seen. But they claimed the Diaghilev reputation anyhow as their birthright.

But now their master had left. There was a war on. It was timely as well as useful to take note of native talent. They all approached the problem with energy and ignorance.

The year before I joined them, Serge Ivanovitch Denham had replaced Colonel de Basil as top boss after an extremely violent quarrel which put the word "choreography" into English law for the first time. Denham's struggles with Massine and de Basil have been going on for years in and out of law courts on two continents, with the dancers changing sides and rushing to whoever was likely to guarantee them six months' food. Nothing, nothing ever stops these three. They survive all, and it is marvelous to see how.[1] Choreographers grow old and tired and are kicked out. Dancers are kept at bare subsistence and they break or droop or marry, but Denham, de Basil and Massine, and now de Cuevas, reorganize,

---

[1] As this book goes to press comes word that Colonel de Basil has not survived. Adversity, starvation, bankruptcy, betrayal, war and exile he overcame, but his exhausted heart laid him low. He died July 27 mourned sincerely by scores of dancers who but for him would never have found a theater, mourned also by the managers and executives whose lives he made so colorful by his astonishing and unorthodox activities. He organized and revitalized the ballet world at a time when it lay in disintegration, and all dancing benefits. If he did not pay his debts, it was because he simply could not. Posterity will remember that he mounted ballets and that they were beautiful.

regroup, rush to new countries or back into old, where some memories are long and others mercifully short, and are once more at their exercises. The glittering "Ballet Russe" is on the Opera House. The crowds pour in. The dancers, underpaid, under-rehearsed and sore in the feet, do their work with haughtiness and verve and the great tradition is carried on.

Hurok, the most powerful impresario in the Western Hemisphere and the smartest, has managed them all in turn. They quarreled with him also but they all needed and used him.

At the same time that I first met Denham, an enormous *coup d'état* had taken place. Hurok and Denham had been engaged in one of those long wrestling matches which ended in a divorce of power and resources. Lucia Chase and Ballet Theatre slipped between the antagonists and Hurok grabbed her and her company. Lucia was enchanted with her deal and the fact that Ballet Theatre was now going to be boosted by Ballet Russe's erstwhile manager. Hurok, I dare say, was pleased to snub Denham, who was being so troublesome, and clinched the victory by enticing Massine away, a crippling loss to the Russians. Massine had been the mainstay of Ballet Russe, and was certainly the biggest box-office draw in the business. Chase had Michael Fokine, the dean and master of all choreographers, as well as the future's hope, Antony Tudor, his hair slightly awry and his nose just a touch out of joint. They all went down to Mexico City to dish up half a dozen new works. That left Ballet Russe without a resident choreographer. Denham held to the belief that the Ballet Russe was not foundered. "I have rid art of that oktoppus," he said, referring with delightful candor to exactly whom I was not sure. He also indicated that he expected to survive the loss of Massine. "We are free to do great and beautiful things." That would be I who had just been frozen out of my home company, Ballet Theatre. I was the great and beautiful future staring at him with gray, appraising eyes over his blotter. I was a whole lot less imposing than the people he was used to trusting. This impression was heightened by his never having heard of me before.

Certainly I had never dealt with anyone like him. He had been a banker, he told me, but he looked like an old-world diplomat, slender, suave and silky. He tiptoed through large circumventions and maneuverings with pussy-cat elegance and, while never losing track of the grave involvements, bent to all the little attentions with the zest of a courtier. There was a sense of timelessness about him, ease and leisure. He almost gave the impression that nothing at all mattered except beauty and the grace of human relationship. His long aristocratic hands lay serene on the desk or fluttered in delicate accentuation, his dark eyes gazed deep, his dead white unwrinkled brow bent in gentle courtesy toward you just as though behind that bland forehead were not a wheel within a wheel within a wheel. The soft voice rose and fell in singsong monotony with the caressing rubato of enthusiasm as he talked of grandiose monetary involvements, or Michelangelo, or the advisability of accepting an insupportable salary. His business exploits were a kind of saraband, and he wore protocol and prerogative like gold lace. The chair he sat in while the company warmed up backstage had his name painted on it and was always placed center-stage square in the middle of rehearsal. He had the right to stand in the wings with his guests no matter how crowded or hectic, or to walk with his guests into any rehearsal. He was always, even on these occasions, a charming conversationalist. He said to me, "Alexandra Danilova is the Russian Ballet. She is The Star, The Ballerina, the only one left in the Grand Tradition, but she rises whenever I enter a room because I am The Impresario. I am a democrat, but that is nice, no?" He considered for a minute the beauty of her deference. "That is tradition," he breathed, like an Amen.

Although the situation I found myself in was ornate and rich with treacherous personalities, I had these advantages:

1. I said just what I meant which baffled the Russians to a standstill and set them to figuring at length what lay behind my seeming naïveté. Nothing lay behind it. But they didn't realize this for several years. I was to them a figure of mystery.

2. They spoke Russian so I could not understand their objections.

3. I thought they were a down-at-heel, shabby company who had got by with hokum for far too long, so I was not hampered by awe or any such restricting emotion.

4. I believed that I could do something good.

5. This was to be my last job so it didn't matter anyway.

"Whom do you want for a composer?" said Denham in his high voice.

"The best, Aaron Copland."

"I have heard this Copland is good."

"You have heard correctly."

"Now, supposing we cannot arrange this with him? Who is your second choice?"

I had fifteen dollars in the bank, and I was now shopping for the world's great composers. I adjusted my sister's hat with a languorous gesture and drawled, "Let us decide that when Copland definitely refuses." And I put my heels hard on the floor to keep my knees from trembling.

"Now, Miss de Mille," Mr. Denham cooed and sighed, "let us do this thing with lyricism and with beauty."

At the mention of this dangerous word I set my teeth. It was going to be a tough fight on money, I could see. "Talk to my lawyer about the aesthetics," I muttered.

"Naturally, naturally." His hand described an eighteenth-century parabola. "But let us not have just American brawn and vim. Let us not have only the American hotcha. There is also lyricism. There is also poetry." (He's going to try to get away with four hundred dollars for the whole job, I thought.) "There is the tender side of life."

"Mr. Denham," I interjected, "have you ever seen a running set?"

"Frankly, no, I have not."

"Or any native American dance not devised by Leonide Massine?"

"To tell truth, no."

"Then," I said, "relax. You have in mind the Cossack version of our native forms, which differs from the Colorado."

"Ah-ha!" said a voice in the corner. A large-domed, bald, egg-shaped gentleman by name David Libidins had seated himself behind me. "A younge lady who knows her mind. This I like. This I like verrry much." And he went into a mouthful of Russian which sounded like hot chocolate and whipped cream mixed with teeth. Libidins was business manager and comptroller. He was enormous. He was male. Part llama, part bull. He was also very smart. Every so often he giggled with a high piercing Russian male giggle that boded no good for someone. At the moment he told me he was writing his memoirs and submitting them not to an editor as one might suppose but to his lawyers, and he was right to do this. It is virtually impossible, he told me, to write three consecutive sentences about the Ballet Russe without infuriating colleagues. Evidently his lawyers were firm. I wish, indeed I wish, they had not been.

"Now, Miss de Mille," he said, "continue. Speak out all what you wish." Later he called me Malinki which means small. I don't know why he took my part. But he did right from the beginning. He said I had a back like Fedor Chaliapin. He also said that Chaliapin's torso when stripped was the finest in the world. But it is my impression he was comparing us dynamically.

Sergei Ivanovitch Denham continued, "Let us have a large red barn for the party scene."

"But, Mr. Denham," I said, "there are no barns in the Southwest. I have a relative who owns eight thousand head of cattle, an average amount. They do not go into a barn at night."

"But a barn is so interesting, so picturesque. Benois once designed me an enchanting red barn. You cannot imagine what an effect was the deep red behind the dancing."

"Square dancing?"

"No, *moujiks,* but the reds were incredible."

"No barn, Mr. Denham." I glanced at David Savielovitch Libidins.

"*Da!*" he said and his ponderous head chopped forward as though decapitating Denham's idea. "It is her cattle. This she knows about." He muttered in Russian. "There will be no barn," he said airily to me.

"We will call it *Colorado Pastorale*." Denham pronounced every syllable separately, even the final *e*, with mellifluous attachment. "The name is so musical." I did not argue the point.

"One thing I insist on," he continued, his voice like the tinkling of spinets, "there must be a clause in the contract that if any other choreographer puts foot in your rehearsal hall, the agreement is void. This I advise from experience. But, above all," he continued in his high hypnotic tone, "let us seek to keep all beautiful and lyric."

I hastened out to hire the toughest lawyer I could find.

On the bus home I met, of all people, Martha Graham! "This is a mighty strange adventure I've embarked on!"

"At last," she cried, "one of us has breached the impregnable. Now, Agnes, you listen to me. Be arrogant."

("They have no dancers in America," said Toumanova to me in '34. "Grahhm has a sort of technique but no ideas.")

"You be arrogant," said Martha in 1942. "You're every bit the artist any one of them is. This they won't know because they don't know art from a split kick, but they will recognize arrogance, and for your sake, for our sakes, show them what it is like once in a way to be on the receiving end. They won't respect you unless you're rude."

I took the pledge. She kissed me. "Remember," she called. I pranced down the street waving the roses in my, or rather Margaret's, hat.

But although he may not have understood all he was bargaining for, it was Denham and Denham only, a Russian and an alien, who gave me my real chance, supported and furthered my efforts and lent the resources of the Ballet Russe at the height of their power. Deakin and Libidins could have urged until kingdom come. Denham listened and Denham agreed.

Aaron Copland, brought by Franz Allers, the conductor, came to interview me. There being only one chair in my studio, Allers sat on that. I sat on the piano bench. Copland lay on my bed, propped up with chintz pillows.

"This is to be for the Russians?" said Aaron with glasses twinkling among the pillows.

I detailed the scenario.

The story centers around a cowgirl who dresses and acts like a man in an effort to stay close to the head wrangler with whom she is infatuated. She succeeds only in annoying all the cow hands and laying herself open to the mockery of the women. In the end she puts on a skirt and gets her — or rather a — man.

There was a pause.

"Well," I said, "it isn't *Hamlet*."

He giggled.

" — but it can have what Martha Graham calls an 'aura of race memory.'"

At this Copland's glasses flashed and gleamed. His body began to vibrate all over with great explosive laughs. "Couldn't we do a ballet about Ellis Island?" he asked, his glasses opaque with light. "That I would love to compose."

"You go to hell!" I replied.

Allers jumped to his feet in amazement. He looked searchingly from one to the other of us. "But what has happened?"

"Mr. Copland and I have just reached a basic understanding," I said.

"Evidently," said Allers, sitting down not enlightened.

"You'll get the scenario by post tomorrow," I promised Copland. "If you like it at all, come to tea."

"Put the kettle on," he phoned at noon the next day.

That afternoon over buttered scones we blocked it out minute by minute. It scarcely deviated by a gesture in the final version. Not that I didn't have my doubts.

The next morning I was on the phone again explaining that, as I knew I could not choreograph lyrically, the twilight scene was to be scrapped.

"Too bad," said Copland. "I've composed it already." This, as

Leonard Bernstein later pointed out, was a patent lie. He had just found something put away in a drawer he thought might serve. I, however, amazed at his speed, dashed to his studio and found the piece lovely. So for better or worse, I was committed to the twilight scene. I had doubts about the end of the story. I had doubts about a possible divergence in style. Copland laid a masterful hand on my arm and proceeded with the work as outlined. From then on he paid no heed to my chattering confusion, giggled merely and got on with the scoring.

The problem of the barn settled, the problem of scenery still confronted us. Denham took me to Pavel Tchelitchev for advice. We found him among drawings of skinned babies' heads and desiccated leaves. "Tell me the plot," he said, folding his long legs and leaning his chin on his slender hand.

I told him.

"This is not an interesting plot. It is not fit for a ballet. Let us think of another plot." And he began to outline several quite different.

"Mr. Tchelitchev," I said, "it is kind of you to concern yourself with the plot of my work, but however unworthy it is too late to change. Mr. Copland has already composed the first section."

"Has he really? That is a pity."

"What we want is advice about a scene designer."

"Ah yes. I myself will not design for you."

"We never supposed you would."

"Well, I won't. But there is Florine Stettheimer. She is not a member of the union, of course, and I don't think she would like doing this, but she is a very great painter, probably the greatest American painter of all time. She will do you sets unrealistically, unlike the West which would be banal. She would paint things you have never seen in your life."

Denham interposed faintly but insistently. "Pavel, please, have you any whisky?"

"I have no whisky. You must excuse me. I will get you a small glass of Coca-Cola."

He talked without cessation in three or four languages and lifted nis hands here and there, sometimes toward a naked young man and sometimes toward a bunch of children hanging by their feet from a very large tree. And I found myself considerably soothed by the reassurance of that much energy flowing, flowing into sound, the comfort of his eyes which beamed with fatherliness.

Denham spoke. "Pavel, please. It is very hot. Perhaps, some tea —"

"There is no tea — I am so sorry. I will arrange about Stettheimer's entering the union."

"Mr. Tchelitchev," I interrupted, "don't you know of someone who would like to paint something we have seen before, an American landscape, for instance? Our ideas may seem commonplace to you."

"They do."

"Yours seem perverse to me."

Denham eyed me with amazement and patted me on the back as our host loped to the kitchen. "Bravo, Agnes, don't let him bully you."

"He's trying to tease us both."

Pavel returned with a glass of plain water. "I think it would be less banal if Nijinska did the cowboy ballet and you did the old Russian fairytale."

"Good God!" I said, forgetting myself.

Tchelitchev was getting bored with his fun. He terminated the interview. "There is an unknown young man, Oliver Smith. He will do. I will personally see that he does a good job for you."

He did call Oliver. He did mean to help. His intentions were kind and practical.

Oliver Smith turned out to be red-headed, six feet three, amusing and gifted, also impoverished and therefore amenable. Together we went with his sketches to Denham, who professed himself enchanted albeit dismayed at the number of backdrops, two more than he had counted on, which was one. He hoped there was something left over from a recent flop, *Igrouchka,* he could make do. He then took fifty cents out of his pocket and told Oliver and me to go buy a good large breakfast and figure out how to do with one drop. We ate a good large breakfast at the Algonquin, spending over two dollars which neither of us could afford, and formally returned to Mr. Denham his four bits together with the announcement that we were standing pat. Libidins was as usual in the corner. "These sketches are good," he said and winked. "Go home now, work. I will fix." As we left the dark Russian had started to flow, interspersed with high yelps of protest from Denham.

Toward Denham I continued to evince a Bismarckian assurance. I might wake in the night shuddering with fear — but I dared not show him a crack in my conceit. A more opinionated and disagreeable girl he had never dealt with. I may have overdone it, but the role was new to me. In any case, the discipline worked. Once the word was secretly got to me that Copland had signed, I put the heat on. The lawyer and he grappled and struck for terms far higher than Mr. Denham hoped. Upshot: five hundred dollars for the work. (It took five months — this guaranteed me twenty-five dollars a week, just about the the ribbon saleswoman's salary I'd hankered after.) Twelve-fifty royalty for the first ten performances of every season, ten dollars for the next ten, seven-fifty thereafter. I was to dance the opening night. He balked at this, but I stood firm, and he yielded at last with the understanding that I would accept the minimum union wage — fifteen dollars. That was my salary per performance for the opening season in New York.

Denham's reputation for driving bargains had not been underrated. Denham also is supposed to be without peer in securing money from wealthy patrons. And this was lucky for ballet.

Ballet being the most expensive form of theater excepting only opera, there being neither federal nor municipal endowment nor any organized group of sponsors like the Metropolitan Opera Board, personal donations are the lifeblood of the project. And there is only one way of procuring these: by begging humbly in graceful, groveling attitudes. The great Diaghilev himself was past master at this. In fact, his genius for raising money was said to match his genius for organizing theater pieces and discovering creative talent. Every great company, except the Sadler's Wells, must beg continuously for funds, de Basil's Ballet Russe, Denham's Ballet Russe, Ballet Theatre, Kirstein's American Ballet (which developed into the New York City Center Ballet Company). None of them can meet their budgets even when selling out. The Sadler's Wells Ballet and the Paris Opéra are, of course, state supported.

I have never seen Denham in the more virtuoso aspects of his function, but I have heard tales of rich old ladies who have given thousands for the privilege of looking at scene designs in Sergei Ivanovitch's office, not buying them, mind you, just viewing them. Far better pictures are to be seen free up the street in well-known museums, but the sense of private favor conferred was irresistible to them. And when I have heard him discoursing on the beauties of his company, the remarkable new talents, the grand repertoire, the enormous background of the stars, the *esprit de corps,* detailing how even the wardrobe mistress had worked for years with almost no salary, which I can well believe, I have dropped my eyes in awe to the rich food the victims had prepared to their undoing. He made them believe they were patrons in the great sense, as necessary to the history of dancing as the Medicis had been to the history of painting. He made them know they were endowing composers and painters as well as choreographers. He gave them the joy of serving, the power of creating. He showed them how they were necessary to the survival of beauty.

Besides the unquestioned satisfaction of making glory possible, there were other stimulating and exotic rewards, being brought back stage, for instance, by Mr. Denham just before the performance. They used to stand with their backs to the curtain while the dancers warmed up. When the ballet began they moved to the wings where they established themselves in the way with a fine view of heavy breathing. Another reward was the privilege of giving parties for the cast to which the dancers came, gaunt, ravenous and exhausted. The guests filled their plates at the superb buffets and their glasses at the champagne buckets and then retired to corners where they talked exclusively to one another, except, of course, the stars who made a social effort. The rest left when they had fed, barely thanking the hostess. The spectacle of white-faced underpaid boys, unable to assume any responsibility themselves, lapping up the cream of rich ladies as though it were their due and the least a matron could offer them as repayment for jumping in the air and clapping their calves together, seemed to me one of the really corrupting aspects of ballet life. But the hostesses were not repelled. In Seattle, Cleveland, St. Louis, Dallas, Fresno, Denver and Detroit, they were grateful to have romance whirl through their dining rooms. And there was always Danilova, who behaved like a great lady and was gracious. And there was Sergei Ivanovitch, princely, attentive and promising of endless backstage visits.

Possibly some American city will, one day, support a lyric theater as cities support a library or an art gallery or a symphony orchestra. But I believe this will be long after our dancing days are done. In the meantime, Mr. Denham takes old ladies out to lunch and the dancers do their own laundry in Pullman washrooms and sleep eight to a hotel room.

I began to show some of the dance steps to Frederic Franklin and Lubov Roudenko — I insisted on privacy — and the three of us behind locked doors tried out the hoe-down. The *régisseur,* Ivan Ivanovitch Yazvinsky, uneasy outside, put his eye to the keyhole and froze with dismay. He rushed to the telephone and warned his master. I was, he said, reducing the Ballet Russe to the status of a night club. All this was going on in the hall right behind me but in Russian so I never knew. Denham lost no time in getting to my lawyer. There must be a clause, he said, guaranteeing him the right of veto, otherwise how could he count on my taste? I might put a mustache on a Rembrandt.

"Never," said I. He was buying my taste and no one else's. He could call the whole deal off if he wished.

With this statement I came of age. This was, I believe, professionally speaking, the first brave and independent thing I ever did.

But this was my last job and I intended to have fun and do exactly what I pleased.

The contract was signed. No veto clause. I had final word on every artistic matter. This was important, for into their stronghold of tradition enforced by an almost Prussian discipline I entered to break down all their cherished habits, to awake instincts curbed and warped by inflexible techniques, to disturb the balance of power, to question their authorities, authorities which had brought them international success, champagne suppers, and glamour — not money, of course, they never expected that, but unstinted adulation.

No doubt they muttered a good deal. Russians do. Luckily, as I have remarked, it was in Russian and no trouble to me.

But they stood whenever I entered the room and allowed me to precede them through the doors, even Danilova, the great ballerina, adored on three continents and with an immortal reputation, even she stood and followed after. I was the choreographer, in my sister's borrowed dress and hat and my sister's shoes, and with a necklace lent by my sister. I knew very well what I was facing. Behind me, too, was a lifetime of discipline, no success, but discipline, nonetheless. In my homemade embattled way, I felt ready. We joined forces.

CHAPTER 25

Rodeo

THE RUSSIANS entrained for the Far West. I went on the same train, but not with them. I had to live on my twenty-five dollars a week and pay my New York rent. I got besides three dollars a day traveling expenses to cover everything — hotels, food, taxis, and so on. Mr. Libidins put into my hands a round-trip transcontinental railroad ticket, first class, which I promptly turned in and rode coach. The difference in fare balanced my budget. I carried my clothes in a light wicker basket to obviate porters' tips. I ate only sandwiches and coffee in cartons. Four and a half days is a long time not to be out of one's clothes, but at the other end was a clean bed waiting at Father's. When we came into stations, I hid behind the luggage until the troupe had cleared the platforms. It would not do for them to see their choreographer coming out of a coach; Massine had traveled in a drawing room.

This was July 1942. At every station groups of drawn and pallid young men came aboard leaving women with obliterated faces and whimpering children on the station platforms. We finally reached the Coast.

I lived with Father and his wife during the time the Ballet performed at the Hollywood Bowl and rehearsed the new works. Pop was now head of the dramatic department of the University of Southern California and as Professor de Mille had made a national reputation as lecturer and director. His role in the building of moving picture form and technique had been historic; now in his later years he was devoting himself to writing and passing on his unique knowledge to serious students of the theater. Clara had joined the motion picture department at U.S.C. and gave courses in scenario writing which she was well qualified to do, having a distinguished career behind her in this medium.

The home they opened to me was quiet, thoughtful, understanding, and very needful to me during the stresses of the time. The days were delivered over to hurly-burly.

The first rehearsal was held in what had been Carmalita's studio, now in the hands of Maria Bekefi. I asked for the men first. If I could break them, I would have the whole company in my hand. As I walked down the flowering drive I heard the music of *Gaité* and a good deal of stamping and shouting. Shoura (Alexandra) Danilova and Freddie Franklin were standing on chairs yelling the counts and clapping. The men, the great thick-muscled men, and the stringy-muscled girls were stamping and swooping and clenching their fists in a miasma of sweat. It was not a very large room and Shoura and Freddie were up to their waists in Parisian abandon. I glanced in and I went pale; clutching my little dancing bag, I crept up the stairs. Madame Bekefi had taught me in '36. "Madame," said I as I knocked at her apartment, "may I come in? I'm frightened."

"Yez, darling, yez. I have made frezsh coffee."

"Coffee for courage?"

"Coffee for courage! Yez, darling. You have not need to be frightened. You will do good."

I was summoned below. *Gaité* was finished but the girls hung about, streaming sweat, their shoes and towels under their arms, very curious. Danilova was collecting her slippers.

"You would like this room empty? No?"

"Please." I nodded faintly.

She clapped her jeweled hands and stilled the hubbub. "Madame would like this room empty. Emediately! Get out," she said with dainty succinctness. "Get out. You! All go." Then she turned to

me and grasped my hand. "Now I go too because that is more con-
venient for you. I have great excitement for this. We hope much.
Bonne chance!" And with a twinkling smile, she walked neatly out
on her long silken, fabulous legs and her turned-out feet, leaving
a breath of delicious and expensive perfume behind her.

I turned deliberately and faced them. There they were — nineteen of them. Male. Great muscled brutes leaning against the
barre and staring with watchful, smoldering eyes. Behind them
were Paris, Covent Garden, Monte Carlo and, in three cases, the
Maryinski. And behind me? A wall. It occurred to me at this
precise moment that with the exception of five soloists I had never
worked with men in my life. Never more than one man at a time.

I took a deep breath. "We are going to begin," I said in a scarcely
audible treble, "with men riding horses in a rodeo. For instance,
if you were riding a bucking horse and were thrown, it would look
like this." And I rode a bucking horse and was thrown the length
of the room on my head.

"Darling!" said Freddie rushing over to me. "Darling, you'll
hurt yourself!"

"Did it look good, Freddie?"

"It looked wonderful! But you'll kill yourself."

"Not me. It's you who are to do it."

The young men, around the room, looked nonplused.

"Well," said Freddie, "no help for it. Come on, boys, let's have
a try. Ee — "

The riding movements were neither realistic nor imitative. I had
worked for a year in London to make them intrinsically beautiful.
When performed correctly they suggested the high vigorous emotions of riding. But they were very difficult because the dancer had
always to look as though he were propelled by an unseen animal.
He hung off balance in the air. He did not jump, he was thrown
or wrenched upwards. His feet never touched earth, it was the
horses' feet that clattered in the pebbles. The very essence of the
movement was shock, spasm and effort.

Alas, although big boys, they had been trained to move like

wind-blown petals. "Raise your arms," I begged them. "You have men's arms, they have striking power, they can control a heavy, moving rope, or the brute furies of an eight-hundred-pound animal."

Up came the delicate wrists and the curled fingers of the eighteenth-century dandy. "Move from the solar plexus and back," I shouted, "not from the armpit. Think of athletes," I entreated. "Think of throwing a ball, from your feet, from your back, from your guts." But it was a long time since they had thrown balls. They had forgotten. They had not used the ground since they were children except to push away from it. Their arms rose up and down but they themselves looked absolutely stationary.

"Don't *plier*. Sit your horse," I implored. "There's a difference." But the strain was too much and they relaxed back into bad second position where they felt eminently at home.

A few Russians lolled on the barre and considered the matter poorly. "It is not dancing," they said. But I had never said it was, and I was delighted to excuse them. They picked up their towels and left in haughty silence. The ranks thinned quickly. I had planned to have eighteen men in the cast. I settled for ten. Those that stayed were ready and able.

For two hours, I rolled on the floor with them, lurched, contorted, jackknifed, hung suspended and ground my teeth. They groaned and strained. I beat them out in impact, resilience and endurance. I broke them to my handling. I broke them technically, which was where they lived and worshiped.

At the end, I suggested we walk. We what? We walk like cowboys. They looked at me in dumfoundment, their clothes matted to their bodies, their hair all on end and dirty from the floor. They walked. "Not that way," I shouted.

By this time I was feeling pretty frisky. "Crotch-sprung, saddlesore, with rolled-over high heels and sweat-stained leather, ill at ease and alien to the ground, unhorsed centaurs."

"Look," I said. "The sun in Colorado beats on your eyes like blows. You can't hold up your heads that way in the sun."

"Why, that's right," said a couple nodding in recognition. They began to squint, their gait slowed, they grew hot and dusty and weathered before me. One could almost, as my sister said later, smell them.

Out of this comes folk dancing, and out of nothing less.

I dismissed rehearsal. The survivors, mostly English and American, thanked me.

Next day they couldn't even walk. They sat in the sun and rubbed one another's muscles with oil. And they all had cracking headaches.

I had won.

Two days later I took on the girls. We walked, giggled, whispered, and looked to the far horizon for two hours. They thought this unreasonable. "Oh, Madame, we will be funny when we have costumes. Please do not concern yourself. We will assuredly be funny."

"You be funny right now on count eight." And I set my lips in a merciless line and waited.

We worked for four hours on a boy kissing a girl at a dance. This was the kind of effort they had put into high jumps or turns. They thought I was perverse. They thought I was insupportable. Well, not all of them, perhaps. Lubov Roudenko was breaking her back for me. She had perpetual headaches from the lurching and bucking. Freddie believed. A few of the American boys and girls, although perplexed, began to hope. Even in rehearsal some of it looked good, even to them. And there was always Freddie barking the counts and snapping at their feet. And dancing, dancing until the sweat poured from his back and head. "Oh, darling," he would say gasping, "this is impossible. Well, there's no help for it. Come on boys, let's try. Ee — "

He was the first great male technician I had ever had the chance to work with and I tried everything I thought the human body could accomplish. He was as strong as a mustang, as sudden, as direct, and as inexhaustible. There was no slacking off at the end of a long effort, no dawdling, no marking. He came into the room briskly, dressed and ready at the first minute of the rehearsal, and he worked full out without a second's deviation of attention until rehearsal finished, and the last lift was as precise and as vigorous as the first. With the exception of Massine, he has the most exact sense of timing of any man in the dance world. (He can pick up a difficult tap routine at a single rehearsal — as quickly in fact as he hears it. Only very great tap dancers can do this.) His verve galvanizes an audience as it does a rehearsal. He is the inner motor of the Ballet Russe, the reason they get through the sheer amount of labor involved in each tour.

I shall not forget my surprise when I first placed my hands on his shoulders for a jump and felt the muscles move across his back and arms as I just went up and stayed up. I shall not forget my wonder at the animal force that lifted and carried me. I had danced alone, or with girls or with actors, but with no one of this caliber technically. I came down like a hysterical baby that had been tossed around by a grownup. I couldn't wait to go up again. Naturally, I didn't let him see my delight. I was Madame, the choreographer. He still called me Miss de Mille. We were very formal always.

Luba Roudenko came to me. She was very happy with the role but her friends had told her she had a great technique and might she please, Miss de Mille, might she please do some *fouettés* in the hoe-down? I said no.

Between rehearsals, I sought consolation from Carmalita. "You can't produce work of integrity this way," I moaned. "Not with a company of strangers in two months."

"Of course not," she said. "But you can try," she added gaily. "Something might surprise you. Not integrity, of course." She looked at me hard. "They are paying you, aren't they?"

"Sort of," I mumbled.

In San Francisco we got into the second scene. In Seattle, the third. All along the way I dropped Russians from the cast.

"Dear Agnes," said Sergei Ivanovitch one night in the wings. "I hear you threw Sasha out of rehearsal today. That is unfortunate.

To tell truth, I am pained. He is a fine young man, a bit impetuous, wild like all young men, but we must be indulgent. Appeal to his class, dear Agnes, appeal to his class." I gasped in astonishment.

"He is a Count, Agnes, a Count."

At this point I threw back my head rudely and simply hollered. Sasha had been surly, insolent, lazy, slow, untalented, demoralizing, tardy and extremely hung-over.

"Agnes," continued Denham persuasively, "I am the last person not to be democratic. I understand very well your ideals. But he is good material."

I said no.

"And now," continued Denham not unreasonably, "may I not see some little part of the ballet?"

I said no.

"Agnes, dear Agnes, you treat me as though I were an outsider, an amateur in this business."

I said no.

Nor would I allow the dancers to watch one another. Whenever more than four got in the same room pandemonium developed. Obviously, no choreographer before had explained clearly. After each suggestion there was a United Nations Assembly at the back of the room. I stamped, screamed and howled for silence. I promised to ask their help when I was stuck. There was a good deal of surprise at this; no choreographer had ever acknowledged the need for help. Again, I criticized my own work sharply. Dumfoundment! All choreographers had hitherto been infallible.

Occasionally I was the one surprised. "Bob! Bob!" I yelled, urging them to dip and curtsy on the beat. The hubbub grew to a roar. "For the love of God, be quiet!" I howled. "And bob!"

"But Madame," said a Russian as spokesman, "we cannot understand who you mean. Which Baub, please?" Four Roberts stepped forward with inquiring faces.

The music gave us trouble; it was difficult.

"No, no, no!" shouted Rachel Chapman, jumping up from the keyboard and beating her fists on the top of the piano. "You are absolutely and entirely wrong. That is not the rhythm the composer vished. I protect the composer. Now listen."

Freddie cocked his head. "She's right, kids. It's syncopated."

Rachel was infallible and exacting. She looked and acted like a Polish lioness. She played terrifically without cease in all rehearsals and in the pit. She and Freddie were the watchdogs of the repertoire. She helped me very much.

Luba Roudenko came to me. She was very happy with the leading role, but her friends had told her she was not showing off her strong technique. Perhaps if she did some batterie and brilliant *chaîné* turns in the hoe-down? I said no.

Rumors drifted up from Mexico. Ballet Theatre was going to have a dazzling repertoire. Fokine himself was down there working hard. My own boys and girls knew they were facing desperate competition and possible bankruptcy. I was to save them. They didn't express this to me in so many words, but it was made quite plain. I was carrying the ball. Somehow I'd become a member of the troupe and when there were no Pullmans to be had and the boys tore the seats apart to make beds for the girls, I bedded down among them three in a row.

Throughout this tour, Danilova, like a princess godmother, threw her arm about me, introducing me to the best restaurants and the most charming hostesses. She had made this trip seven times annually and inasmuch as she and Massine were the biggest box-office names in ballet, she was in a position to introduce me where and as I had never been introduced before. "Our choreographer," she would say, pushing me ahead of her in Margaret's dress into a salon.

We traveled from city to city while the ballet performed its summer tour. Sometimes we stayed a week and sometimes one night. We spent a great deal of time together on the trains.

What does the Russian Ballet look like on tour? Different from what you've been led to believe. Most of the girls and boys are simply, even poorly, dressed. They have no money. In fact, they have borrowed months ahead on next season's contract in order to get through their two months' vacation. They live like indentured servants. The stars are smart. They look like stars. But they travel without maids. Danilova has a faithful follower who maids for her; Slavenska has her mother.

The stars travel in Pullman berths with the company. Denham travels in a compartment, and Massine when he is with them sleeps and eats apart. He is the reverse of chummy even with his lifelong companions. But of course, at this time, he is absent in Mexico building up the Ballet Theatre repertoire.

The girls usually sit mending their tights or sewing the ribbons into their shoes or darning the ends of their blocked point slippers to preserve the satin from floor friction. The care and preparation of tights and slippers as well as the cost of the tights devolve upon each dancer personally.[1] The girls have to wash their tights at each wearing to make the silk cling, so the washroom is full of pink legs swinging in the train vibration. The girls talk shop, intrigue and knitting patterns. Never anything else. Never, although war, flood, strikes, elections and plague pass over them. Never. They talk technique and what so-and-so's mama said to Mr. Denham last night. The older men play poker in three or four languages. The younger men look out of the window and hold hands. Some few read. Not many. They eat five or six meals a day. They are always hungry. They take cat naps, like animals, wherever they drop.

Mia Slavenska sits coiffed and perfumed with a Bruckner score opened on her smart tweed knees. The topaze on her hand is enormous and gives her a sense of reassurance as she leans her exqui-

---

[1] The company pays for the slippers five dollars per pair; a pair lasts for about a week. In the last century a ballerina had a new pair for each act of her ballet. These were unblocked silk with a sole like paper. Taglioni threw hers out after a single use as the stage of the Opéra was kept purposely dirty to prevent slipping. The stiffening of the toes introduced the need for a breaking-in process, very tedious to the dancer. Pavlova frequently asked her best girls to break in her shoes, although hers were Italian and relatively soft. She carried literally hundreds of pairs and selected and chose with a kind of nervous obsession. The breaking-in of the hard-blocked American slipper is a real labor and terrible on the knuckles of the feet. The fastening of a slipper requires the same care a surgeon gives his gloves. Markova glues her slippers on her feet around the heel, slips the ankle ribbons through a loop at the back and sews them fast with needle and thread. She has to be cut out of her shoes.

sitely manicured forefinger against her lovely brow and contem-
plates choreography. Miss Twysden, Danilova's companion, biographer and helper, knits Danilova's practice tights and discourses on
the inferiority of all other companies. The inferiority of all other
ballerinas she considers axiomatic. But she is a lady bred and cannot say what she thinks with Slavenska contemplating in the next
seat, and with Slavenska's mama staring at her with a hard gaze.
Libidins progresses down the car greeting his wards. Slavenska
leaves off her intellectual pursuits, smooths the coils of her sun-red
hair, straightens the seams on her stalwart smooth legs and corners
him. She has been waiting to explain that if she doesn't dance more
Giselles she will be distraught and she details what that condition
implies in Yugoslavia. David Savielovitch manages to turn the talk
into reminiscences of Chaliapin. Mia is distraught. Both voices
rise. But no one can compete with his reminiscences. Libidins was
once an old-style basso in a provincial Russian opera company.

A great deal has been written about the ballet's glamour. This is an
elastic word. In a recent play, *Look, Ma, I'm Dancin'!* and in the film
The Red Shoes, the impression is made that they are a hard-working, healthy group of boys and girls rather like a traveling university. Nothing could be farther from the truth. Hard working
they are to the point of slavery, and gay frequently. But healthy?
Not very. Raddled with sexual insecurity, financial instability, ambition, jealousy and terror, they are herded from one engagement to
another locked within the frenzied confines of their group for ten
months at a stretch. They never stop anywhere en route long
enough to make outside contacts. Intrigue assumes Renaissance
proportions. Romance is a kind of round-robin tournament, and
psychosis the hallmark of every experience. Most of the men are
homosexual. Most of the women are sex-starved. Occasionally
there is a nervous breakdown and a girl is unloaded at some station
and left behind in a Midwestern hospital. Occasionally someone
has a temper tantrum and beats up his girl friend or his wife, forcing her to seek succor in adjacent bedrooms. Next morning they
are all doing *pliés* in a row in perfect decorum.

There are a few gay harlots in the old tradition, very few, for the girls simply haven't the energy. And there are a few happy marriages. These stand like rocks in the currents of emotional chaos.

But it is the bewilderment of exhaustion and transience that clouds most spirits and energies. Janet Reed said to me once, later, when I was traveling with Ballet Theatre, "Last night I came out of the theater and I couldn't remember what city I was in or which way to walk toward my hotel. It turned out to be Cleveland."

So they jog on together locked in the stewing, untidy cars. On arrival everyone frantically stuffs belongings into bags and boxes. Down come Slavenska's furs from the case on the rack. Slavenska's cat is put in a basket by Slavenska's mama. Danilova unpins last night's orchids from the back of her seat. The poker players settle their debts rather loudly. Wet wash is stuffed into hatboxes, knitting into the cosmetics. All, girls and boys, load up and stagger out. There are not arms enough for gallantry and no one can afford a porter; the girls lug their own suitcases. The car looks like an abandoned picnic ground. The porter, untipped, is not charmed.

They pour out of the train chattering, swearing, calling. In the rear or well in advance, Sergei Ivanovitch Denham and David Savielovitch Libidins trundle in dignity down the platform complete with briefcases, porters and neat luggage.

The company mobs the taxi racks, eight to a car, and goes off in search of lodgings. The stars, of course, have hotel reservations, but the *corps de ballet* have to rustle their own rooms. This sometimes takes two or three hours. They sleep always two to a room, sometimes six or eight. One person registers for each group; one person only attempts to pay.

Once settled in they assemble at the theater for replacement rehearsal. The usual breakage necessitates constant last-minute substitution. They snatch a malted milk at six and start warming up for the evening performance. They eat dinner at midnight. They eat in hash houses or drugstores except when they are being fed champagne and French cuisine by leading hostesses.

The next morning sees them either on a train or taking class with the best local teacher. As there are only six cities in the United States in which ballet can play a week's stand, this procedure is followed two or four times weekly — room hunting and all.

For this they were paid $45 a week,[2] the basic minimum wage for a *corps de ballet* dancer in 1942. Soloists received anything up to $300. Markova and Dolin received the highest fees in the business, $400 and $450 respectively (their salaries have multiplied since then). The basic wage for a scene shifter or grip was $121 and for a pit musician $140.

Every evening I do a barre with the boys and girls hanging on to the costume trunks. I change my practice clothes in the star dressing room shared by the two great ladies of the troupe. They sit at opposite tables, fitted out with their dainties, and they quarrel delicately and precisely over precedence, choice of roles, and the other paraphernalia of their trade. Mia's mama rummages in her trunk. Twysden, the lady helper, knits and practices scorn with unmodified English assurance.

Behind every great star there is usually a sad quiet woman mending or knitting. Some of them are quite horribly young women. Being a ballet mother is a métier in itself and different from any other function in the theater, and they develop occupational symptoms like extreme aggressiveness, extreme nervousness, extreme jealousy, and as regards their own persons, extreme selflessness. They spent their youth sitting in smelly practice studios; they spend their middle age standing in the wings. They are drudges and do all manner of menial and selfless service forever underfoot, in daily oblivion. A few of the ballet boys have mothers too. These are rarer, but I believe more formidable.

The hour before performance is a visiting time in a ballet theater. Outsiders are not welcome, but the girls and boys go back and forth between dressing rooms, gossiping, chatting, relaxing, letting go

[2] Since *Oklahoma!* and the opening of a new competitive market, the basic minimum wage has risen from $45 to $75 a week. The basic minimum wage for a dancer in a dramatic or Equity show has risen from $45 to $75 a week. The salaries of musicians and crew have risen correspondingly.

the outside, integrating more and more closely within their group. They seem to be wasting time. Actually they are undergoing a change. They are warming up, quieting down, cutting off from daily life. None of them will stay away from the theater and miss this hour; it is very important to them.

I visit the corps to go over tomorrow's notes with some of my girls. The corps girls dress in barrack rooms at long trestles. Their tutus hang overhead like large inverted flower corollas. They make up nearly always stripped to the waist, the complicated tapes which pull up their tights dangling loose from their thighs. They are a very pretty sight as they lean forward to apply their enormous false eyelashes or put the markings around their eyes as elaborate and formal as a Japanese actor's mask. Their hair is greased flat and nailed to the head with bobby pins so that they could be shaken like a rat in a terrier's mouth and not a strand would be loosened. With the foliage of tarlatan fluff overhead, the candles for mascara twinkling in front of the glasses, and the naked pearly young bodies stretching and moving, the scene suggests a kind of grotto. They have the most beautiful bodies in the world and they are all pre-adolescent. There is not a hip or a bust among them. But that's all right. It's better for dancing and they all, whenever it suits them, have babies with the greatest aplomb, showing that every-one, but chiefly Mother Nature, is wrong. Between the nymphs move Madame Pourmel and wardrobe women with freshly ironed costumes. They say nothing. Their tired, raw fingers zip and hook and fasten. Their faces are bleached and faded. They are reminders of what lies ahead.

I hang around mostly backstage during performances. I rarely go front for the pertinent reason that from this aspect the spectacle is depressing, and I think it helpful at this moment not to become depressed. If I have spoken of all this with excitement it is because I know toward what the dancers are striving and what lies behind them. And because I have grown enormously attached to them. The plain fact is that from where the audience sits the perform-ances are often poor; they are under-rehearsed, paltry and tired, and rely for their success on the glittering efforts of a few great soloists and the splendid heritage of their name. Is this company just another dingy troupe of acrobats? Does their fascination rest chiefly on nothing but good press agenting? What distinguishes them from any traveling stock company?

Stand backstage at curtain rise and you will see. Their three-hour preparations are completed. They are ready now in full costume and make-up. They try steps nervously, complaining of the floor, complaining of the new batch of shoes, invocating the Madonna while cracking their tights, scolding the conductor while rosining their slippers, having indigestion from a too cheap dinner behind the electrician's box, having love and heartbreak with finger pirouettes, receiving Denham's benediction center-stage like a lump of sugar. The boxed-in space hums with pandemonium in three Slavic languages, peppered with French. The lights raise the heat to baking point. There is a sudden quiet from the pit and then a roll of drums. The company stops talking and stands. The girls smooth out their tarlatans. The boys run softly in place easing their insteps. The stage manager made up for *Scheherazade* continues to whisper to the electrician. The national anthem is being played — not their national anthem, a good proportion of them are homeless. They stand this way for "The Marseillaise," "God Save the King," "Maple Leaf Forever," "The Star-Spangled Banner." Nearly every one of them was born in a land whose anthems they will not hear in a hurry. The orchestra starts the overture. They move into place. They spit over one another's shoulders. They do this every night throughout the tour. They say *"Merde"* or *"Ni poukha ni péra"* or whatever three times. They cross themselves three times right shoulder first and touch the wood of the floor. Denham takes up his folding chair and moves to the wings. The lights turn blue. Everyone's mouth goes suddenly purple; their eyes glitter unnaturally. The grease in their hair takes on bright blue reflections. "I beginning," yells Yazvinsky. "Kourrtain!" The curtain moves up. There is a rush of air from the front.

And they are Sylphides, and the music is Chopin. This is their native land. Every head is bent to the line. Every breath is bated. From toe tip to trembling fingers they are at attention. They move down the stage, these scrapping youngsters, in the oldest living tradition of our theater.

They share all the characteristics and faults of other theater folks with this difference: behind each turn of the head and footfall stand a lifetime of effort and three hundred years of experimentation. There is a glory carried by these poor, dingy, travel-worn waifs. The cost of this effort is isolation and abnormality. It constitutes blood sacrifice; they are dedicated people. They are bound together in common need like blitz victims. They are bound together by training and heritage. They are bound together, poor, deluded fools, by pride. Notwithstanding they are treated like bastard members of a family and are given the disadvantage of every doubt in all practical matters — in dressing-room arrangements, newspaper releases, legal documents, leases, charge accounts, sales agreements, savings and lending, and insurance policies — they are most unnaturally proud. They think they are doing the most difficult and interesting work in the theater.

❧

July moved into August, August into September. The United States lost the Aleutians. Rommel had all but reached the Nile, the Japanese were hard upon New Zealand. We knitted and rehearsed and gossiped back across the continent in cars that were shunted aside to let trainloads of tanks take the right of way, and trainloads of men, some in uniform, but all with intent lost faces. In New York we settled to three weeks of straight rehearsing, six hours a day. At night I prepared the final plans.

All of America was quickening, was affirming itself, was searching its heart. There was high challenge in every face one met. My soldier was far away preparing himself for overseas duty, and I did not know from week to week what he was doing or where he would be next. I used to stand in my studio in the hot summer nights and it seemed to me I could feel the quickening energy around me, the gathering of the force of remembering. If in the face of this enormous self-recognition I could hold up one tiny token of our common life, I felt I was not entirely wasteful of the time.

In some ways this was the happiest period of my adult life. I worked tranquilly between lives. I hoped not greatly; I feared nothing. It was very like the delicious expectant moment when one knows one is about to fall in love but has not yet hazarded the furies and commitments of the enterprise. I was in love with the haunting legends of my land. I was in love also with a soldier. And somehow the one became mysteriously a symbol for the other. I opened the great French windows of my studio to the New York night and walked and walked in the warm dusk lit only by the windows across the way, and played the lovely Texas songs Copland had set and thought of the prairies I had crossed as a child, the prairies where my young man was even then growing up. I thought of the men leaving, leaving everywhere — generation on generation of men leaving and falling and the women remembering. And what was left of any of them but a folk tune and a way of joining hands in a ring? And I searched my heart for the clues to remembering.

In the morning I screamed for three hours at the Russians to shut up and be simple, and in the afternoon I screamed for three more hours to be quiet and be simple. We finished the ballet in ten days.

Luba Roudenko came to me. I said no.

Then came the show rehearsal. Denham, Libidins, Franz Allers, Irving Deakin, Yazvinsky, with their wives, and my mother attended. No one had as yet seen any of it. The company assembled in immaculate black tights and white shirts. "Who told them to do this?" I asked delighted. Tradition. They stood quietly. They did not even whisper. They danced without a fault.

There was a cry from the spectators at the end. Libidins roared loudest. "Thanks God, Agnes, Malinki. Thanks God. What a ballet! Ham and eggs! Let me kiss you!"

"What's that?"

"Ham and eggs! *Scheherazade, Gaité, Rodeo:* ham and eggs. Our meal ticket for the next season!" Denham kissed me. Mrs. Denham kissed me. Allers kissed me. Mother kissed me. This was the first time she had seen any of the ballet. She was a trifle giddy.

"Now," I said turning to the dancers, "we will really get to work." But the room was empty. They had left on their vacation.

Since I was to dance the *première*, I used the time to brush up on my own dancing. I had practiced every night with them before performances and they were considerably alarmed. Before God, I was no technician. I shut myself in a studio and labored on the comedy. But I broke training for three days, borrowed thirty bucks from Mother and dashed out to Nashville, Tennessee — sitting up, of course. There being no seats available, I spent a good part of the trip in the men's washroom. There were two other women there, a crying child and some very disgruntled sailors for company. I went complete with the records Copland had made me. I could not buy or hire a gramophone so for the first time in my entire career I made use of Cecil de Mille's name and borrowed a machine in the local broadcasting studio. In this confined space I danced out solo the entire ballet, rodeo, love scenes, hoe-down and running set for my corporal. He thought it looked promising which was what I wanted to hear.

The company reassembled three weeks later. Massine was about. Because of overlapping contracts he found himself the husband of both groups. Ballet Theatre was housed also in the Metropolitan and their two-week season preceded ours. The two companies of dancers passed one another on stairs, in dressing rooms, rehearsal halls, lavatories, with the chill reserve and uncommunicative politeness of enemy officers about to join issue in a contest for survival. The following season they were most of them working for the opposite group and passed their former bedmates with the same hostile condescension. This behavior is a ballet tradition as old as the five positions and dates from the time when the French despised the Italians and both decried the Russians and Danish. Even within Russia, there has always been ugly feeling between the Moscow and St. Petersburg schools, and considering that the dancers always ended up in the same theater, it made for a liveliness of atmosphere.

Ballet Theatre opened for the first time in the Metropolitan Opera House with the full panoply of Hurok's forces. They produced their *pièce de résistance,* Massine's *Aleko.* Outside of Chagall's superb sets, it had a dubious success. Then followed Massine's *Don Domingo,* which was a real bust. The members of the Ballet Russe were not gallant in their comments. I tried to keep my mouth shut but I couldn't help figuring that none of this hurt me. Then followed *Helen of Troy,* but Fokine had died of pneumonia in mid-rehearsals and his work, later pulled together by Lichine, was at its first performances in bits and pieces. We stood at the back of the theater and watched with grisly gratification. We rushed to whisper in rehearsal halls and behind costume trunks.

Sevastianov's curt dismissal still smoked in my vitals. He had also, while in Mexico City, sold or destroyed the sets and costumes for *Black Ritual,* something for which I have never to this day forgiven him.

We rehearsed upstairs at night while they went through their repertoire below.

Our season began. The same audience returned in the same evening clothes. One noted the same cheering, the same lining-up on the lobby stairs to see who had come, the same promenading of dress and manner and presence, the same greetings, the same wandering, inattentive eyes, the same babbling of technical jargon by would-be initiates, the same drinking away of half the ballets in Sherry's bar by the real initiates, to wit: Mr. Hurok and his weary staff. During the American season one half the group murmured praise, the other half scorn — the parts were reversed the next week. It made no great matter. It all happened between dinner and supper. Differences may have been noted by the people who were there because they loved dancing. Their opinion has always been less conspicuously expressed. But the young men prowling at the back of the auditorium, including the youth with spangles in his hair, were undisturbed. From their point of view nothing had changed.

I was spending a great deal of time at Karinska's — the costume executant — watching the fittings. Kermit Love, the designer, practically lived there. He said he stayed the nights too which is possible, though for what purpose I have yet to ascertain. He claimed he had the pants dyed and dried on his own legs so that they would look sun-faded and worn.

On Monday before the opening we showed the ballet to Aaron Copland and I, not Lubov Roudenko, for the first time danced. Massine practiced a barre at the back of the room throughout. He had no more business in that room than Lucia Chase, but bald curiosity compelled him to stay. Deakin came up to me at the start and whispered, "I see Bela Lugosi in fourth position back there." I didn't mind. I had so grown in confidence I didn't mind. There were only five guests, but there was a small ovation at the end. Massine came to the front of the room without comment to take charge of the next rehearsal, his *Rouge et Noir*. He sat on a chair with his back to the mirror.

During the hoe-down I had kicked off one of my slippers, and it had shot under the chair on which he was sitting. To retrieve it I had to get down on my hands and knees and fumble long-armed behind his feet. He did not move. He looked down at me with his staring enormous expressionless eyes. "I see you have done a lively ballet!"

"Haven't I?" I said, wiping the dirt off my hands and straightening up. "Yes, I think maybe I have."

We had an orchestra reading. Aaron Copland sat in the front row. I sat beside him until about the twelfth bar; then I shot up and down the aisle. The cleaning women wiping the red velvet seats stood up now and then to listen. Some of the dancers came between the crack of the great gold curtain to hear what their cues sounded like on the instruments.

Then, the afternoon of the opening, we had dress rehearsal. That is, the scenery was up, Oliver's lovely sets. Because of union prices, we only had one hour. There was no time to figure out entrances or exits or spaces. But those surprising ballet dancers figured everything for themselves. This was the moment experience paid off.

They solved on the instant every spatial and directional problem. I kept all my entire wits on myself and my own performance. Out in the red velvet auditorium in the endless scallops of empty seats sat Denham and Libidins and apart, very small and alone in a black tricorne, sat Mother.

I believe I didn't eat.

I was in the theater at six. I shared a star dressing room with Nathalie Krassovska. I had my costumes because I had personally gone to Karinska's and taken them away. I checked over every detail — bow, boots, belt, hat — again and again. Only two costumes this time, not fourteen. I did a careful barre. I put on my make-up. And then who should come into my dressing room and sink into the armchair but Mrs. Massine. She conversed with Krassovska in Russian, but as I stripped and redressed, she cast long appraising looks at my body. And she was a great beauty with the elegance and arrogance of a woman who has known since girlhood that things would come easily to her.

Kermit Love appeared pallidly in the door. "I'm so distressed," he sighed.

"Why?"

He hesitated. "They have made the collar to Milada's dress badly and you know how prettily I designed it."

"Oh, Kermit, for God's sake."

He faded away. Kermit lied like a gentleman. There was not a costume in the house, Milada's or anyone's. It was a tradition of Karinska that her clothes arrive piecemeal in a flotilla of taxis during the evening, some still with bastings and pins, and a half score of seamstresses in attendance to do last-minute sewing on dancers in the wings. The clothes were worn without trial of any sort. It is a tribute to her expertness that no accidents ever resulted. The wear and tear on the cast's nerves was, however, simply dreadful. Karinska has executed three ballets of mine. I have never had anything like complete costumes at the dress rehearsal. Why does anyone hire her a second time? Simply, she is without peer in her field.

Mrs. Massine did not stop talking for a minute. On and on and on she chattered. In Russian, thanks God, but noisily. I had only a few minutes to make my peace with heaven. *Rouge et Noir* had been on for a quarter hour. I stepped to the door partly dressed. Danilova beckoned me across the hall. "Agnes, I can help you with your hair. I will show you how to fix so it not come loose. These little secrets I learn through many years." She sat me at her dressing table and got to work with pins in her mouth. On the night of my debut Alexandra Danilova maided me — hairnets, barrettes, bobbies, elastics and ribbons.

Rouge et Noir was over. I went back to my room. Mrs. Massine raised languid amused eyes to my taut face. "Are you nairvous?" she drawled.

"I am," I said. "I am sick at my stomach."

"Good luck! Success!" she said punctiliously.

I turned to her quietly. "I hope we have success. The success or failure of my life depends on the next half hour. And I hope, for the company's sake, there is success. Much depends on this ballet for them, too. If I have failed them they are in a bad way. And they have worked hard, harder than you can imagine."

Under the façade Mrs. Massine like most people has a heart. She was confounded. "As you say," she murmured, "for all — success."

I walked onto the stage. Everyone I knew was out front. Mother had seen to that. She herself was in a box in black lace. Beside her sat Mary Meyer and Edward Johnson and Margaret. The refugee German of the violets and Martha Graham and Mary Hunter were there, and although I didn't know it until later, John Andrews from the Rambert Company, now an officer in His Majesty's Navy with six of the staff of his corvette. They made a fine blue and gold effect in a box complete with a bunch of red roses. And in another box, not by accident, sat Richard Rodgers, Oscar Hammerstein II and Theresa Helburn of the Theatre Guild. I had heard they were contemplating a play on Western cowboy life and I thought I could do good dances for them.

Mother alone was not nervous. "This is the first time I have not had to worry about the box office," she said serenely. "And I didn't have to spend the afternoon trying to impress my friends into coming."

The house was sold out.

Behind the gold curtain we stood in our cowboy pants, I among my men, nearly every one of whom has since become an important soloist. Beside Franklin stood Harold Lang, Casimir Kokic, James Starbuck, Robert Pagent, and David Tihmar, and waiting in the wings for a walk-on was Maria Tallchief, and beside her Betty Low, Dorothy Etheridge, Milada Mladova, and Vladimir Kostenko, who was to play Jud in the *Oklahoma!* ballet for six years. We were in our pants because the Karinska cabs had begun to arrive filled with hysterical seamstresses and pins. There was a great rustling of tissue paper in the wings. On one side flowers were being unwrapped, on the other, dresses and hats no one had ever seen. There was also a great deal of whispering as to who was to put on what. Behind every piece of scenery the company in tights and dressing gowns crouched watching, head on head, with painted and elongated eyes like the larvae of insects. On folding chairs behind the tormentor sat Danilova and Slavenska, crossing themselves, spitting, and looking on me with shining eyes. Franz Allers, the conductor, kissed me. "Here we go, Malinki," said Libidins. "Ham and eggs!"

Denham gave his blessing.

"I'm going in," said Allers, and he left to enter the pit.

Freddie spat over my shoulder and bumped his knee against my rump. He didn't say anything. He was tightening his belt and figuring out the spacing within the new set. His eyes darted back and forth. I moistened my lips. This was a terrible moment, but I had company. I was no longer alone. There were men standing all around me — very great dancers. I looked at their thighs and their shoulders and the intensity of their faces, and I knew I would never again be alone.

The large descending octaves sounded from the brass, sharp as sunlight on rocks. We flexed our insteps and breathed deep. The gold folds contracted. The music was suddenly clear under our feet. The naked, living dark yawned.

"This is it, kids," said Freddie, without moving his lips.

If it is possible for a life to change at one given moment, if it is possible for all movement, growth and accumulated power to become apparent at one single point, then my hour struck at 9:40, October 16, 1942. Chewing gum, squinting under a Texas hat, I turned to face what I had been preparing for the whole of my life.

This was not a great performance; we gave better later. Neither was it a great ballet. The style, as I always feared, did break. But it was the first of its kind, and the moment was quick with birth.

There was applause on my first exit. An unexpected bonus. There was applause or response on every phrase. Did the audience laugh on count eight as I had promised in July in California? They laughed, not just female titters, but real laughing with the sound of men's voices, and the laugh turned into handclapping. This happened again and again. The dancers were elated but not surprised. I had promised them laughs. The pantomime was spaced to accommodate them.

There were mishaps. At one point, Kokic grew confused with his new costumes and failed to make an entrance, leaving me to improvise a love scene, without partner, alone, and exposed for sixty-four bars of music on the Met stage. Lines were crooked. Some of the girls clapped off beat. It didn't seem to matter.

The pace of the performance rushed us like a wind. The audience were roused and urging us on. Great exchanges of excitement and force and gaiety were taking place all around. The dancers rushed and whirled, grabbing the right person, because the right person was there, though unrecognizable in an unexpected dress and hair-do. And throughout the pace which was too quick for me, beyond my understanding, faster than could be savored or appreciated, was Freddie's hand, Freddie's arm, Freddie's strong back, propelling, pushing, carrying, and Freddie's feet like bullets on the wood. It was beyond endurance. It was beyond help. It was slipping away too fast, too fast. Also my collar was too tight.

"Freddie," I said at the back of the stage, "I'm fainting. Loosen my collar."

"No time, duckie. Here we go."

And as though we were blown out of the mouth of a gun, he propelled me to the footlights. We separated. Bob, bob. (Which Robert, Madame?) All the trumpets and horns threw their shafts between us. We hung on the brink. The music tore open. We rushed. We clashed. We were lifted. And all the girls had faces like stars with their hair dropping over the boys' shoulders. The great curtain fell. There was dust in my nostrils from the dusty lining of the curtain. It was over. It was done. And I had made so many foolish mistakes. So many hasty things gone wrong. Once more I had been incapable of the perfect effort. "Oh, Freddie," I said gasping, "what a stinking, lousy performance. We must rehearse like demons tomorrow."

I looked at him wistfully but we were walking forward and we were all holding hands and bowing. A large bunch of American corn was put in my arms tied with red, white and blue ribbons. More flowers came, more flowers. The Russians did things this way. They also clapped and called out. Hadn't I stood grinding my teeth at the back of the house for years while they cheered bogus nonsense? We bowed and bowed. At the eighth bow, I looked into the pit. The fiddlers were beating their bows on their instruments. The others were standing up yelling. No one gets the union boys to do this easily. I looked at Freddie in amazement. "Freddie," I said, "this is not a claque. This is not Libidins's contriving."

"Darling, darling," said Freddie, kissing me, "this is an ovation. This is the real thing. Take it." He pushed me forward, and all the company backed away to the edge of the stage and stood there clapping.

We had twenty-two curtain calls.

The grips and members of the company helped me carry my flowers to the dressing room. They filled half the floor space. The doorman could not hold my friends in check.

In the hall between dressing rooms, I met Massine. He bowed

formally, and then apparently thought he must say something. He stared at me with his binocular eyes. "You have done a character-istic ballet." I struggled to follow this. "And in Europe I think it will have success." We bowed.

Mary Meyer sat at my dressing table crying and crying. "I can't stop," she said, mopping her nose. "It isn't that this is the most wonderful ballet I've ever seen. I've seen better. It's just that I can't stand you making a success after all these years."

"Aren't you proud of her?" said the friends to Mother. And Annie drew herself up to their shoulders and looking at them steadily with her penetrating blue eyes answered, "I've always been proud of her. Always. When no one hired her. I'll go home now and start the coffee."

And in the lobby Billy Rose was marching up and down shouting, "But where has she been? Why haven't we known about her? How could we have overlooked this talent?"

And Terry Helburn was phoning in a wire to Western Union: WE THINK YOUR WORK IS ENCHANTING. COME TALK TO US MONDAY.

I did some phoning of my own. I called Officer-Candidate School at the Aberdeen Proving Grounds and spoke to a soldier. "It is a success. It has made a furore."

"Oh," he said, "that does not surprise me. I knew it would."

He knew it would! He'd known me six months and seen nothing of my work at all. He took this evening for granted. Well so, miraculously, did my mother. But she had waited fourteen years, had sewn costumes, sold bonds, nagged at her friends to attend her girl's concerts, run errands, done without all luxuries, and hoped, and hoped, and hoped, steadily and without default in the face of reason and proof unlimited that her efforts would meet with no success. She was home now, serving coffee and chocolate cake and salad to all and sundry. This time the doors were wide open. Any-one could walk in.

C H A P T E R   2 6

The Contribution

WE HAD BREACHED the bulwarks, Tudor above all, then Ashton, de Valois, Eugene Loring, and I lastly. Two years later Jerome Robbins with *Fancy Free* was to confirm the new tradition. (George Balanchine, whom many consider the greatest living ballet choreographer, was no revolutionist. He worked in the direct line of development from a classic premise.) How did we differ? Beyond the individual works and the personal style, had we really made a new tradition?

Ballet gesture up to now had always been based on the classic technique and whatever deviated from this occurred only in comedy caricatures. The style throughout, the body stance, the walk, the run, the dynamic attack, the tensions and controls, were balletic even when national folk dances were incorporated into the choreography.

We were trying to diversify the root impulse and just as Gershwin impressed on the main line of musical development characteristics natural to his own unclassical environment, we were adding gestures and rhythms we had grown up with, using them seriously and without condescension for the first time. This is not a triviality; it is the seed and base of the whole choreographic organization. If dance gesture means anything, it means the life behind the movement.

The younger choreographers believed that every gesture must be proper to a particular character under particular circumstances. (In the classic ballets the great solos could be interchanged with no confusion from one ballet to another.) Tudor developed the story-telling quality of his choreography to such a degree that each gesture, formed out of the emotional components of the moment, is almost as explicit as though the dancers spoke. The new choreographer does not arrange old steps into new patterns; the emotion evolves steps, gestures, and rhythms.

And for this reason, the line between dancing and acting is no longer clearly marked — though by acting I do not mean realistic imitation. Consider the role of Hagar in *Pillar of Fire* (created by Nora Kaye) — a frustrated woman who gives herself to a man she does not love through fear of spinsterhood. Her turns are an agony of spirit, her repeated balances and falls a bewilderment and frustration, her leaps a striving for release. A sailor beside me, seeing her throw herself into the arms of a man she did not love, groaned aloud. He had, as it happened, just witnessed a passage of technical virtuosity very nearly beyond the scope of any other living dancer. But he was not aware of this and did not clap. He did not cheer. He groaned and said, "Oh, my God!" He could recognize trouble when he saw it.

Hagar's gestures were chosen with prayer and fasting. Antony Tudor worked with his dancers like research students shut away for months. He traveled with them, danced with them, practiced beside them day and night. Nora Kaye was rehearsed for a year, exploring with the choreographer every possible psychological overtone. He brooded over her, informed her so clearly with his idea that it is impossible to say where composition ends and performance begins. The fluttering of her eyelids, the smoothing of a dress, the pause and turn of head, the drawing in of breath, were as firmly set and as inviolate as a series of sixty-four pirouettes.

Contrast this with Massine's method, where the human bodies are used merely as units of design, grouped, lumped, and directed into predetermined masses. But as performers the dancers were called upon to go it blind and fell back on their own resources. And their resources were the classic technique and the Petipas and Fokine repertoire. The young man, for instance, who played the wolf in *St. Francis* was at work on the role for two weeks before he discovered that he was portraying a carnivorous animal and not an Italian adolescent. Frequently, the cast was not even clear about the plot of the ballet they were spending a summer in creating. And when Massine left the company and his enormous vitalizing influence was removed the gestures wore down through sheer unthinking repetition to the point where the performers could not have themselves explained what they were doing. Anything was permitted as long as toes were pointed and arms kept moving.

Between Fokine and Tudor stand Proust and Freud as well as Graham, the Ballets Jooss, and Mary Wigman. And lastly, it must never be forgotten that the new generation of choreographers is almost entirely English or American and our cultural heritage is different from the Slavic or Germanic folklore that influenced our forebears. We dance what we know about. The sailor watching Hagar recognized his own kind of misery. He does not particularly recognize himself in *Swan Lake*. Mind you, the sailor likes *Swan Lake*. But *Fancy Free, Pillar of Fire*, and, I think, *Rodeo* talk to him. Animals, birds, magicians, FATE, LOVE, BEAUTY, DEATH, and, above all, MAN, have largely disappeared. I, for one, had grown weary of MAN.

By the time I composed *Rodeo* I had crystallized a technique of composing. It was in essentials the same method I had fumbled with in my early pantomimes, but it has routined itself with the subsequent Broadway practice into a true discipline.

To make up a dance, I still need, as I needed then, a pot of tea, walking space, privacy and an idea. Although every piece I have done so far for a ballet company is a *ballet d'action* or story ballet, I have no preference for this type — quite the contrary — I think the lyric or abstract ballets more pleasing and much more enduring, but my knack has been for dramatics.

When I first visualize the dance, I see the characters moving in color and costume. Before I go into rehearsal, I know what costumes the people wear and generally what color and texture. I also, to a large extent, hear the orchestral effects. Since I can have ideas only under the stress of emotion, I must create artificially an atmosphere which will induce this excitement. I shut myself in a studio and play gramophone music, Bach, Mozart, Smetana, or almost any folk music in interesting arrangements. At this point I avoid using the score because it could easily become threadbare.

I start sitting with my feet up and drinking pots of strong tea, but as I am taken into the subject I begin to move and before I know it I am walking the length of the studio and acting full out the gestures and scenes. The key dramatic scenes come this way. I never forget a single nuance of them afterwards; I do usually forget dance sequences.

The next step is to find the style of gesture. This is done standing and moving, again behind locked doors and again with a gramophone. Before I find how a character dances, I must know how he walks and stands. If I can discover the basic rhythms of his natural gesture, I will know how to expand them into dance movement.

It takes hours daily of blind instinctive moving and fumbling to find the revealing gesture, and the process goes on for weeks before I am ready to start composing. Nor can I think any of this out sitting down. My body does it for me. It happens. That is why the choreographic process is exhausting. It happens on one's feet after hours of work, and the energy required is roughly the equivalent of writing a novel and winning a tennis match simultaneously. This is the kernel, the nucleus of the dance. All the design develops from this.

Having established a scenario and discovered the style and key steps, I then sit down at my desk and work out the pattern of the dances. If the score is already composed, the dance pattern is naturally suggested by and derived from the pattern of the music. If it remains to be composed as it does in all musical comedies, the choreographer goes it alone. This, of course, is harder. Music has an enormous suggestive power and the design of the composer offers a helpful blueprint.

All I know about dance composition I learned from folk dances. These are trustworthy models because they are the residuum of what has worked; there is no folk dance extant that did not work. I had first become aware of the importance of folk dancing when Dr. Lily Campbell asked me to reconstruct medieval singing games for her class in English Drama. I have studied folk forms since where possible. It must be remembered that outside of Louis Horst's classes in preclassic dance forms, choreography is taught nowhere and there are no texts on the subject. I learned by trial and error as did all my colleagues.

Through practice I have learned to project a whole composition in rough outline mentally and to know exactly how the dancers will look at any given moment moving in counterpoint in as many as five groups. As an aid in concentration, I make detailed diagrams and notes of my own arbitrary invention, intelligible only to me and only for about a week, but they are not comparable in exactness to music notation.

At this point, I am ready, God help me, to enter the rehearsal hall.

I don't believe any choreographer ever overcomes his terror of the waiting company. Imagine a composer facing the New York Philharmonic with his score projected in his head, not a note on paper, and the task before him of teaching the symphony by rote to the waiting men. He could start by whistling the main theme to the first violins.

Well, there they stand, the material of your craft, patient, disciplined, neat and hopeful in their black woolens. They will offer you their bodies for the next several weeks to milk the stuff of your ideas out of their muscles. They will submit to endless experimentation. They will find technique that has never been tried before; they will submerge their personalities and minds to the blindest, feeblest flutterings of yours. They will remember what you forget. They are pinning all the hopes of their past practices and future performings on the state of your brains. There they stand and consider you as you walk into the room. If they know you and are fond of you, it's easier. But at best, it's a soul-challenging moment.

The choreographer is apt to be short-tempered and jumpy at these times; he has not only to face the psychological problems of mastering and guiding a group of human beings, but all the problems of composition simultaneously. I take comfort in hot coffee. With the friendly warmth of a carton between my hands and the steaming rim to hide my face in, and the piping hot reassurance in my stomach, I can just manage to step out on the floor and make a suggestion. Dancers very quickly learn to hand me coffee before they ask a taxing question such as "What do we do next over here?" I find a ring of cartons waiting around my chair in the morning.

It's a good idea to give the company for a beginning something definite and technically difficult to get their feet down on. The minute they start to sweat they feel busy and useful. Like Tudor, I always try to start with two or three dancers I know who are sympathetic to my suggestion, and I have learned to have the rehearsal planned through to the end, preferably on a piece of paper in case I dry up mentally. Standing and scratching one's head while the dancers cool off in their tights, and then put on extra sweaters, and then sit down on the floor, and then light cigarettes and start to talk, is what one wishes to avoid. No group of workers in the world is slower to lose faith or interest, but they are human. While you are struggling to find the exact phrasing they get tired in the back of their knees. And when you ask them to get off the floor and try the jump in the eighteenth variation they rise creaking. Then you grow hot with anger that you cannot solve the problem and punish their bodies for your own stupidity, forcing them to do it again and again and again, pretending that it is their lack of performance quality that invalidates the idea. But no one is fooled. Neither you nor they. You scold them. And your company quietly grows to hate you. They are now more or less useless for your purposes. If you were working with marble you could hack at it for a year without any deterioration of material. If you were writing a book you could lay down your pen, take a walk, take a nap, have some coffee and come back to find your manuscript just as you left it. But dancers stand with patient drawn faces waiting for your brains to click.

One could simply terminate a rehearsal and wait for a more fruitful moment. But after all, the dancers are there to work, the hall is rented, the pianist hired and attentive.

There are, however, the times when one scrapes absolute bottom. The manner in which he deals with these moments is the exact measure of a choreographer's experience. Balanchine dismisses a rehearsal without any ado at all and goes home. If, on the other hand, he likes what he is doing, hell can break loose around him and he pays not the slightest mind. Short of hell he nearly always is surrounded by a roomful of chattering, knitting, practicing dancers and visitors. Massine holds the entire company in the room. They sit for hours sometimes while he wrestles with one or two soloists. If he gets stuck he keeps it to himself as he never explains a single thing he is doing to anyone he is working with. Martha Graham sends her group from the room and has it out with God. I cannot endure the sight of one person sitting down waiting. A sense of guilt and tedium oppresses me exactly as though I were failing a guest. I, therefore, allow in the room with me only the people I am working with, never any visitors, and inside the rehearsal room no one may sit down or chew gum or smoke. I have to keep myself geared to such a pitch that if I relax or allow the dancers to relax the rehearsal for all effective purposes is over. Outside in the waiting room or hall they may do as they like — drink, chew, eat, gossip, play cards. This pertains to the beginning weeks. When the composition stands by itself on the floor and is no longer a matter of hypnotism between me and the group, everything is easier.

But with all the good planning possible, there comes sooner or later the inevitable point of agony when the clock dictates and one must just set one's teeth and get on with it. Then one wrings the ultimate out of one's marrow. The astonishing fact is that it is there to be wrung.

The dancers themselves frequently help. For the very reason

they are human and have wills and imaginations and styles of their own, their manner of moving will suggest an infinite number of ideas to the choreographer. They can evoke where clay and canvas cannot. The minute the choreographer moves a tentative hand or places a foot forward, they are behind him imitating. The stimulus of their interest will excite him. He will improvise beyond his expectations. He may not know exactly what he has done. But bright-eyes has seen; the gesture is immediately reproduced. The choreographer can then turn around and watch his idea on someone else's body. This he can correct and edit. A sensitive performer needs only a hint, a breath, and he is off, the rhythms generated in his body helping to push the design ahead.

When I have verified certain ideas on my test dancers (if I get two or three good gestures in two hours I consider the morning well spent. Half a dozen pages of notes can boil down to three jumps filling in all about five seconds of time), I call in the group and teach them together, using the first performers as models.

Sometimes the solo figures are developed first and the group patterns blocked in behind like the orchestration to a melody. Sometimes when the soloist has simple dramatic or storytelling movement the group is set first and the soloist added. In these cases I go to the back of the theater where I can get a perspective of the stage and add on the soloist by shouted direction. Bambi Linn is so responsive to group movement that she can interpret instructions invented on the moment and screamed out while the dance is in full progress.

Big designs are largely headwork and must be visualized in advance. Obviously a large group is too disparate an instrument on which to improvise — until it is aroused.

Such times are memorable. They usually occur when the group is exhausted after hours of work, late in a studio at the dinner hour or at night in the theater when everyone else has gone home. There, in absolute privacy and with no impatience to be gone to other concerns, working together in perfect community of understanding, the moment comes. And quite simply every single performer knows what to do as though he were inside the composer's head. In this art, the interpreters are present at the actual moment of creation and if they share the labor they also know some of the glory. They are grateful for this and stand abashed and wondering. And so, by God, does the choreographer.

Choreographers have notoriously poor memories. And for a group that has no documentation of their work this is unfortunate. Possibly they keep in mind as I do the variants to each step. This tends to be confusing. Certainly most dancers remember through their muscles and as a consequence can remember only what they have themselves performed. Music is an enormous memory aid, But where the original dancers cannot be brought together for purposes of revival much of the original detail is always lost. Some works disappear entirely with each change of personnel. All of Martha Graham's early group compositions, for instance. There was nothing like these great works in all of dance literature. Nor will she ever compose in this vein again. We have suffered an irreparable loss.

Even in the more durable ballet companies when the choreographer is absent personal idiosyncrasies of style gradually work alterations that in a few years make the dance unrecognizable. In a repertoire of twenty-five or thirty ballets every role is remembered by heart. All the choreography of the old classic ballets is handed down from generation to generation entirely through tradition. But in this case the task is not too difficult. As they were composed in the exact idiom that is taught daily in every ballet class and as the steps and positions are rigidly prescribed there is less chance for variation.

Without the aid of a camera, however, it is almost impossible to preserve the more experimental modern choreography. Very few choreographers have used moving pictures to record their work, largely, I suppose, because of the cost.

Given a fair chance, the dancer will remember, and fairly accurately, the documentation of the work. Learning everything by rote, retaining the entire repertoire in his head, he is probably the quickest learner and the most retentive in all the performing arts.

In the spring of 1948, on the opening day of Ballet Theatre's season at the Metropolitan Opera House, Nora Kaye, one of the company's two ballerinas, was taken without warning to the hospital with virus pneumonia, three hours before the curtain rose. She had no understudy in *Lilac Garden*. Alicia Alonso had performed it twice six years previously and not at all in the interim. She used the supper hour to refresh her memory under Tudor's coaching, opened the bill with a Balanchine piece, went back upstairs to the rehearsal hall during *Tally-Ho* and then four hours after the first frantic phone call performed the work in question, a role of real intricacy and twenty minutes' duration without a single mistake. Bear in mind there was no score for her to study. This prodigy of memory is in a class with the Toscanini legend; but he has all his needed scores on his library shelves.

A more spectacular example occurred this spring (1951). In the first movement of William Dollar's *Chopin Concerto*, Norma Vance, first soloist, hurt her foot and was unable to continue. Paula Lloyd, working in the corps, who had merely watched the solo rehearsals, stepped in a few bars later and finished the ballet to the end without rehearsal of any kind. What's more she maintained her place in the ranks simultaneously stepping in and out of the solo role as need arose. It was this extraordinary act of professionalism that prompted Virgil Thomson to remark beside me, "These are the most highly trained people in the theater, far, far better disciplined than opera singers."

❧

The circumstances which governed the creation of *Rodeo* were not unusual; nearly all ballets are composed just this way — with the company in full motion. If there were difficulties there were also enormous advantages not to be found in other forms of the musical theater. In the first place, the company was a unit and had worked together for years. Furthermore, they were all dancers with a uniform training and discipline. The cast of a musical play on the other hand I knew would be made up of a heterogeneous group, dancers from various schools, actors, singers, acrobats, all ages and sizes. If I did the new Rodgers-Hammerstein show I was going to have to face this situation. And there would be other problems as well. In a ballet company choreography is the essential element and the choreographer complete, total boss toward whom all artists bend their will in the interest of a common success. The drawbacks, not enough money, not enough rehearsal time, and always exhaustion, do not overbalance the advantages of scope and power.

In a musical play all would be different: the dances would have to suit the book; they would have to build the author's line and develop his action, adding an element not obtainable through acting or singing and necessary if for no other reason than their dynamic effect. The problem of preserving character, period atmosphere and style would be a tough one since the bulk of the play would be performed realistically in a style as divorced from dance gesture as speaking is divorced from singing. Transition was accordingly going to have to become a fine art, for if the audience could not be swung from dramatic dialogue through song into dance and back again without hitch, the dance would be destroyed. The choreographer was going to have to learn surgery, to graft and splice.

Furthermore, in this medium the dance director was no longer boss or anything like. By tradition the composer was tyrant although Oscar Hammerstein was to prove shortly that the author of the book might be equally important. The director had some say and also the producer, but the dance director not much. The designers were never charged to protect the dancing. They were told only to fill the stage with color, to see that the girls looked lovely whether they could move or not, to favor the star and to do something sufficiently splashy to get more shows to design. If the dancing was hobbled or overweighted, it never reflected on anyone but the choreographer. The duration of numbers would be strictly limited — because of course for every minute of dancing there would be one less minute of singing or acting, something the composer, author and director never forgot. Besides it had been estab-

lished long since, had it not, that the general public was less interested in dancing than in anything else?

Compared to a ballet schedule, the rehearsal time, five weeks,
seemed unlimited, but I knew from past heartbreaking experience
better. I would get the dancers, it is true, for seven hours a day
(the Equity maximum) for one week, and they would not be rehearsing any other ballets or performing at night. But the second
week they would be called for the staging of songs and crowd
scenes, and the third week they would be taken constantly for
costume fittings. The fourth week would be cut up with run-
throughs of the whole play and the fifth devoted entirely to traveling to the out-of-town theaters and dress rehearsals. If the
dances weren't largely completed by the end of the second week, I
would be sunk. This was a harsh time sheet.

But every aspect was challenging. If I had to fit dances to the
story, the story itself might suggest much. If the score were good
and the songs witty, they might help further and the music would
be composed to the dancing right in the rehearsal hall and orchestrated only after the dance was completed. I could order exactly
what I wanted at the moment on the spot. The other members of
the creative staff might be more powerful but they were not ungifted.
One did not have to take full responsibility alone. One had great
collaborators. And there was money for anything reasonable one
needed, and one could pick one's cast at will. And last and most
wonderfully, the curtain would not go up in New York until all had
been brought to shining, lustrous perfection. Not a single risk
would be tolerated. Not one.

I'd broken my neck in the musical theater several times before
but I'd learned quite a lot in the process. I had had to learn to
adapt myself to emergency, time and human frailty, and to accept
men in the theater — in particular, managers. I had had to discipline myself to avoid risk, to stop providing myself with an alibi
for (or means to) failure. I had had to learn the difference between
the bearable fatigue and the unbearable, the fatigue of fear. The
first can be cured by a night's sleep; the second kills. I had had to

find the strength to fail and fail and keep thinking, to come up at last with the idea that works. This is what men pay salaries for — more even than for good taste and vision. I felt quite confident. I did not, in fact, have a qualm, which, considering my history, is inexplicable. Richard Rodgers, who did not know my history, had qualms. He recognized clearly the crucial difference between the two media. Hammerstein hoped for the best, and Lawrence Langner, who had seen a good deal of my work, thought I might bring something fresh to the production.

But even after the success of *Rodeo*, I just barely succeeded in getting the new Rodgers-Hammerstein-Theatre Guild show. Indeed I had heard nothing official until I met Oscar Hammerstein, by chance, in a New York drugstore and knocked a plate off the counter in my haste to speak to him. Dick had qualms, he said. I continued pressing until Dick capitulated.

When I started my tour with the Ballet Russe I had the promise of the dances for the musical version of Lynn Riggs's play *Green Grow the Lilacs*. For I was to tour with the Ballet Russe de Monte Carlo as guest star.

On the first night I had received $27.50, a combination royalty and performance salary. Libidins gave it to me in cash in a dark corner of the stage, knowing that I needed the money badly and that the Ballet Russe checks were slow in coming. He whispered to me that they wanted me to travel with the company right across the continent and dance in all the big cities, and for this I was to get something like a salary.

So, on the tour in my suitcase went a blank copybook labeled *Lilacs* with pages entitled "Ballet" — "Many a New Day," "Cowmen and the Farmer," "Kansas City," "Jud's Postcards," and as I sat happily in hotel bedrooms, I made notes —

"Laurie sits under a tree thinking. She is worried. Downstage left she appears to herself dressed in her own dress, but with a wreath on her head. The music changes to 'Beautiful Morning.' She is moving about in her morning and taking possession of her world. She is to be a bride."

CHAPTER 27

Beautiful Morning

I REJOINED the Russians in Chicago and wishing to spend Thanksgiving with my soldier who could procure only sixteen hours away from O.C.S., I had relinquished the *première* in that city, and took over only after Rudenko had introduced the work. And this was a strange thing: I had spent my life longing to get on the great stages and now that I could at last, I was passing up the opportunities quite carelessly and it seemed to me the only possible course of action.

We traveled west to San Francisco, the city of my mother's birth, the city where *Progress and Poverty* had been planned and written. The great hills sloped down to the water, the hills about which my mother had talked all her life, now green with the first rains, and silky with mists from the wine country. The mists lay on the water where the enormous transports waited, and on the docks alongside the army trains unloaded and unloaded and unloaded. I sat on a cliff and watched the gulls wheel up. "Please God," I said, "let him not be sent to the East." A submarine net stretched across the harbor, the gulls screamed and dipped. There were the clank of machines and chains and the grating of wheels on new tracks. The gulls rose in a scattering whorl from before the War Memorial Opera House (World War I Memorial). The gulls had been my grandfather's favorite bird, Mother always said, the sailor's bird. Gulls meant land ahead. The great late harvest moon lifted and hung, and inside the Opera House we danced for auditoriums of men that were saying good-by. We danced our folk piece, reminding ourselves and them a little of what we had grown up with.

"*Rodeo* is refreshing and as American as Mark Twain," wrote Alfred Frankenstein in the *San Francisco Chronicle*. "It is much the kind of ballet that Mark Twain might have written if his mind had run to ballets. . . ."

By the time we reached Los Angeles, we were in good order. Opening night was for me an unprecedented return. What higher satisfaction could there be than to go back after all the troubles with the most famous ballet company extant, in my own work, a score by our leading composer, brilliant *décor*, and for my partner a great virtuoso?

The Philharmonic Auditorium (where as a child I had heard all my first symphonies, where I had dreamed through musical matinees of doing solos on this very stage) was packed to the roof. The orchestra played splendidly. We danced and acted as never before, and my father sat throughout hearing the laughs turn into hands, hearing the hands turn into calls. I faced about at the end, dripping and breathing and spent, my arms filled with carnations and roses, toward the wings and there, in the exact spot I had stood as a girl waiting to see Anna Pavlova, there under the great column spots stood Pop, smiling and radiant. He was waiting for me. And around about him stood the scouts from the big studios, and the agents, and the musical movie producers. Pop smiled wryly and nodded. Gray and patient, not so tall as before, doubting and trusting with the same smile, his beautiful brown eyes burning black with attention, he nodded and smiled. Haven, fortress, alpha and omega! I dropped the flowers and was gathered home. His suit still smelled of cigar smoke. He still cleared his throat and chuckled as he patted my hair awkwardly.

"My daughter," he said, "you have come a long way. I am so proud." He could not go on. The agents and scouts moved aside and left us. We stood quietly together. My grease paint came off all over his suit lapel.

"There now," said Pop, "this is a good job. You can be well pleased. Go speak to your friends. I'll drive you home."

Pop's adoring university students came loyally in droves and the English department from U.C.L.A., all now devoting their gifts to teaching young officers to write simple declarative sentences with subjects and predicates, and my classmates in uniform, and Warren who got leave from ship welding and was about to be married, and Carmalita, and Richard Pleasant, a captain in the artillery, who kissed my hand and took me dancing.

I waved aside the studio scouts by explaining I had to go East to do a Broadway musical about early life in the West. I talked a little about the new job to Father. He took all my personal episodes very quietly. He trusted in the natural course of events I'd marry and that some instinct would keep me from making a fool of myself. We talked entirely about work. But now I no longer cried; I argued and chivied with considerable belligerence. When I grew too heated he retired into his beer.

I parted with the ballet in Los Angeles and hurried to New York.

I went for my first interview very firm and determined. Hammerstein seemed understanding but as I had found out, one never could tell. First, I informed him, I must insist that there be no one in the chorus I didn't approve. I sat up quite straight; as I spoke I looked very severe. "Oh pshaw!" he murmured. He was sorry to hear I was going to take that attitude — there was his regular girl, and Lawrence Langner had two, and Dick Rodgers always counted on some. For one beat, I took him literally, there being no trace of anything except earnestness in his face, and then I relaxed on that score for the rest of my life.

I heard the enchanting music. At these auditions, Oscar always read the role of Aunt Eller. Certainly it has never been played so well since. I remember the gasp that went around the room after "Beautiful Morning." Dick looked up from the keyboard and smiled abstractedly. He and his assistant, Margot Hopkins, together at double pianos, always accompanied auditions. They played very many these days. They were having a dreadful time raising money.

I advised them to drop from the score "People Will Say We're in Love," a song shortly to become one of the most lucrative hits of the century.

There were conferences and casting. My contract with the Guild called for a meager cash payment and no royalties, and I was to get no further rights of any kind. After all costs were paid off, they promised I should receive an additional five hundred dollars.

A great reservoir of talent had been gathering in the studios for years waiting for some sort of chance, and I had been watching the young dancers mature in daily practice. The *Oklahoma!* line-up was accordingly without parallel. But just for appearance' sake, we took in two chorus girls. They seemed terrified at the vigorous company they found themselves suddenly in and sat or stood locked close together from pure loneliness. The rest were dancers. I obtained the leading role for my good friend, the beautiful Katharine (Katya) Sergava, late of Ballet Theatre. There was a deal of heated argument during the choosing of the chorus. Helburn and Rouben Mamoulian wanted slim legs above all. I wanted talent and personality. Rodgers wanted faces, but was inclined to stand by me on many occasions. His idea and my idea of a face, I found, had frequently to do with the character in it. Oscar wasn't around. Langner was in Washington. We finally chose all but three. Mamoulian rejected my candidates categorically. "They're certainly not pretty. They can't act. Possibly, they can dance. That's your department. They're useless to me."

Two of them were my pupils. I knew they could act. All three could dance. I staged my first tantrum. "If I don't have them, I'll quit the show."

Mamoulian shrugged. "Then just keep them out of my way."

Their names were Joan McCracken, Bambi Linn, and Diana Adams.

The Guild was on the verge of bankruptcy. We worked in their old theater on 52nd Street which they did not clean for economic reasons. Mamoulian took the stage. I worked below in what had been the foyer and way above in what had been costume and rehearsal rooms, and with the assistance of Marc Platt and Ray Harrison I kept three rehearsals going at once. I was like a pitcher that had been overfilled; the dances simply spilled out of me. I had girls and boys in every spare corner of the theater sliding, riding, tapping, ruffling skirts, kicking. We worked with tremendous excitement, but always under great strain. For the first three days Richard Rodgers never left my side. He sat with fixed surgical attention watching everything. This made the dancers nervous, but it was I who really sweated. He did not relax until the third afternoon, when smiling and patting me on the shoulder he gave the first intimation that on this show I would not be fired.

Rodgers is not only a very great song writer, he is one of the most astute theater men in the world. He concerns himself zestfully and relentlessly with every detail of production. Nothing escapes his attention and he takes vigorous and instant action. This might be interfering if he were not sensitive, sensible and greatly experienced. He knows also when to keep his hands off. Mamoulian and the Guild frequently said, "It can't be done." It was always Rodgers who urged, "Let's see."

Our director, Rouben Mamoulian, provided daily challenge. He was used to complete, unquestioned authority and total obedience. As a choreographer in a ballet company, I was used to the same. But here I was no longer Madame the choreographer. I was the dance director in the basement, and although I began work with a respect for him that amounted to hero worship, we immediately ran head on in jurisdictional disputes. I think I can confidently say I would have gone down under the conflicting opinions if Richard Rodgers had not lent me his incomparable knowledge and authority as running interference. Due to his jealous care, my work came shining through for whatever it was worth.

But we all got increasingly nervous. I lost my temper at every thwarting. And when Terry Helburn started interrupting rehearsals to show unfinished work to prospective backers in her frantic efforts to raise money, I blew every fuse I had. Hurling my pocketbook at her head, I shouted and denounced and was dragged off screaming by Marc Platt one day and held under a faucet of cold water until I quieted down.

Once, when my ballet was unnecessarily interrupted, not by Miss Helburn this time, during a run-through, I gave a scream of anguish and hurled myself on Oscar Hammerstein's bosom. He was taken quite unaware and looked down startled at the hysteria on his waistcoat, but it was the comment from the rear rows that really surprised him. "Agnes," said Mother peremptorily, "control yourself."

I snapped up as though a ruler had been applied to my hand. I trust Oscar got over his surprise. I've continued to hurl myself on the same spot for years now. His is the largest and most receptive bosom in the Western Hemisphere.

All the dances in the show were set within two weeks. I set double the amount that was kept. I put the ballet together on the second Sunday when everyone else was home resting and we showed it intact the next night at the first run-through. The cast seemed impressed.

The youngest member of the troupe, Kenneth LeRoy, came down with German measles and retired temporarily from rehearsals, but not before he had infected nine or ten of us. Due to the length of the incubation period, however, we were not made aware of this until we reached Boston. I developed a lethal cough.

We worked feverishly, frantically. I had no other interest, my soldier having gone to Omaha. I wrote him constant bulletins. Of course, he really did not know what I was talking about, not having seen any of my work, nor any ballet at all for that matter. I wrote anyway.

A. de M. to W. P. *N.Y. February 23, 1943*

They sent me home in the afternoon, so I've napped and redone one dance, and now I must go to sleep again because I've just got to get well. Besides all the work to do, there's disorganization, demoralization and confusion while I lie at home coughing.

I'm well again. There was no chance of any rest so nature coped. I blew my lungs in and out of my mouth like a bubble for a week. Now I don't. And I can laugh without paroxysms of the diaphragm, though Libidins asked me last night if I were studying *Traviata*. Nearly all the important dances are done, only bits and pieces left. I never worked so fast in my life. I've set forty minutes of straight dancing in less than three weeks. The company raves. Rodgers put his head on my shoulder this afternoon and said, "Oh, Aggie, you're such a comfort in my old age." And Marc Platt, my leading dancer, said this evening, "In all soberness, I never worked with anyone I respected more." Katya has made a hit. I've discovered two girls who are going to be sensations, my two leading men *are males* and also the stage manager, so rehearsals are lively and gay. We live in the basement. I see sunlight only twenty minutes each day. The dust from the unvacuumed Guild rugs has made us all sick, and I put away three Thermos bottles of coffee an afternoon. I look awful. Thin, old, and hard. A rumor came down from upstairs, where the grownups work, that Mamoulian (Mamoo, he is called) did something good at eleven-thirty.

Hurok sent for me. He wants two ballets and he wants them this summer.

Libidins sends you greetings. *Rodeo* plays every night to howling success. I asked how the performances were. "In my opinion, pretty lousy, but it seems to make no difference."

Suddenly the five weeks of rehearsal were gone and we had to leave for New Haven. I had coughed and cursed and quarreled. I had run from the stage to the basement and back to the roof. Everyone was worried, At lunch, Celeste Holm held forth on what was wrong with the playing of the comedy scenes. At dinner, I groused about the ensembles. We worried and groused and fretted. I knew the show had possibilities of greatness, but it was being wrecked, wrecked, wrecked. I myself was doing only a hack job.

It could be nothing else since I was composing so fast and easily. I wrote my father as much. He said to stop talking and get on with it. There was only one man who rode the froth quietly and failed to turn a hair.

"Do you know what I think is wrong?" said Richard Rodgers as we sat on the stage one midnight. "Almost nothing. Now why don't you all quiet down?" He has learned to worry since, although he has persuaded himself that he never really frets. But that is one of his really endearing vanities. He has become one of the most nervous rehearsers in the business. In 1943, with a great deal at stake, he was blithely sanguine. As for me, I was convinced we were failing, but my deep concern lay elsewhere. Every night at eleven, I turned on the war news, drank one glass of sherry and wrote a long letter west.

So we traveled to New Haven on Tuesday afternoon and now everybody's temper went absolutely to pot. I began to become aware of Oscar Hammerstein, who had stayed up to this point almost exclusively in the book rehearsals. He sat through the endless nights quietly giving off intelligence like a stove. He never got angry or hasty or excited, but when people were beating their heads on the orchestra rail made the one common-sense suggestion that any genius might think of if he was not at the moment consuming himself. Lawrence Langner expounded. Terry Helburn snapped and badgered and barked at our heels, with a housekeeper's insistence on detail. Mamoulian created in spite of the hour and other people's nerves. But Oscar just quietly pointed the way.

To W. P.   *New Haven, March 10th*

We're working around the clock now. Thursday we open. Dick Rodgers took my hand in his yesterday and said, "I want to thank you for doing a distinguished job."

There's hell ahead and unless we pull the show up very quick we're sunk. On Fridays, I have hysterics . . .

Kurt Weill and both ballet companies (Ballet Russe and Ballet Theatre) are crawling up and down the back of my neck. I've grown old like a stick but Katya says in Boston she will help me shop and buy a trousseau. I looked at myself in a full-length mirror and received the surprise of my life. I've lived off Italian food (next door to the Guild) and sandwiches for five weeks and done literally nothing but sit on my behind and shout, but miraculously the coughing has shaken off the fat I expected to accumulate. I'm as slim as a boy through the shank. The behind I dreaded simply is not there. Oh jubilation!

When you phone, make it collect. The Guild pays my bills up to $10.00 a day.

New Haven, March 13th

You haven't been getting my letters so you haven't followed what's been going on. All Broadway shows are simply fierce during rehearsals, but this one has been insanity. And only Dick Rodgers has kept me from flouncing out. That and the fact that my life is grounded now and none of this nonsense can touch me . . . Oh yes . . . and the night of the dress rehearsal when I was ordered off the stage for the second time while I was placing dances and then twenty minutes were taken to show boys how to bang pots in a chivaree (something they'd rehearsed steadily for three weeks), I blew a fuse and was dragged out by the stage manager and given coffee and I talked about how I never, never would forgive and suddenly I found myself talking about how I loved you and I talked and talked. And he was smiling at me and I stopped embarrassed and said, "This has nothing to do with the rehearsal." And he said, "But now you can go back to it and run it." And I said, "Now I can run the world." And we skipped back and did. And the next night the first dance stopped the show cold and Dick Rodgers standing beside me threw his arms around me and hugged and hugged.

Half of the audience on opening night was from New York. "The wrecking crew," Ruth Gordon has called them. Agents, backers, theatrical lawyers, first-night hounds, all came up, liked a few things enormously and left early to catch the train and take the news back that it was, on the whole, definitely not a success.

March 14th

Today both Langner and Helburn came to me and thanked me and volunteered the promise of more money than my contract called for. They're going to give me a bonus.[1]

Kurt Weill came to see the show this afternoon. He doesn't think it's good. (It's not but it may succeed.) But he still wants me to do his show, so that's something.

To dinner and back to the God damn theater. Oh for a movie instead! But you'll take me to a movie, won't you?

I hoped to spend the trip to Boston reading a detective story but I reckoned without the Guild. They hired a drawing room on the train. We all crowded into it and in three and one half hours rewrote the play, chiefly the second act. I was ordered to produce a small three-minute dance in twenty-four hours. I did. But the skin came off the girls' ribs from continuous lifting, and I couldn't seem to stop throwing up. The first night in Boston with the new script was pretty rocky and the press only fair. But funny thing, people went home down the sidewalks singing, and they wanted to come back. No one seemed very excited but suddenly we were sold out.

Lawrence made a list of everything to be done on a yellow pad with a program. The various departments were allotted time on stage exactly like astronomers scheduled for the hundred-inch telescope. Lawrence policed the theater with a large watch in his hand and there was no reprieve possible from his "I'm very sorry, my dear." Every night after the show sharp council was held. I have never seen a group of people work harder and faster except perhaps the same group during the *Carousel* tryout. The entire play was reorganized in two weeks and new long numbers staged — the entire *Oklahoma!* number, for instance.

At this point the play was called *Away We Go*. There were con-

[1] $50 a week augumented four years later to a small percentage.

ferences about a change of title. *Oklahoma* was suggested but it
didn't seem like a very good title. Lawrence declared himself satisfied if an exclamation point was added. Would people go to see
something with a plain, geographical title, we asked. Armina,
Lawrence's wife, had been born out there and she thought, with
great fervor, they would.

In pure exhaustion, I decided one evening to forego dinner and
have a nap instead. I was barely bedded when the phone rang.
Maria had broken out in spots and no understudy was ready. An
hour later I was on stage in Maria's dress and bonnet. Next day
I came out in spots.

Boston, March 23rd

So now I have German measles and can stay at home and
write you more letters. This morning's message swept me
through rehearsals with great gusto, well spotted out as I grew
momentarily. Katya is now having acute nervous indigestion.
Terry is in bed with ice bags on her head. Mrs. Hammerstein
runs a temperature that won't stop. But there are others
nothing happens to. If only this were real measles, I'd have a
brand-new skin all over me and when you saw me in that
you'd die — brand new all over, pale, translucent, pink, like a
baby's stomach.

I'm going to read a detective story now and then I'm going
to fall asleep dreaming of the clothes I shall buy to ravish you
with. I want your battalion to gape with envy and Prude's Ag
to become synonymous with all that's provocative, an Omaha
byword. Mamoulian said to me last night at dinner, "Why is
it all great dancers never give a damn how they look?"

Boston, March 26, 27

I've had three beautiful days doing nothing, sleeping,
eating, with Katya and Johnny, receiving flowers, sleeping,
reading the Constitution of the United States and a Perry
Mason mystery, sleeping, trailing around the Ritz in my brown
velvet dressing gown to midnight conferences with the bosses
who wanted to cut my work without my concurrence, sleeping, thinking of meeting you in ten days — afternoon or eve-

ning and this time could you meet the train? And what should I wear to delight you the most? Receiving phone calls from my kids, hourly reports — Margit had fever but Vivian had done extremely well in her place, Marc had bruised the bone in his foot, Ray would do the "bells" for him, Marc was proceeding very well with rehearsals on *Kansas City* (phone call from Marc as I write this — Joan McCracken passed out cold during performance). So I continued doing nothing. Tomorrow I go back to the slaughter. All the bosses (except Johnny and I) believe we have a smash hit. The houses are selling out. I don't care at all — at all. I sit by the window and hear a wonderful old bell tolling the hours in a beautiful old church tower. And April seems imminent in the buds on Boston Common.

March 27

Thank you for breakfast gay and good because of your wire. I rushed to the theater in singing spirits. Marc had all but fractured his foot and was ordered not to dance for a week. McCracken's attack had been nervous exhaustion resulting in suffocation — no less. Margit fainted every time she jumped, two of the leads and one of the best girls out of every number. The matinee went on today in good order. This is a remarkable troupe. The actors are dumfounded. They've never seen such stamina before; they've never worked with real dancers.

My memory of this time is chiefly a sense of well-being and excitement, lying in my luxurious Ritz bedroom, listening for the sound of the wheels on the little serving tables as breakfast arrived, possibly with the letter from the West. The snow fell lightly. There were daffodils and apple blossoms in the lobby and the old bell tolled in the church near the Common. Much was going to happen — very much. I was going to be married, for one thing.

During the last dress rehearsal in New York, some musician struck a wrong note — Diana Adams's face contracted with pain. It was not annoyance or amusement, it was agonized concern.

Richard Rodgers saw the expression and marveled. That look had never crossed a chorus girl's face; he was aware (as were not all of us?) that responsible artists had entered the ranks. Diana's expression marked the beginning of a new era. I remember going up to the Ballet Arts School the day of the opening and finding her and Bambi Linn sweating through two classes. I ordered them home to rest but I had to enlist the help of the teacher to make them leave the floor.

The first night was by no means sold out. The Guild subscription had fallen very low. I had ten front-row balcony seats and I didn't know whom to give them to. I think a couple remained empty. I stood at the back beside Rodgers and the staff. Oscar, who was calm, sat with his wife.

Marc's foot was very bad, but he said if he lost his leg he would dance the opening so a doctor anesthetized it. He danced on a frozen leg and foot. He had to be cut out of his boot afterwards.

I stood at the back in Margaret's black evening dress. Rodgers held my hand. The curtain went up on a woman churning butter; a very fine baritone came on stage singing the closest thing to lieder our theater has produced. He sang exquisitely with his whole heart about what a morning in our Southwest is like. At the end, people gave an audible sigh and looked at one another — this had seldom happened before. It was music. They sat right back and opened their hearts. The show rolled.

At intermission, I bucked the tide of spectators and fought my way to the stage door. Marc's leg was in a terrible state. I got a bottle of brandy for him. Upstairs Kate Friedlich was crying because she had torn two ligaments from her heel but she insisted on continuing. I got some brandy for her too. Luckily Marc's doctor was on hand to cope.

The barn dance opened Act II. Marc Platt in an ecstasy of excitement rode the pain to triumph. Virile, young, red-headed and able, he looked like Apollo and moved like a stallion. The audience roared. "Oh, Agnes," said Rodgers, "I'm so proud of you. I hope this opens the doors."

"Dick, Dick," I said melting into his arms, "I love you. Thank you." Then the rehearsal accompanist started beating us on the back and shrieking, "Will you two stop courting and look what's happened to the theater?"

They were roaring. They were howling. People hadn't seen girls and boys dance like this in so long. Of course, they had been dancing like this, but not just where this audience could see them.

I took Mother to Sardi's for a sandwich. Some critic, I think it was Wolcott Gibbs, crossed the restaurant to shake hands. "I want to congratulate you. This was most distinguished." I chewed on in a sort of stupor.

The morning press next day was only fair. *Brigadoon*, for instance, got better. I was back in the theater at noon rehearsing Marc's understudy. Indeed it was years before any of us realized and perhaps the final word should be from Douglass Montgomery bringing the pattern full circle. Dug wrote four years later from London where he had become a star and thus described the reopening of the bombed Theater Royal, Drury Lane:

". . . How I wish you could have been there. It really was the 'New World' speaking. In my long youth of theatre-going, I have *never, any place,* seen, heard and felt an atmosphere such as there was during the intermission. Tired eyes were clear again. Trivial, unhealthy people were temporarily genuine. Unexpected types were 'discovering' dancing. Quite patently a strong, fresh breeze had been cleaning their faces. From you, keed. I was full of rememberings — and gladness — and pride.

"And how well I felt I understood the style. Once upon a time I was growing along with its growing pains. Yes, I read and hear you've surpassed it since — but not for me. In short, and as always — I love you."

But after the New York premiere, certain minor indications of change began to be felt. In Omaha, while making my wedding plans, the phone started ringing, Hollywood calling. "Have you signed with M-G-M? Well don't. Paramount is interested." The lieutenant and I tried to talk about things engaged people talk about. New York calling: "Sam Goldwyn is really interested."

"How much was that last for?" he asked.

"Seven hundred and fifty dollars a week to begin with."

"That's a lot of money," said the lieutenant. "I don't think I can keep pace with this."

"But I only want to be with you and do good dances. I don't think I'll do such good dances at Paramount."

"That's a lot of money to say no to," said the lieutenant. The phone rang again. He said, "It's likely I'll be busy for some time. While I'm away you might as well keep occupied. Do one more show. Get it out of your system. Then you'll be ready to quiet down."

I spoke to my mother. First I told her I was going to get married soon, and then I told her about the Hollywood money. "I can pay you back everything. I can help now. I can be a real help."

"What are the terms?" she asked.

"A seven-year contract . . ."

"Never," she shouted through the phone. "Never, not for any money. Your freedom is not to be bought for anything in the world. Not for money. Keep your freedom. It is beyond price. You must be able to choose. Do not consider the money. Think only of the kind of work you want to do. Don't ever speak to me about paying back."

Oh, Annie! Spoken like your father's girl! She had done without every possible luxury to keep me going, a woman aging and sickening fast. I listened to her as I had grown used to doing. When she spoke, the bugles called. That she gave advice that was also profitable was not known to either of us at the moment.

When I returned to New York, the deluge was upon me. Everyone in New York and Hollywood wanted me to do the *Oklahoma!* ballet for his new show or picture. But I was buying a trousseau.

This was the first time in my life I had taken more than a sporadic interest in clothes. They piled on my bed now, white on snowy white, ruffle on starched ruffle, crisp ribbons, button on silk —

Mother was sewing petticoats and dressing jackets — the kind of lingerie she had had — not costumes.

All through my packing I heard the phone ringing. Agents, reporters, pressmen, musicians, dancers — all now wanted to talk to me urgently. My number was, of course, listed as it had been for years. How was I going to get time to study? To plan my new good works? To keep to myself and think? The clamor was frightening.

The ship had come to port — but to what port? Was this what I had intended and wanted?

I saw *Rodeo* again. Due to lack of rehearsals and replacements, it was unrecognizable. I had succeeded all right. Now I did the cold reckoning without the hysteria of failure to underscore my concern. The work wasn't good enough. All changed, all passed. There was no way of ensuring lasting beauty. Verily, I wrote in water and judging my work with a dreadful dispassionate vision, perhaps it was as well. I spoke to Martha Graham on the pavement outside of Schrafft's restaurant. She bowed her head and looked burningly into my face. She spoke from a life's effort. I went home and wrote down what she said:

"There is a vitality, a life-force, an energy, a quickening that is translated through you into action and because there is only one of you in all of time, this expression is unique. And if you block it, it will never exist through any other medium and be lost. The world will not have it. It is not your business to determine how good it is nor how valuable nor how it compares with other expressions. It is your business to keep it yours clearly and directly, to keep the channel open. You do not even have to believe in yourself or your work. You have to keep open and aware directly to the urges that motivate you. Keep the channel open. As for you, Agnes, you have a peculiar and unusual gift and you have so far used about one third of your talent."

"But," I said, "when I see my work I take for granted what other people value in it. I see only its ineptitude, inorganic flaws, and crudities. I am not pleased or satisfied."

"No artist is pleased."

"But then there is no satisfaction?"

"No satisfaction whatever at any time," she cried passionately. "There is only a queer divine dissatisfaction, a blessed unrest that keeps us marching and makes us more alive than the others. And at times I think I could kick you until you can't stand."

I kissed her and went west to my bridegroom.

Index